BRITISH JEWRY
BOOK OF HONOUR

PART 2

British Jewry
Book of Honour

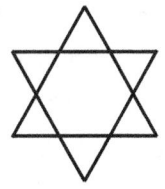

Edited by
REV. MICHAEL ADLER, D.S.O., S.C.F., B.A.

Organiser
MAX R. G. FREEMAN

Part Two
Illustrations

The Naval & Military Press Ltd

Published by
The Naval & Military Press Ltd
Unit 10 Ridgewood Industrial Park,
Uckfield, East Sussex,
TN22 5QE England
Tel: +44 (0) 1825 749494
Fax: +44 (0) 1825 765701
www.naval-military-press.com

© The Naval & Military Press Ltd 2006

In reprinting in facsimile from the original, any imperfections are inevitably reproduced and the quality may fall short of modern type and cartographic standards.

INDEX
TO
THE ILLUSTRATIONS

PORTRAITS OF FALLEN OFFICERS

Name	Plate
Abrahams, Lt. A. C. L.	155
Abrahams, Major M.	114
Alexander, 2nd/Lt. G. R.	10
Arnholz, Lt. R. H.	10
Arnold, Lt. A. L.	42
Aron, Lt. F. A.	155
Bamberger, Capt. C. D. W.	106
Bamberger, 2nd/Lt. W. E. W.	106
Barnett, Lt. V. B.	220
Barnett, Lt. V. B.	297
Barron, Lt. L.	34
Baswitz, Capt. A. (M.C.)	114
Beer, Lt. A. H.	155
Benjamin, Capt. H. S.	106
Benjamin, Capt. J. A.	204
Benzecry, Lt. S.	155
Bernstein, 2nd/Lt. M. L.	157
Bingen, Lt. C. A. M.	42
Bloom, 2nd/Lt. B.	52
Bowman, 2nd/Lt. C. H.	45
Brooks, 2nd/Lt. F. J.	362
Cansino, 2nd/Lt. J. H.	44
Capper, Capt. E. R. (M.C.)	114
Caro, 2nd/Lt. J. P.	34
Cleef, Lt. H. V.	362
Cohen, 2nd/Lt. E. (M.C.)	44
Cohen, 2nd/Lt. G. H.	51
Cohen, Lt. Moss (M.M.)	10
Cohen, 2nd/Lt. M.	52
Cohen, 2nd/Lt. S. M.	42
Cook, 2nd/Lt. N. G.	10
Coote, 2nd/Lt. P. E.	204
Cullen, 2nd/Lt. R. N.	237
Danziger, 2nd/Lt. C. W. J.	155
Davis, Capt. C. J. B.	44
Davis, Lt. H. N.	45
Davis, 2nd/Lt. H. P.	45
Davis, 2nd/Lt. L. E.	155
Davis, Capt. Leigh J.	106
Davis, Capt. L. J. (War Mem.)	273
De Pass, Lt. F.A. (V.C.)	1
De Pass, Lt. W. H. D.	362
Dundon, 2nd/Lt. S. J.	34
Emanuel, Lt. O.	44
Ezra, Capt. D.	220
Fine, 2nd/Lt. S.	106
Fink, 2nd/Lt. S. J.	42
Fleet, 2nd/Lt. L.	213
Frankenstein, 2nd/Lt. C. J.	52
Frankenstein, 2nd/Lt. O. R.	45
Franks, 2nd/Lt. B. A.	45
Frece, 2nd/Lt. C. R. de	204
Freeman-Cowen, 2nd/Lt. C.	34
Friend, 2nd/Lt. J.	45
Goldseller, Lt. L. D.	106
Gollin, Capt. E. B.	44
Gosschalk, Lt. E. M.	42
Green, Capt. E. M.	52, 297
Greenwood, Lt. I. H.	213
Grossmann, 2nd/Lt. V. D.	44
Haldenstein, Capt. F. W.	114
Harris, Lt. H.	45
Harris, Capt. N. L. (M.C.)	52
Hart, Capt. C. L.	297
Hart, Capt. Cecil L.	362
Hartman, Nurse E.	52
Henriques, Lt. P. B.	204
Henriques, Lt. R. L. Q.	52
Henry, 2nd/Lt. A. R.	51, 297
Henry, Lt. C. C.	155
Herman, 2nd/Lt. R. (War Mem.)	273
Heumann, Capt. R.	106
Hitner, Lt. V. J.	237
Holt, Capt. L.	362
Hurstbourne (Hirschbein), 2nd/Lt. W. H.	42
Hyams, Lt. A. H.	213
Hyman, 2nd/Lt. E. H.	34
Hyman, 2nd/Lt. R.	52
Isaacs, 2nd/Lt. B. C.	10
Isaacs, 2nd/Lt. F. H.	114
Jacob, Lt. V. V.	44, 297
Jacobs, 2nd/Lt. D.	51
Jacobs, 2nd/Lt. J. (Yorks Regt.)	52
Jacobs, Sub-Lt. T.	51
Jeffreys, Capt. A.	52
Joseph, 2nd/Lt. W. F. G.	34
Joseph, 2nd/Lt. W. G. A.	220
Josephi, Lt. E. H.	204
Josephs, 2nd/Lt. J.	51
Joyce, 2nd/Lt. P. S.	10
Kahn, 2nd/Lt. E.	297
Katz, Lt. S. G.	157

	Plate		Plate		Plate
Kesminsky, Lt. M. E.	- 362	Moses, 2nd/Lt. V. S.	- 237	Selby, 2nd/Lt. M. G.	- 362
Keyzor, 2nd/Lt. H. L. A.	42	Myer, 2nd/Lt. Denzil G.		Sherek, Lt. P. -	- 106
King, Lt. S. - -	- 213	A. - - - 114, 297		Simon, Capt. E. C.	- 220
Klean, 2nd/Lt. M. G. -	42	Myer, Major E. A.	- 220	Simons, Capt. L. (M.C.)	45
Klemantaski, 2nd/Lt. L.		Myers, Lt. A. F. -	- 155	Slowe, 2nd/Lt. A. -	10
A. - - - -	51	Nathan, 2nd/Lt. W. S.	42	Smith, 2nd/Lt. C. Owen	204
Kohnstamm, 2nd/Lt. J.	- 237	Ohlmann, 2nd/Lt. G. A.		Solomon, Capt. A. -	- 297
Kohnstamm, Capt. N.	- 237	L. - - -	- 10	Solomon, Lt. A. -	- 237
Krauss, 2nd/Lt. D. E.	- 220	Paiba, Lt. E. J. A.	- 106	Solomon, Capt. A. M.	- 237
Lan-Davis, Flight/Lt. C.		Piza, Capt. D. -	- 237	Solomon, 2nd/Lt. E. J.	220
F. - - -	- 51	Polack, Lt. B. J. -	- 362	Solomon, 2nd/Lt. L.	
Langdon, Capt. W. M. -	44	Polack, Lt. E. E. -	- 362	(K.O.S.B.) -	- 220
Levene, Lt. N. N. -	- 34	Posener, 2nd/Lt. P. J.	- 114	Solomon, 2nd/Lt. L.	- 297
Levene-Davis, Cadet J.		Raphael, 2nd/Lt. H. G.	- 213	Solomons, Lt. Bert	- 155
H. - - -	- 204	Reese, 2nd/Lt. A. (M.C.)	106	Solomons, Lt. L. B.	- 155
Leveson, Lt. R. M. -	- 157	Rodney, 2nd/Lt. W. B. -	10	Sonnenberg, Lt. M. C.	- 237
Levi, 2nd/Lt. F. J. -	- 45	Rosenbaum, Lt. L. B. -	45	Spielmann, Capt. (H.L.I.)	51
Levi, 2nd/Lt. H. -	- 213	Rosenthal, 2nd/Lt. A. -	10	Spiers, Lt. A. L. C. -	362
Levy, 2nd/Lt. A. M.	- 213	Rothband, Capt. J. E.	- 114	Stern, 2nd/Lt. L. H.	- 44
Levy, Lt. J. - - -	220	Rothschild, Major Evelyn		Stern, Lt. S. - -	- 213
Lewinstein, 2nd/Lt. H.	- 213	A. de - - -	220	Stuart-Smith, Lt. P. J. -	34
Lezard, Capt. A. G. -	42	Rozelaar, Capt. S. L. -	51	Styer, Cadet W. H. 237,	297
Lewis, 2nd/Lt. H. -	- 362	Rudell, 2nd/Lt. E. A. -	220	Telfer, Lt. C. W. -	- 44
Liebson, Capt. S. A.		Salaman, 2nd/Lt. E. -	42	Telfer, Lt. H. A. 44, 297	
(M.C.) - - -	45	Samuel, 2nd/Lt. E. B. 114,	297	Tobias, Capt. L. M. -	42
Lifetree, 2nd/Lt. E. H. -	213	Samuel, 2nd/Lt. G. B. -	114	Ullman, Lt. D. M. -	- 204
Lion, Lt. N. I. - -	34	Samuel, Lt. Gerald G. -	10	Valentine, 2nd/Lt. M.	- 362
Lury, 2nd/Lt. G. H. -	51	Samuel, Lt. G. G. -	- 64	Van Den Bergh, Lt. J. H.	237
Lyone, Lt. A. M. (M.C.)	220	Samuel, Major L. -	- 44	Van Den Bergh, Capt.	
Marks, Lt. Arthur S. -	10	Samuel, Capt. W. G. -	155	Seymour H. J. -	237
Marks, 2nd/Lt. I. D. -	34	Schaffer, Lt. H. -	- 213	Van Der Linde, 2nd/Lt.	
Marks, Lt. J. (D.L.I.)	- 52	Schiff, Capt. M. E. H. -	52	M. J. T. - - -	34
Marks, 2nd/Lt. J. A.	- 114	Schonfield, Capt. E. -	114	Van Der Linde, 2nd/Lt. S.	34
Meza, Capt. J. de -	- 106	Sebag-Montefiore, Capt.		Wolffe, Lt. B. - 89, 106	
Michaelis, Lt. G. M.	- 51	R. - - -	51	Woolf, Lt. W. R. M.	- 155
Montague, Lt. R. H.	- 213	Segal, 2nd/Lt. M. -	45		

FALLEN NON-COMMISSIONED OFFICERS AND MEN

Aarons, Pte. M. J. -	- 27	Abrahams, Pte. M.		Alexander, Pte. D.	- 196
Abelson, Pte. J. -	- 139	R.A.M.C.) -	- 36	Alexander, Pte. H. -	- 196
Abrahams, Pte. A.	- 139	Abrahams, Rfn. M.		Alexander, Pte. M.	- 197
Abrahams, Pte. D.	- 151	(K.R.R.C.) -	- 54	Allen, C.P.O. E. -	- 293
Abrahams, Pte. H. (K.		Abrahams, Pte. S. (Lon-		Allonowitz, Pte. L.	- 58
L'pool Regt.) -	- 26	don Regt.) -	- 27	Althusen, Pte. M. 116, 151	
Abrahams, Pte. H. (R.		Abrahams, Pte. S. (R.		Altman, Pte. L. -	- 107
Berks Regt.) -	- 316	Scots Fus.) -	- 36	Andrade, Pte. W. A.	- 27
Abrahams, Pte. H. A.	- 150	Abrahams, Pnr. S. -	- 112	Anker, Pte. A. -	- 20
Abrahams, Pte. I. (2/10th		Abrahams, Rfn. S.	- 112	Annenberg, Pte. A.	- 150
London Regt.) -	- 60	Abrahams, Rfn. W.		Annenberg (Ashberry),	
Abrahams, Pte. I. (N'land		(R.B.) - -	- 36	Pte. B. - -	27
Fus.) - -	- 316	Adler, Sgt. P. (M.M.)	274	Annenberg (Ashberry),	
				Tpr. R. - -	27

INDEX TO THE ILLUSTRATIONS

Name	Plate
Apter, L/Cpl. S.	276
Aronheim, Pte. S.	197
Aronson, Pte. M.	276
Asher, Cpl. S.	107
Averback, Spr. J.	331
Avner, Pte. M.	276
Baker, L/Cpl. H. R.	107
Balchin, Gnr. W.	150
Balon, Pte. I. E.	172
Bamberg, Sgt. M.	176
Bankofsky, Pte. A.	118
Barback, Pte. M.	268
Barmes, Gnr. W.	151
Barnard, Sgt. L.	180
Barnard, L/Cpl. S.	276
Barnett, Rfn. B.	256
Barnett, Pte. D.	112
Barnett, Pte. E. B.	118
Barnett, Cpl. H.	151
Barnett, Pte. M.	107
Barnett, Rfn. M.	226
Barnett, Rfn. R.	66
Barnett, Cpl. S.	270
Barney, Pte. J. G.	119
Baron, Pte. O.	125
Baronovich, Pte. L.	58
Barzoloi, Pte. L.	107
Baum, L/Cpl. H. H.	205
Baumgard, Pte. S.	125
Bazinski, Rfn. S.	285
Becker, Pte. Joe	205
Becker, Pte. J.	205
Becker, Pte. W.	107
Beckerwick, Cpl. M.	293
Belcher, Gnr. C.	139
Belman, Pte. A. M.	284
Bender, L/Cpl. J.	150, 172
Benjamin, Rfn. A.	172
Benjamin, Pte. C.	135
Benjamin, Pte. H.	205
Benjamin, Pte. H. B.	308
Benjamin, Pte. L.	285
Benjamin, Rfn. P.	275
Benjamin, Pte. P. D.	164
Benjamin, Bdr. S. O.	300
Benson, Pte. S.	274
Bentley, Rfn. J. (M.M.)	245
Benzimra, Pte. A. J.	150
Berkson, Sgt. M. E.	172
Berliner, Pte. H.	151
Berman, Pte. B.	112
Berman, Pte. L.	255
Berman, Pte. M. (R. Scots)	284
Berman, Pte. P.	139
Bernard, Pte. F.	205
Bernard (B. Levy), S/Sgt. L.	164
Bernhard, Pte. A.	107
Bernstein, Pte. A.	276
Bernstein, Pte. H.	20
Bernstein, Pte. J.	128
Bernstein, Pte. L.	176
Bernstein, Tpr. S. A.	107
Berson, L/Cpl. D.	292
Berson, Pte. W.	308
Berzance, Dvr. L.	176
Best, Pilot D.	308
Beyfus, Pte. C. S.	262
Beyfus, Rfn. H.	308
Bishop, Pte. S.	20
Black, Sgt. D.	111
Black, Pte. M.	308
Blacker, Pte. P.	107
Blackman, Pte. J.	107
Blackman, Cpl. M.	150
Blackstone, Pte. M.	171
Blaubaum, Pte. E.	245
Blint, Pte. M.	151
Blok, Stoker M.	20
Bloom, Gnr. H. (R.H.A.)	66
Bloom, Rfn. J. (R.B.)	262
Bloom, Gnr. J. (R.F.A.)	292
Blostein, Pte. P. (M.M.)	58
Bluestone, Pte. M.	66
Boam, Pte. C.	255
Bober, Pte. H.	139
Bogard, Rfn. J.	150
Bogard, Pte. M.	255
Boller, Pte. J.	205
Bomberg, Pte. I.	66
Boock, Sgt./Major B.	314
Boodson, Cpl. L.	157
Booker, Rfn. J.	251
Boss, Rfn. N.	157
Braham, Pte. C.	112
Brick, Pte. B.	107
Brodie, Cpl. M.	285
Brown, Pte. H.	118
Brown, Pte. M.	186
Buck, Rfn. A. I.	157
Burns, Pte. M.	151
Butman, Pte. J.	308
Caminer, Pte. A.	112
Canton-Cohen, S/Sgt. J.	3
Carmel, Pte. M.	67
Carolten, Pte. R.	204
Cassell, Pte. C. A.	150
Cassonman, Pte. N.	139
Cats, L/Cpl. L. V.	12
Cave, Pte. E. M.	54
Chalfen, Pte. J.	197
Chart, Pte. B.	285
Chesney, Pte. D.	107, 242
Chesses, Dvr. W.	60
Claff, Pte. R.	67
Clarke (Cohen), Pte. H.	139
Cohen, Cpl. A. (Leics. Regt.)	12
Cohen, Rfn. A. (London Regt.)	186
Cohen, Pte. A.	238
Cohen, Pte. A.	245
Cohen, Pte. A. A.	54
Cohen, Sgt. A. G.	18
Cohen, Rfn. A. J.	285
Cohen, Pte. B.	3
Cohen, Tpr. D.	66
Cohen, Cpl. D. (M.M.)	197
Cohen, Pte. H. (Aus. Inf.)	150
Cohen, Pte. H. (Cheshire Regt.)	150
Cohen, Pte. H.	221
Cohen, Pte. I.	139
Cohen, Pte. I. (Ches. Regt.)	58
Cohen, L/Cpl. J. (London Regt.)	12
Cohen, Pte. J. (King's Liverpool Regt.)	58
Cohen, Rfn. J.	60
Cohen, Pte. J. (Manchester Regt.)	238
Cohen, Gnr. J. (R.G.A.)	300
Cohen, Rfn. J.	300
Cohen, L/Cpl. J. I.	60
Cohen, Sgt. L.	66
Cohen, Rfn. L.	139
Cohen, Pte. L.	221
Cohen, Pte. M. (R. W. Fus.)	18
Cohen, Drummer M.	197
Cohen, Pte. Myer	204
Cohen, Pte. O.	229
Cohen, Pte. P.	67
Cohen, L/Cpl. P. (King)	133
Cohen, Pte. S. (Aus. Inf.)	245
Cole, Cpl. H.	186
Collins, Pte. B.	150
Collins, Pte. B.	221
Collins, Pte. D. G.	112
Collinsky, 2nd A/M. J.	151
Collock, Pte. M.	151
Comor, L/Cpl. M.	30, 293
Conquy, Q/M/S. J. S.	66
Cooper, Pte. A.	151

614 INDEX TO THE ILLUSTRATIONS

Name	Plate
Coor, Pte. P.	197
Cornblatt, Pte. S.	139
Corper, Gnr. W.	238
Cossack, Pte. H.	186
Cossack, Pte. M.	12
Coster, Pte. J.	276
Coster, Pte. H.	171
Couplan, Spr. J.	122
Couplan, Sgt. M.	122
Cowan, Petty Officer A.	179
Cowan, Pte. A.	221
Cowan, Rfn. L.	197
Cristoll, Pte. H. S.	12
Crook, Cpl. M.	112
Croop, Pte. M.	171
Cushelson, Gnr. J.	197
Da Casta, Rfn. J.	112
Dainow, Pte. G.	122
Daskel, Pte. A.	309
David, Rfn. J.	151
Davidson, Pte. E. H. L.	186
Davidson, Pte. H. M.	262
Davies, Pte. B.	139
Davies, Pte. S.	186
Davis, Rfn. D.	58
Davis, Pte. D. K.	300
Davis, Cpl. J. I.	172
Davis, Pte. M.	163
Davis, Pte. N. (Grave)	9
Davison, Pte. S.	112
Deitz, Pte. M.	229
Delinsky, Dvr. I.	285
Diamond, Rfn. A.	150
Diamondstone, Pte. J.	112
Dion, Pte. Jack (M.M.)	112
Dion, Pte. J.	151
Dobkin, Rfn. J.	135, 221
Downs, Sgt. F.	186
Dreebin, L/Cpl. H.	122
Dreezer, Pte. J.	139
Eagle, C/S/M. N.	275
Eckstein, Pte. D.	133
Edgar (Ettinger), Pte. B.	275
Elias, Cpl. B.	157
Ellis, Pte. N.	269
Ellis, Pte. S.	269
Ellison, Pte. P. S.	133, 269
Ellison, Pte. S. J.	269
Emden, Pte. J.	221
Erdman, Cpl. H.	276
Falk, Pte. B.	316
Falk, Pte. H.	118
Falk, Pte. L.	261
Farbstein, Pte. L.	262
Fearn, Pte. B.	316
Felperin, A/M. M.	301
Ferner, Cpl. A. (D.C.M.)	164
Fifer, Pte. R.	171
Figgins, Rfn. J.	316
Filar, Pte. H.	187
Fineberg, Pte. S.	125
Fink, Pte. S.	292
Finkelstein, Pte. A.	214
Finkelstein, Pte. H.	316
Finstein, Pte. S.	180
Fisher, Pte. W.	210
Fishman, Gnr. M.	180
Fitelson, Spr. H.	316
Fordanski, Pte. C.	316
Foreman, Pte. M.	269
Forstein (Foster), Pte. J.	133
Foster, Pte. G. J.	262
Fox, Rfn. D.	63
Fox, Rfn. S.	111
Franklin, Rfn. F.	180
Franklin, Pte. H.	256
Franks, Rfn. A.	292
Franks, Pte. I.	164
Franks, Pte. L. E.	63
Freedman, Pte. J.	171
Freedman, Pte. M. (N'land. Fus.)	125
Freedman, Pte. M. (M.M.)	316
Freeman, Pte. M. I.	164
Freiner, Pte. M.	26
Fresco, Rfn. M.	214
Friedlander, Pte. H.	4
Friend, Pte. J.	269
Fromer, Sgt. H.	214
Fuchsbalg, Pte. M.	133
Gabriel, Pte. H. M.	163
Gabrielson, Cpl. M.	157
Galinsky, Pte. A.	309
Galinsky, Pte. H.	244
Galinsky, Pte. H.	309
Galinsky, Pte. M.	245
Gallewski, L/Cpl. M. (M.M.)	18
Gans, Pte. J.	12
Garbutt, Cpl. L.	186
Gardner, Pte. J.	164
Garrett, Pte. G.	20
Geffen, Pte. E.	292
Geller, Cpl. H.	187
Gerber, L/Cpl. E.	244
Gerber, Pte. J. S.	197
Gerlisky, Pte. L.	67
Gilbert, Bdr. H.	19
Gilbert, Pte. S.	262
Gillies, Cpl. M.	221
Gillis, Pte. J.	183
Ginsberg, Pte. D.	111
Ginsberg, Pte. J.	164
Ginsberg, Pte. S.	60
Ginsberg, Pte. S.	122
Glasberg, Pte. J.	67
Glassman, Cpl. A.	245
Glassman, Pte. Dan	66
Glasstone, Cpl. I.	204
Glatt, Pte. L.	3
Gofberry, Pte. H. H.	229
Gold, Steward D.	38
Gold, Pte. J.	67
Goldberg, L/Cpl. A.	164
Goldberg, L/Cpl. A. J.	238
Goldberg, Pte. D. J.	54
Goldberg, L/Cpl. H. (Grave)	9
Goldberg, Pte. L. (Essex Regt.)	18
Goldberg, Pte. L. (Canadians)	238
Goldberg, Sgt./Major S.	244
Goldenberg, Pte. J.	244
Golding, L/Cpl. J.	18
Goldman, Cpl. A.	163
Goldsmith, Pte. B.	262
Goldstein, Pte. A. (M.M.)	197
Goldstein, Rfn. B. (R.B.)	261
Goldstein, Pte. B.	309
Goldstein, Rfn. D.	238
Goldstein, Pte. E.	229
Goldstein, Gnr. E. H.	18
Goldstein, A/B. I.	20
Goldstein, Pte. M.	60
Goldstein, Rfn. P.	197
Goldston, Rfn. L. E.	67
Goldstone, Rfn. P.	111
Goodfriend, Rfn. H.	187
Goodman, Gnr. J.	183
Goodman, L/Cpl. L.	135
Goodman, Pte. S.	19
Goodman, Pte. S.	300
Gordon, Rfn. B.	12
Gordon, Pte. I.	163
Gordon, Sgt. M. M.	170, 276
Gordon, Pte. N.	3
Gorfunkle, Spr. H.	300
Gosschalk, Rfn. L. B.	163
Green, Pte. A. B.	276
Green, Pte. A. P.	228
Green, Pte. G.	261
Green, Gnr. I.	163
Green, Pnr. L.	183
Green, Rfn. M. M.	276
Green, Rfn. W.	309
Greenbaum, Cpl. B.	157

INDEX TO THE ILLUSTRATIONS 615

Name	Plate
Greenberg, Pte. S.	187
Greenberg, Pte. P. M.	238
Greenbury, Pte. W.	3
Greenwald, Pte. L.	163
Greyman, Pte. S.	169
Grodner (Lewis), Pte. C.	163
Grodzinsky, Pte. H.	12
Grouse, Pte. A.	163
Grouse, Sgt. R. C.	18
Grower, Pte. A.	245
Guterman, Pte. A.	244
Haft, Pte. I.	261
Haft, Cpl. S.	169
Hamburg, Pte. N.	19
Hamburg, Pte. S.	36
Harbour, Pte. I	210
Harris, Pte. A. (R.A.M.C.)	36
Harris, Cpl. A.	228
Harris, Pte. J.	196
Harris, Pte. L. (W. Yorks Regt.)	26
Harris, Pte. S. E.	19
Hart, Rfn. D.	17
Hart, Rfn. H.	54
Hart, Cpl. H. E.	228
Hart, Pte. M. (M.G.C.)	316
Hart, L/Cpl. R.	36
Hart, Rfn. S.	293
Hayman, Desp. Rider E. P.	187
Heilbron, Bdr. V. (M.M.)	20
Heller, Pte. D.	36
Hepstone, Pte. J.	116
Herman, Pte. H.	169
Herman, Rfn. J.	26
Herman, Cpl. S.	183
Herman, Pte. S.	196
Hershon (W. D. Harris), Spr. I. J.	228
Hewson, Pte. J. R.	27
Hillier, Pte. A.	26
Hillier, Dvr. C. J.	26
Hockin, Pte. B.	36
Hoepelman, Pte. H.	196
Hornick, Pte. M.	197
Hovsha, Gnr. H. R.	228
Hyams, Pte. P.	36
Hyman, Dvr. A.	228
Hyman, A/B. A. L.	293
Hyman, Pte. S.	36
Hurwitz, Pte. L.	196
Isaacs, Pte. A. (Worcs. Regt.)	301
Isaacs, Pte. A. A.	132
Isaacs, Pte. E. E.	119
Isaacs, Pte. I. E.	204
Isaacs, Gnr. J. (R.F.A.)	63
Isaacs, Pte. J.	261
Isaacs, Rfn. J.	292
Isaacs (Field), Pte. M.	125
Isaacs, Pte. N.	256
Isaacs, Pte. S. E.	163
Isaacs, Cpl. S. M.	58
Jackoff, Sig. M.	4
Jacks, Pte. A.	301
Jackson, Pte. I.	171
Jacobs, Pte. A.	38
Jacobs, Pte. A.	262
Jacobs, Pte. A. J.	54
Jacobs, Tpr. A. L.	27
Jacobs, Rfn. D. (K.R.R.C.)	27
Jacobs, Pte. D.	316
Jacobs, Sgt. G. (D.C.M.)	27
Jacobs, Rfn. H. (K.R.R.C.)	118
Jacobs, L/Cpl. H. M.	171
Jacobs, L/Cpl. I.	128
Jacobs, Pte. I. E.	163
Jacobs, Pte. J.	54
Jacobs, Spr. J.	261
Jacobs, Tpr. J.	308
Jacobs, A/B. Louis	226
Jacobs, Pte. N.	119
Jacobs, Sgt. R. B.	4
Jaffe, Pte. I.	262
Jay (Jacobs), Rfn. M.	268
Jessel, Pte. H.	268
Jonas, Pte. F. J.	221
Joseph, Sgt. E.	38
Joseph, L/Cpl. J. O.	261
Julius, Pte. C.	221
Kaisser, Pte. S. L.	122
Kalminsky, Pte. J.	12
Karker, Cpl. S.	11
Karlish, A/B. A.	276
Katz, Pte. C.	244
Kaufman (Elias), Pte. E.	270
Kavarsky, Pte. J.	128
Kay, Pte. I. M.	11
Kaye, Gnr. S. (M.M.)	244
Kitchenoff, Pte. W.	164
Kitofski, Pte. W.	122
Klein, Pte. I	255
Klein, Sig. J.	300
Kopinsky, Rfn. J.	284
Kossick, A/B. Louis	214
Kossick, Pte. L.	244
Kossick, Pte. R.	244
Krailsheimer, Pte. J. S.	244
Krell, Pte. J.	309
Krohn, Pte. H.	132
Krohn, Pte. S.	284
Kutchinsky, Pte. A.	132
Kyte, Pte. A.	186
Lappin, Pte. M.	122
Larvey (Levy), Pte. S.	256
Latsky, Pte. W. J.	118
Latter, Pte. A.	183, 255
Lavender, Pte. A.	270
Lazarus, Pte. B.	256
Lazarus, L/Cpl. H.	256
Lazarus, L/Cpl. J. B.	119
Lazarus, Pte. M.	300
Lazoff, Pte. S.	38
Lea (Levy), Rfn. I.	186
Lehmann, Pte. R. R.	111
Leibovitch, Pte. M.	229
Leizerbram, Pte. P.	229
Lensnor, Pte. I.	226
Leschinsky, Pte. M.	171
Letzky, Pte. C.	111
Levene, Spr. I.	4
Levenson, Rfn. H.	187
Leventhal, Pte. L.	133
Levey, Pte. I.	269
Levey, L/Cpl. J.	229
Levi, Pte. E.	11
Levi, L/Cpl. H.	19
Levine, Pte. B. (Royal Warwicks)	183
Levine, Pte. B. (D. of C.L.I.)	12
Levine, Pte. C.	63
Levinson, Pte. A. D.	256
Levison, Pte. S. S.	132
Levy, Pte. A.	11
Levy, A/M. A.	179
Levy, Rfn. A.	309
Levy, Sgt. A. I.	171
Levy (L. Bernard), S/Sgt. B.	164
Levy, Pte. B.	221
Levy, Sgt. B. M.	132
Levy, Pte. C.	171
Levy, Pte. D.	238
Levy, L/Cpl. F. S.	18
Levy, Pte. G. (R. Scots)	301
Levy, Pte. G. N.	18
Levy, Pte. H. (S. Wales Borderers)	169
Levy, Sgt. H. (R. Scots Fus.)	268
Levy, L/Cpl. H.	270
Levy, Rfn. H.	229
Levy, Pte. H. M. (War Mem.)	273

INDEX TO THE ILLUSTRATIONS

Name	Plate
Levy, L/Cpl. J.	4
Levy, Pte. J. (Tank Corps)	118
Levy, Pte. J. (R. West Surrey Regt.)	119
Levy, Pte. J. (London Regt.)	125
Levy, Rfn. J.	180
Levy, Pte. J. (R. Fus.)	238
Levy, Rfn. J.	309
Levy, Pte. L. (Welsh Regt.)	3
Levy, Pte. L. (Hants Regt.)	63
Levy, Pte. L. (S. Wales Borderers)	285
Levy, Rfn. L. L.	63
Levy, L/Cpl. P. M.	128
Levy, Pte. R.	275
Levy, L/Cpl. R. A.	18
Levy, Pte. S.	292
Lewis, Pte. A.	12
Lewis (Grodner), Pte. C.	163
Lewis, Gnr. H.	125
Lewis, Pte. H. (M.G.C.)	180
Lewis, Pte. H. (R. Fus.)	255
Lewis, Rfn. H.	275
Lewis, Rfn. H. R.	133
Lewis, Pte. J.	171
Lewis (Isher), Pte. M.	20
Lewis, A/B. M. C.	133
Lewis, Pte. N.	292
Lewis, Pte. S.	19
Lichtenstein, Pte. M.	238
Lichtenstein, Pte. M. H.	11
Lightstone, Rfn. L.	301
Lightstone, Cpl. S.	179
Linde, Sgt. A.	255
Lion, Rfn. A. J.	12
Lipchinsky (Lipman), Pte. S. R.	269
Lipman, Pte. I.	285
Lipman, Pte. J.	38
Lippman, Pte. S.	180
Lipshack (Phillips), Pte. M. W.	11
Lipson, Pte. S. W.	183
Lisbona, Pte. N.	157
Littman, Pte. S.	183
Littmann, Pte. Sol. (M.M.)	172
Livingstone, Pte. J.	255
Loftus, Pte. A.	301
Lotsky, L/Cpl. A.	268
Louis (Sugar), Pte. P.	4
Loveguard, L/Cpl. C.	292
Lubel, Pte. H.	66
Lubinsky, 2nd A/M. J.	284
Lubinsky, Pte. M.	300
Ludski, Pte. E. B.	3
Lumer, Rfn. J.	309
Lurie, Pte. I. (War Mem.)	273
Lyons, Rfn. S.	133
Macaborski, Cpl. A.	172
Mack (Kurtzman), Sgt. W.	176
Maginsky, Pte. S.	176
Magnus, Rfn. M.	308
Malinsky, Pte. S.	245
Malkin, Pte. J.	269
Malnick, Pte. G.	128
Malnick, Rfn. J.	308
Manhoff, Pte. J.	180
Marcus, Pte. H.	11
Marienberg, Pte. A. G.	11
Marks, Pte. C. A.	176
Marks, Pte. G. C.	300
Marks, Pte. H. (Scots Guards)	128
Marks, Pte. H. (Middlesex Regt.)	172
Marks, Pte. J.	293
Marks, Pte. L. (S. Lancs. Regt.)	284
Marks, L/Cpl. L. G.	255
Marks, Pte. M.	256
Marks, Pte. R.	238
Marks, Pte. S.	268
Marks, Pte. W.	176
Marks, Pte. W.	245
Markus, Pte. H. (War Mem.)	273
Marquis, Pte. G.	111
Marshofsky, Pte. A.	285
Mason, Pte. I.	66
Mazerkoff, Rfn. B.	128
Mazerkoff, Pte. M.	20
Meisel, Pte. H.	276
Meltzer, Pte. S.	58
Mendelsohn, Tpr. F.	187
Mendelson, Gnr. M.	179
Mendes da Costa, Pte. B.	268
Mendoza, Pte. V. M.	262
Michael, Pte. S.	205
Michaels, Dvr. D.	269
Miller, Rfn. E.	261
Montsoff, Pte. H.	256
Monty, Sgt. J.	285
Morack, Pte. M.	119
Morell, Pte. I.	179
Morris, Pte. A. (K. L'pool Regt.)	11
Morris, Pte. N.	63
Morris, Gnr. S.	38
Morris, Sgt. S.	268
Moscovsky, Pte. H.	63
Mosely, Pte. M. S. C.	119
Moses, Cpl. I.	128
Moses, Gnr. L.	275
Myers, Pte. G.	172
Myers, Pte. H. T.	284
Myers, Sgt. J.	180
Myers (Smith), Pte. L.	171
Myers, Pte. P.	205
Nagavkar, Pte. R.	270
Naphtali, Pte. H.	270
Nathan, Pte. C.	132
Nathan, Pte. J.	135
Newhouse, Pte. M.	66
Newman, Pte. S.	268
Newman, Rfn. S.	275
Norman, Pte. C.	3
Norris (Nossek), Cpl. G.	270
Novinski, Pte. I.	270
Novitsky, Pte. H. M.	38
Nunes Vaz, Rfn. L.	238
Nyman, Pte. H.	60
Nyman, Rfn. J.	270
Page (Rosenthal), Cpl. J.	63
Pampel, Rfn. A.	179
Paterson, Cpl. R. F.	269
Pattie, Pte. H.	229
Pearlman, Pte. J. (R.E.)	118
Perlberg, Pte. M.	11
Perlman, L/Cpl. M.	301
Pestka, L/Cpl. L.	214
Phillips, Pte. A. (R. Fus).	11
Phillips, L/Cpl. A.	268
Phillips, Pte. B. (London Regt.)	255
Phillips, Pte. D.	179
Phillips, Pte. J.	261
Phillips (Koninsky) Pte. L.	132
Phillips, L/Cpl. M.	60
Phillips, Tpr. M.	58
Phillips, Pte. S. (R. Fus.)	269, 274
Phillips, Pte. S. (R. Warwicks)	275
Phillips, Rfn. S.	285
Pinto, Sig. H. E.	132
Pinto, Pte. L.	245
Pivansky, Pte. A.	118
Plater, Tpr. J.	301
Polakoff, Rfn. J.	63

INDEX TO THE ILLUSTRATIONS

	Plate
Polikoff, Pte. I.	300
Pomerance, Pte. S.	132
Pomerantz, Pte. J.	293
Posenor, Pte. A.	275
Primack, Pte. M.	119
Primhak, Pte. N.	275
Prins, Pte. A.	245
Racionzier, Pte. H. F.	54
Rapaport, Pte. P.	26
Raphael, Pte. H. C.	125
Raphael, Sgt. S. F.	125
Raport, Pte. M. D.	19
Rasky, Pte. L. S.	196
Reckler, Pte. L.	3
Reinfleisch, Pte. A.	118
Reuben, Pte. E.	316
Revensky, Pte. H.	196
Rissidore, Gnr. F. D.	226
Robinson-Moliver, Pte. S.	60
Rogalek, Pte. M.	36
Rood, L/Cpl. M.	262
Roomz, Pte. M.	244
Rose, Pte. A. S.	36
Rose (Rosenbaum), Pte. W.	54
Rosen (Rosenberg), Pte. L.	26
Rosenbaum, Pte. A.	118
Rosenbaum, Gnr. A. (R.G.A.)	122
Rosenbaum, Pte. S.	27
Rosenbaum, Pte. S.	262
Rosenberg, L/Cpl. D.	18
Rosenberg, Pte. I. (K.O.R.L.)	26
Rosenberg, Pte. L.	196
Rosenberg, Pte. M.	27
Rosenberg, Pte. S.	228
Rosenbloom, Pte. H.	284
Rosenthal, Pte. A.	/19
Rosenthal, Tpr. A. K.	19
Rosenthal, Pte. C.	111
Rosenthal, Pte. G.	60
Rosenthal, Pte. H.	293
Rosenthal, L/Cpl. H.	300
Rosenthal, Pte. L. M.	196
Ross (Rosenberg), Pte. H.	176
Rothblatt, Pte. S.	244
Rothkugel, Pte. M.	122
Rowson (Rosenbaum), Rfn. D.	196
Rubinstein, Pte. P.	118
Russell (Rosenbaum), Pte. A.	157
Sackshiver, Rfn. J.	256
Salaman, A/B L.	214
Sampson, Sgt. A. F.	270
Samson, Rfn. I. S.	292
Samuel, Rfn. S.	54, 205
Samuels, Pte. P. (R. Fus.)	284
Sandall, Pte. D.	20
Sanders, Sgt. G. J.	128
Sandys, Pte. J.	133
Sanofsky, Pte. S.	176
Sarfaty, Sgt. J.	214
Savitz, Gnr. J.	293
Saxon, Sgt. M.	111
Schaffer, Pte. E.	229
Schein (Warner), Pte. J.	275
Schilling, Pte. H.	26
Schilling, Rfn. R.	214
Schneider, Pte. S.	308
Schneiders, 1st A/M. A. M.	58
Schonewald, C/Q/M/S. S.	67
Schwartz, Pte. B.	26
Schwartz, Cyclist E.	180
Schwartz, Pte. I.	63
Schweitzer, Gnr. P.	38
Segal, Pte. N.	255
Seigar, Cpl. P.	133
Selcovitch, Pte. H.	293
Seline, Pte. J. J.	308
Selman (Solomons), L/Cpl. B.	38
Selman, L/Cpl. H. D.	164
Seramber, Pte. C.	187
Shalgosky, Pte. B.	292
Shall, Sgt. I.	128
Shapero, Pte. C.	179
Shatgofsky, Pte. H.	54
Shatz, Pte. M.	205
Sheare, Gnr. S.	19
Shenow, L/Cpl. W.	119
Sherman, Rfn. S.	63
Shibko, Cpl. I.	255
Showman, Pte. S.	205
Silver, L/Cpl. A.	180
Silver, Pte. J.	293
Silverman, Rfn. H.	284
Silverman, Rfn. P.	196
Silverstein, Pte. L. B.	301
Sillberg, Pte. M.	187
Simlo, Pte. R.	125
Simmons, Pte. B. E.	20
Simons, Flight/Sgt. A. S.	187
Singer, Rfn. P. P.	66
Slifkin, Pte. I.	256
Slonemsky, Spr. J.	284
Smollen, Pte. D.	58
Sniders, Pte. S.	309
Sobel, Sgt. M.	67
Solomon, Pte. F.	301
Solomon (Sullivan), L/Cpl. H.	172
Solomon, Pte. J. (Warwick Regt.)	26
Solomon, Sig. J.	214
Solomon, Telegraphist M.	38
Solomon, Pte. M.	293
Solomon, Pte. N. C.	176
Solomons, Sgt. A. (Middlesex Regt.)	11
Solomons, Pte. A. (R. Dublin Fus.)	285
Solomons, Rfn. H. (1/12th London Regt.)	292
Solomons, Pte. I. (R. Fus.)	111
Solomons, Rfn. I. (R.B.)	163
Solomons, 2nd A/M. J.	38
Solomons, Sgt. L.	183
Solomons, Pte. M. (Worcester Regt.)	132
Solomons, Pte. M. (London Regt.)	157
Solomons, L/Cpl. M.	183
Solomons, Pte. S.	205
Solomons, Pte. T.	268
Spear, Pte. M.	308
Spero, Pte. J.	128
Spero, Rfn. M.	179
Spilg, Pte. W.	187
Spurling, Rfn. M. W.	179
Staal, Pte. E.	172
Stahl, Sgt. J.	183
Stander, Spr. B.	270
Steinberg, Pte. A. (W. Yorks. Regt.)	132
Steinberg, Pte. I.	187
Steinberg, Pte. M. L.	176
Stern, Stoker W.	20
Sternheim, Pte. A. H.	308
Stibbe, Pte. M.	54
Stodel, L/Cpl. I. A.	270
Stone, Pte. H.	183
Stott, Rfn. J.	27
Strauss, Rfn. A. L.	176
Strauss, Pte. R. A.	284
Sugarman, L/Cpl. M.	180
Sultan, Gnr. J.	38
Susman, Pte. J.	119
Swede, Pte. J. A. M.	256
Sykes, Pte. R.	125
Tasch, L/Cpl. F. G.	210
Taylor (Schneider), Sgt. D.	122

Tennenbaum, Pte. J. - 4	Van Ryn, Rfn. D. - - 214	Woolf, Rfn. H. (R. Irish Rifles) - - 261
Tennens, Rfn. J. - - 4	Van Thal, Rfn. M. - - 133	Woolf, Pte. H. B. - - 245
Tobias, Pte. J. - - 18	Vinefsky, L/Cpl. A. - 128	Woolf, Pnr. H. L. - 228
Tobias, Rfn. J. - - 164	Wagner, Cyclist H. - 182	Woolf, Pte. J. - - 3
Tompofsky, Rfn. M. (M.M.) - - - 164	Wallack, Pte. M. - - 229	Woolf, Rfn. J. (K.R.R.C.) - - 119
Trachtenberg, L/Cpl. M. I. - - - - 122	Wein, Pte. M. - - 301	Woolf, Pte. M. - - 60
	Weinberg, Pte. H. - 4	
Tragheim, Rfn. E. - 172	Weinberg, Pte. W. - 4	Woolf, Rfn. N. - 111
Tragheim, Pnr./Cpl. E. - 221	Welt, Pte. H. - - - 3	Woolf, Pte. R. - - 275
Travers, (Tragheim), Rfn. E. - - - - 221	White, Pte. J. R. - - 186	Woolf, Pte. S. (K.R.R.C.) - - 214
	Whitefield, Sgt. C. S. (M.S.M.) - - 268	
Tresman, L/Cpl. H. J. - 214	Winstone (Wainstain), Pte. J. - - - 179	Woolfson, Pte. S. - - 3
Trotskey, Pte. S. R. - 301		Woolman, Pte. A. - - 4
Truefitt, Tpr. C. J. - 111	Wise (M. Simcovitch), Pte. H. - - - 60	Woolman, Rfn. E. - 229
Tubb, Pte. J. - - - 67		Wyler, Rfn. J. M. - 179
Vanderlind, Pte. M. S. - 67	Wise (Cohen), Pte. R. - 58	Wyne, Pte. J. B. - - 261
Vander-Molen, Pte. S. - 125	Wollman, Pte. M. - - 186	Zimmerman, Pte. H. - 19
Van-Engle, Pte. S. - - 4	Woodrow, Pte. A. - 67	Zimmerman, Rfn. J. - 228
Van Leer, Bdr. A. - - 309	Woolf, Gnr. B. G. - 261	Zimmerman, Pte. M. - 228
Van Locken, Pte. J. N. - 132	Woolf, Rfn. B. J. - - 125	Zimmerman, Pte. N. - 228
Van Praag, Sgt. B. - 119		Zimmerman, Pte. S. - 228

OFFICERS

Abensur, Sub/Lt. M. - 250	Barnett, Capt. - - 90	Blumberg, 2nd/Lt. M. - 215
Abrahams, Major A. (O.B.E.) - - 343	Barnett, Lt. H. - - 335	Boas, Lt. Harold 177, 201, 265, 339
Abrahams, Lt. A. - - 305	Barnett, Major M. - 339	
Abrahams, Major A. C. (C.B.E.) - - 252	Barnett, 2nd/Lt. - - 90	Boodson, 2nd/Lt. H. - 31
	Barney, 2nd/Lt. L. V. - 207	Breckman, Capt. J. 305
Abrahams, Lt. M. - 215	Barney, Sub/Lt. S. D. 305	Breckman, 2nd/Lt. S. - 352
Abrahams, 2nd/Lt. S. - 356	Barton, Lt. G. (M.C.) - 192	Brilliant, Capt. & Adjt. L. 356
Abram, 2nd/Lt. A. - 337	Beatty, Capt. - - 90	Briscoe, Lt. M. - - 175
Adler, Rev. M. (D.S.O., S.C.F.) - 56, 116, 170, 222, 249, 313	Beddington, Lt.-Col. E. H. L.(D.S.O., M.C.) 337	Brown, Lt. - - - 90
		Brown, Lt. H. - - 160
	Beddington, Lt. H. L. V. 109	Caminer, 2nd/Lt. D. - 160
Adler, Capt. S. M. - 198	Beddington, Lt. W. R. - 215	Cassell, Lt. M. C. - 109
Afriat, Capt. J. - - 31	Bentwich, Major N. de M. - - - - 234	Cather, Capt. - - - 90
Alexander, Lt. M. - 343		Chaikin, Capt. B. - - 352
Ancill, Lt. G. C. - - 345	Benzimra, Lt. F. J. (M.C.) - - - 352	Chart, 2nd/Lt. A. - 356
Andrade, Lt. V. R. - 222		Cohen, Lt. B. M. - - 258
Ansley, Capt. S. S. (M.C.) - - - 332	Bernstein, 2nd/Lt. A. - 339	Cohen, Lt.-Col. C. Waley (C.M.G.) - - 69
	Bernstine, Lt. I. L. - 61	
Arnold, Capt. M. P. - 347	Besso, 2nd/Lt. A. - 43	Cohen, Col. D. de Lara - 43
Arnold, Lt. - - - 90	Besso, Lt. M. 175, 215	Cohen, Major Sir Herbert B., Bart. - - 254
Aserman, Lt. C. (M.C.) 222	Bingen, Lt. E. A. - - 109	
Aserman, 2nd/Lt. D. - 222	Blaiberg, Capt. E. - 252	Cohen, 2nd/Lt. J. - - 352
Attwell, Lt. H. - - 332	Blaiberg, Lt. H. - - 252	Cohen, Capt. J. M. - 305
Balaban, 2nd/Lt. I. M. (D.C.M.) - - 198	Bloom, Lt. H. - - 279	Cohen, Capt. Lionel L. - 252
	Bloom, 2nd/Lt. J. - - 279	Cohen, Lt. M. (M.C.) - 341
	Bloom, Flight Cadet M. - 279	Cohen, Lt.-Col. S. C. S. - 198

INDEX TO THE ILLUSTRATIONS

	Plate
Cohen, Capt. Sefton	278
Cohen-Henriques, Lt. L. V.	279
Collins, Lt. A.	198
Colt, Capt. M.	175
Conway, 2nd/Lt. F. J.	192
Cooper, 2nd/Lt. B.	31
Coussin, Lt.	90
Cowan, Lt. A. R.	222
Cowen, 2nd/Lt.	90
Cross, Lt.	89
Daltroff, Lt. E. M.	89
Davis, Lt. C. M.	222
Davis, Lt. D. L.	222
Davis, Capt. E. D. Pinder	198
Davis, Major E. J.	222
Davis, Capt. H.	61
Davis, 2nd/Lt. K.	108
Davis, Lt. P. W.	61
Davis, Capt. S. (M.C.)	305
Diamond, Lt. S. (D.C.M., Croix de Guerre)	279
Drapkin, 2nd/Lt. J. A. (M.M.)	69
Dreyfus, 2nd/Lt. M.	109
Drucquer, Lt. M. W.	250
Dulberg, Capt. J.	198
Duparc, Capt. S.	332
Dutch, Major H. (M.D., T.D.)	254
Ellis, Capt.	341
Emanuel, Lt. P. H., F.R.G.S.	175
Enoch, Major C. D.	252
Epstein, Lt. M. G.	61
Evans, Lt.	89
Ezekiel, Sub/Asst.-Surg. A.	61
Fallon, Lt. D. (M.C.)	153
Feldman, Capt. I.	343
Finklestone, 2nd/Lt. M. J.	227
Finsburg, 2nd/Lt. M. G. (M.C.)	215
Flatow, Lt. E. W.	215
Flatow, 2nd/Lt. E. W.	198
Fligelstone, Lt. B.	339
Fligelstone, 2nd/Lt. T. H. (M.C.)	69, 339
Frampton, 2nd/Lt. G. M.	215
Frankenburg, Capt. S.	43
Frankenthal, Rev. I. (C.F.)	332
Franklin, Capt. E. A.	250
Franklin, Lt. Paymaster J. A.	250
Franks, Cadet B.	207
Franks, Capt. & Q/M. L. L.	192
Franks, Lt. I. A.	341
Fraser, Lt. H. J.	258
Freedman, Capt. L.	345
Freeman, Lt. A. H. D.	250
Freiman, Lt. N. B.	207
Friend, 2nd/Lt. S.	160
Gee, Capt. R. (V.C., M.C.)	1
Geffen, Rev. L. (C.F.)	43
Geffen, Capt. M. W.	345
Gilman, Lt.	90
Gluckman, Lt. B.	108
Gluckman, Lt. P.	108
Gluckstein, Capt. I. M.	61
Gluckstein, Lt. I. V.	279
Gluckstein, Lt. L. H.	352
Gluckstein, Major M. (O.B.E.)	175
Gluckstein, Lt. S. M. (M.C.)	345
Golbie, Capt. J. M.	175
Golding, 2nd/Lt. A.	356
Goldreich, Lt. R.	279
Goldstein, Capt. A.	347
Goldstein, Capt. H. (M.C.)	265
Goldston, Capt. J. J.	305
Goldston, Rev. N. (C.F.)	347
Goodman, Lt. D.	356
Gordon, Lt. C. T.	222
Grave, 2nd/Lt. J. A.	345
Green, Lt. G.	218
Grossmann, Lt. E. E.	109
Guest, Capt. L. Haden (M.C.)	327
Guttman, Capt. W. M. (M.C.)	279
Hanbury, Lt. A.	254
Harris, Capt. (38th R. Fus.)	89
Harris, Lt.	90
Harris, Lt. (38th R. Fus)	89
Harris, 2nd/Lt. A. C. R.	347
Harris, Lt. C. E. R.	347
Harris, Lt. C. L. R.	347
Harris, Lt. E.	43
Harris, Lt. G.	305
Harris, Capt. Hershel	250
Harris, Lt. I.	218
Harris, Lt. J. M.	207
Harris, Capt. L. G. R. (M.C.)	347
Harris, Lt. S.	43
Harris, Capt. S. H.	218
Harris, Capt. S. H. R.	347
Hart, Lt. J.	69, 234, 312
Harwitz, Lt. W.	160
Heilbron, Lt.-Col. E. J.	337
Heilbron, Lt.-Col. I. M. (D.S.O.)	198
Henriques, Capt. B. L. Q.	252
Henriques, Capt. P. Q.	343
Henriques, Major W. Q.	343
Hopkin, Major D. (M.C.)	90
Hyams, Capt. (38th R. Fus.)	89
Hyams, Capt. G. F.	341
Hyman, Lt. C. P.	345
Hyman, 2nd/Lt. G.	175
Instone, Capt. A.	192
Isaac, Capt. H.	153
Isaacs, Major B.	279
Isaacs, 2nd/Lt. C.	234, 312
Isaacs, 2nd/Lt. G.	234, 312
Isaacs, Capt. L. I.	192
Jabotinsky, Lt. V.	207
Jackson, Lt. E.	218
Jacobs, Lt.	90
Jacobs, Capt. C. (M.C. and Bar)	222
Jacobs, Lt. E. E.	258
Jacobs, Lt. G. J.	69
Jacobs, Lt. H. L. (M.C.)	192
Jacobs, 2nd/Lt. Julius	109
Jaffe, Surg. Sub/Lt. H. N.	250
Jaffe, Capt. & Adjt. I. (38th R. Fus.)	69, 254
Jaffe, Lt. I.	89
Jay, 2nd/Lt. S.	218
Joels, Capt. J.	258
Joseph, Lt. B.	279
Joseph, Adjt. F. A.	207
Joseph, Capt. H.	352
Joseph, Capt. M.	116
Joseph, Capt. M.	250
Joseph, Lt. R.	250
Joseph, Lt. S.	341
Joseph, Capt. S. C. (D.F.C.)	302
Joseph, Capt. V.	339
Julian, Capt.	89
Katz, Lt. J.	339
Kauffmann, Lt. B. M.	332
Kaum, 2nd/Lt. G. E.	160
Kaye, 2nd/Lt. M. M.	339
Kemper, Major J. (O.B.E.)	161, 345
Kerin, Capt. C. S.	109
Keysor, Lt. L. (V.C.)	1
Keyzor, 2nd/Lt.	90

INDEX TO THE ILLUSTRATIONS

Name	Plate
Kingsley, Lt. H. H.	207
Kisch, Capt. E. R. (M.C.)	254
Lang, Lt. Paymaster A.	279
Lawrence, Lt. H. P.	258
Lazarus, Lt. J.	347
Lazarus, Capt. L.	250
Lazarus, Lt. L. H.	218
Lazarus, 2nd/Lt. R. H.	207
Lesser, Capt. A.	56
Levene, Capt. L.	222
Leventon, Capt. J.	252
Levin, Rev. W. (C.F.)	258
Levey, Lt.-Col. J. H. (D.S.O.)	215, 313
Levy, Lt.	90
Levy, Lt. A. (M.G.C.)	339
Levy, 2nd/Lt. I. E.	252
Levy, Lt. Myer	218
Levy, Lt. S.	352
Levy, Lt. Selig	160
Lewis, Capt. M. (M.C.)	339
Lewis, Capt. W. (M.C.)	175
Lewis-Barned, Lt. de S.	64
Lightstone, Lt.-Col. H. (D.S.O., M.C.)	339
Lindo, Lt. G. S.	341
Lipsey, Lt. S. M.	332
Lipson, Rev. S. (S.C.F.)	364
Lissack, Lt. M. S.	254
Littman, Lt. H.	345
Loewe, Lt. H.	253
Lotheim, 2nd/Lt. S. (M.C.)	343
Lotinga, Lt. C. G.	337
Lubelski, Lt. W. W. (M.C. and Bar)	252
Lumley-Frank, Capt. J.	332
Lynes, Lt. J.	258
Lyons, 2nd/Lt. A.	218
Lyons, Capt. A. M.	305
Margolin, Lt.-Col. E. (D.S.O.)	90
Marks, Lt. A. E.	207
Marks, Lt. E.	43
Marks, Lt. H. H. (M.C.)	222
Marks, 2nd/Lt. J.	337
Marks, Lt.-Col. J. S.	305
Marks, Lt. L. C.	61
Marsden, Lt. C.	218
Marsden, Lt. C.	258
Marsden, Lt. Chas.	108
Marsden, 2nd/Lt. Claude	108
Mendes, 2nd/Lt. H. C.	61
Mendoza, Capt. A. L.	352
Messulam, Lt. R. M.	215
Michael, 2nd/Lt. M. A.	250
Michaelis, Lt. A. L.	332
Michaelis, Lt. R. L.	305
Mindel, 2nd/Lt. N. I.	312
Mocatta, Capt. C. H.	356
Monash, Lt.-Gen. Sir John (G.C.M.G., K.C.B., G.C.O. Australian Corps)	Frontispiece
Montague, Lt. Hon. S. A. S.	343
Montefiore, Capt. W. Sebag (M.C.)	341
Morley, Capt. A. S.	356
Morris, Lt. A. E.	192
Morris, Lt. H.	89
Morris, Capt. N.	192
Mosenthal, Major H. R.	254
Moss, Capt. A.	332
Moss-Vernon, Capt. S. R. (M.C.)	222
Murphy, Lt.	90
Murphy, 2nd/Lt.	90
Myer, Capt. M. Alex.	250
Myers, Capt. A. P. (M.C.)	258
Myers, Lt. J. P.	254
Myers, 2nd/Lt.	90
Nathan, Capt. A.	332
Nathan, Lt. G.	23
Nathan, Lt. G.	207
Neill, Capt.	89
Nevill, Lt.	89
Newport, Lt.	90
Ockman, Capt. T.	352
Olsberg, 2nd/Lt. A.	337
Oppenheim, Major G. P.	160
Patterson, Lt.-Col. J. H. (D.S.O.)	89
Pearce, 2nd/Lt. H.	153
Pezaro, 2nd/Lt. L.	339
Phillips, 2nd/Lt.	90
Phillips, Lt. P. F.	356
Pinna, 2nd/Lt. C. de	192
Polack, Lt. A. F.	175
Pool, Lt. M. L.	61
Posener, 2nd/Lt. W.	345
Price, Lt. W. (M.C.)	352
Pyser, 2nd/Lt. M.	323
Racionzer, Capt. J. L.	90
Rapaport, 2nd/Lt. L.	175
Reid, Capt.	90
Rich, Lt.	90
Rich, 2nd/Lt. J. M.	254
Richardson, 2nd/Lt.	312
Ripley, Capt.	89
Robinson, Lt. A. A. (M.C., D.F.C.)	218
Robinson, 2nd/Lt. N.	109
Rosenbaum, Flight Sub/Lt. L.	343
Rosenbloom, Lt. H. C.	250
Roskin, Capt. H.	278
Rothband, Capt. B. H.	337
Rothschild, Major J. de (D.C.M.)	97
Rowe, Lt. F.	258
Rubin, Lt. H. de V.	90
Rubinstein, 2nd/Lt. M.	314
Sabel, Capt. P. P.	332
Salaman, Dr. R. N.	90
Salmon, 2nd/Lt.	90
Salmon, Capt. B. A.	207
Salmon, Lt. H.	343
Salmon, Major I. (O.B.E.)	341
Salmon, Capt. J.	192
Salmon, Lt. M.	332
Salomon, Capt. S.	343
Samuel, Capt. B. B.	175
Samuel, Lt. Conrad	352
Samuel, 2nd/Lt. E. H.	198
Samuel, Lt.-Col. F. D. (D.S.O.)	215
Samuel, 2nd/Lt. J. C.	337
Samuel, Capt. H. B.	192
Samuel, Capt. S. (M.D.)	327
Samuel, Capt. W. S.	337
Samuel, Lt. W. S.	341
Samuels, 2nd/Lt. S. M. (M.C. and Bar)	43
Samuelson, Capt.	90
Sassoon, Lt. D.	356
Saunders, Lt.-Comdr. R. (D.S.O.)	302
Saxton, Lt. G.	345
Schonfield, Major W. (T.D.)	61, 79
Schottlander, Capt. A.	252
Seligman, 2nd/Lt. L. B. (M.C.)	160
Selinger, Lt. E.	347
Shueerson, Lt. Liova (O.B.E.)	227
Shortt, 2nd/Lt. J.	61
Silverman, Rev. H. P. (C.F.)	160, 304
Silverstone, 2nd/Lt. A.	254
Simons, Capt. S.	252

INDEX TO THE ILLUSTRATIONS

Name	Plate
Simmons, Lt. D. H.	337
Simonson, Capt. P. W.	341
Singer, Capt. C.	252
Sington, Surg. H.	279
Smalley, Capt.	90
Smythe, Lt.	89
Sniders, Lt. A.	341
Solomon, 2nd/Lt. H.	43
Solomons, 2nd/Lt. L. P.	207
Spero, Surg.-Lt. G. E.	347
Spero, Midshipman L. P.	347
Spero, Capt. S. (Croix de Guerre)	341
Spielman, Major C. M. (M.C.)	61
Spiers, Capt. K. L. (M.C.)	305
Spira, Capt. S. M.	207
Stern, Lt.-Col. Sir Edward (K.B.E., C.M.G.)	356
Stern, Lt.-Col. Sir Edward D.	343
Stiebel, Lt. A.	305
Stone, 2nd/Lt. B.	90, 254
Stone, 2nd/Lt.	69
Strump, 2nd/Lt. R.	109
Symonds, Capt. H.	198
Symonds, Lt. M.	89
Thomas, 2nd/Lt. S.	343
Trumpeldor, Capt. J.	354
Tuck, Capt. D.	43
Tuck, Major R.	215
Turiansky, Lt. M.	227
Tuteur, Capt. & Adjt. M. P.	356
Van Den Bergh, Lt. D.	192
Vyner, 2nd/Lt. F.	160
Wacholder, Capt. A.	356
Waley, Major E. (O.B.E.)	97
Webber, Lt.	234, 312
White, 2nd/Lt. A. A.	109
White, 2nd/Lt. E. V.	218
White, Lt. R. E.	43
Whitworth, Capt. (D.S.O.)	190
Wolf, Lt. C. M.	159
Wolf, Capt. E. M. (M.C.)	159
Wolf, Capt. G. M. D.	159
Wolfensohn, Lt. H.	69, 89, 90, 97, 254
Woolf, Capt. B. M. (M.C.)	175
Woolf, Capt. H. M. A.	345
Wurm, 2nd/Lt. A. L.	31
Zlotnik, Lt. S.	353

N.C.O.'S AND MEN

Name	Plate
Aaron, Sgt. C.	166
Aarons, Sgt. L. L.	127
Abolafia, Intertr. O. S.	333
Abraham, Pte. J.	124
Abrahams, Pte.	71
Abrahams, Pte. A. (R.M.L.I.)	147
Abrahams, Cpl. A.	136
Abrahams, S/Sgt. B. S.	351
Abrahams, L/Cpl. C.	62
Abrahams, Pte. C.	342
Abrahams, Sgt. D.	335
Abrahams, Pte. D.	355
Abrahams, L/Cpl. E.	306
Abrahams, Cpl. Israel	277
Abrahams, Pte. J.	140
Abrahams, Pte. J.	116
Abrahams, L/Cpl. Jack	277
Abrahams, Pte. J. (St. John's Amb.)	277
Abrahams, Sgt. J. (R. West Kents)	310
Abrahams, Q/M/S. Julius	277
Abrahams, Phys-Trg. Inst.	277
Abrahams, Pte. H.	363
Abrahams, Pte. L. and friend	291
Abrahams, Pte. Sid	277
Abrahams, Pte. S.	318
Abrahams, Pte. S.	110
Abrahams, Sgt. T.	149
Adler, Pte. B.	320
Adler, Rfn. D.	243
Aitkin, Pte. A.	346
Aizen, Pte. M.	330
Albert, Cpl.	320
Albert, Pte. D.	243
Alexander, Dvr. B.	338
Alexander, Pte. H.	333
Alexander, Cyclist J.	335
Alexander, Sgt. L.	342
Allan, Pte. S.	355
Altman, Pte. D.	346
Ampel, Pte. S.	325
Annenberg, 2nd A/M. J.	298
Annenberg, Spr. J.	318
Annenberg, L/Cpl. M.	136
Annenberg, Pte. M.	136
Ansell, Sgt. L. G.	126
Appleton, Pte. A.	310
Apter, Pte. J.	354
Aronheim, 1st A/M. A. D.	334
Aschman, Sig. J.	310
Aschman, Sgt. R.	342
Ash, Pte. B.	16
Ash, Sgt. M.	310
Ash, Pte. M.	338
Ash, Pte. V. (R.A.S.C.)	24
Ash, Gnr. V. (R.F.A.)	28
Asher, W/O. Cecil	235
Ashfield, L/Cpl. J.	306
Bader, Pte. C.	314
Bader, Pte. H.	212
Bader, Dvr. M.	311
Bader, Pte. M.	314
Bagola, L/Cpl. Lo.	86
Baker, Pte. A.	22
Baker, Pte. A.	267
Baker, Gnr. H.	246
Baker, Pte. J.	350
Baker, Orderly J. C.	124
Baker, L/Cpl. L.	334
Baker, Sgt. M. (D.C.M., M.M.)	32
Bakesef (3 brothers)	8
Barnard, Sig. A.	357
Barnard, Pte. A.	23
Barnard, Pnr. H. J.	182
Barnard, Tpr. L.	310
Barnard, Gnr. P. L.	333
Barnard, L/Cpl. S. D.	140
Barnes, Pte. J.	23
Barnett, Pte. A.	108
Barnett, Pte. (later Lt.) H.	335
Barnett, Pte.	71
Barnett, 2nd A/M. H.	338
Barnett, Pte. L.	55

	Plate		Plate		Plate
Barnett, Cpl. M.	152	Bernstein, Pte. M. B.	5	Boss, Pte. P.	333
Barnett, Pte. M.	240	Bernstein, Pte. S.	87	Boss, Pte. R.	194
Barnett, Pte. M.	108	Bernstein, Cpl. S. H.	165	Boss, Pte. S.	24
Barnett, Pte. N.	108	Bernstein, Pte. W. S.	143	Bowick, Pte. P.	156
Barnett, Pte. S. C.	48	Bernstine, Dvr. H.	310	Bowson, Pte.	344
Barnett, Pte. S.	108	Bernstock, Pte. H. C.	69	Boyars, L/Cpl. G.	294
Barnett, Art. Mech. W.	267	Bernstock, Pte. J. H.	116	Braham, L/Cpl. M.	50
Baroque, L/Cpl. D.	31	Bernstock, Pte. P.	69	Braham, Pte. S.	28
Barsofsky, Pte. M.	357	Berstein, A/M.	53	Brandt, Pte. L.	149
Bass, Pte. A.	154	Bes, Sgt. C. L. D.	342	Breckman, 2nd A/M. R.	127
Bass, Pte. A.	173	Besso, 3rd A/M. E.	199	Breslau, Rfn. H.	190
Baswitz, Sgt. J.	143	Besso, Pte. V.	141	Bresler, Pte. J.	272
Beards, Sgt.-Major M. B. (D.C.M.)	59	Bierman, Pte. A.	174	Brest, Cpl. R.	154
Beck, Pte. J.	199	Birinberg, Pte. L.	351	Brightman, Pte. H.	251
Beck, Cpl. S.	148	Black, L/Cpl. B.	110	Brill, Pte. S.	350
Becker, Pte. N.	124	Black, Sig. P.	212	Brilliant, Tpr. H.	48
Beenstock, Pte. A. E.	235	Black, Sgt. M. (M.M.)	195	Brilliant, Rfn. N. M.	166
Behrman, L/Cpl. A.	115	Blasenstein, C/S/M. C.	230	Brock, C/P/O. M. J. E.	37
Bein, Pte. H.	189	Blatkin, A/M. D.	48	Brod, Rfn. H.	168
Beirman, Pte. M.	320	Blatt, Sig. M.	235	Brodie, Pte.	283
Bell, Pte. A.	242	Blendis, Pte. A.	87	Brodie, Pte. A.	272
Bell, Pte. J.	310	Blendis, Spr. S.	87	Bromberg, Pte. A.	271
Benjamin, Rfn. B.	16	Blendis, Pte. S.	87	Bronkhorst, Sgt. M. J.	317
Benjamin, Pte. H.	36	Blitstein, L/Cpl. H.	363	Brookstone, Pte. M.	162
Benjamin, Sgt. J.	16	Blitz, Pte. A.	189	Brotman, Pte. H.	156
Benjamin, L/Cpl. L.	22	Block, Sgt. B.	86	Brown, Pte. A.	344
Benjamin, Spr. M.	350	Block, Pte. J.	246	Brown, Pte. C.	131
Benjamin, Pte. N.	280	Blom, Cpl. H.	110	Brown, Pte. H.	7
Benjamin, Pte. S.	146	Blom, Cpl. H.	170	Brown, Gnr. H.	342
Benjamin, Engineer S.	330	Bloom, Pte. A.	24	Brown, Cpl. J.	131
Bennett, Cpl. J.	315	Bloom, Pte. A.	168	Brown, L/Cpl. J.	335
Bennett, Pte. J.	247	Bloom, Spr. C.	188	Brown, Pte. J.	143
Benoliel, Pte. M. H.	115	Bloom, Pte. J.	168	Brown, Tpr. K.	124
Bentata, Pte. J.	22	Bloom, A/B. L.	6	Brown, Pte. M.	191
Bentata, L/Cpl. A. L.	247	Bloom, Dvr. L.	162	Brown, Pte. S.	240
Bentwitch, Pte. I. H.	348	Bloom, 2nd A/M. M.	154	Burnett, Pte. D.	324
Benzimra, Pte. I.	212	Bloom, Pte. P.	188	Bye, Pte. A.	154
Berg, Pte. E.	80	Bloom, A/B. S. G.	202	Cahm, Cpl. S.	166
Berg, Sig. M.	323	Bloomfield, Pte. N.	363	Caller, Pte. P.	224
Berg, Cpl. R.	48	Blumenthal, Pte. J.	24	Campbell, Spr. J.	206
Berg, 2nd/Cpl. S.	323	Blush, Pte. L.	116	Cansino, Sgt. D.	235
Bergman, Pte. P.	22	Boas, Pte. B. S.	346	Caplin, Pte.	130
Berlinsky, Pte. J.	48	Boekbinder, Pte. H.	335	Carey, Pte. J.	363
Berman, Pte. J.	317	Bokofski, Pte. J.	230	Carlish, Pte. A.	116
Berman, Dvr. J. (Lieberman)	148	Boock, Dvr. E.	314	Carlish, Dvr. A.	303
Berman, Pte. L.	154	Boock, Pte. H.	314	Carmel, R/S/M. J.	86
Berman, Pte. M.	333	Boock, Sgt. L. M.	342	Carpel, Dvr. L.	143
Berns, L/Cpl. J.	346	Boock, L/Cpl. S.	314	Carr, Cpl. S.	333
Bernstein, Gnr. E. M.	165	Boodson, Sgt. D.	190	Carson, Pte. A.	130
Bernstein, Cpl. F.	50	Boorman, Pte. A.	306	Carson, Pte. V. G.	363
Bernstein, Pnr. H.	342	Boorman, Cpl. D.	22	Cash, Pte. H.	350
Bernstein, Sgt. J.	264	Boorman, Cpl. H.	247	Casher, Gnr. C.	303
Bernstein, Pte. L.	5	Boorman, Gnr. S.	355	Cassal, Cpl. H.	144
		Borisoff, Pte. M.	330	Chalfen, Sig. B.	318
		Bortnoski, Pte. L. J.	22	Chalfen, A/M. I.	166
		Boskin, 1st A/M. A.	348	Chapin, Pte. D.	147

INDEX TO THE ILLUSTRATIONS

Name	Plate
Chart, Pte. L.	174
Chelen, Pte. M. J.	350
Chelminski, Pte. M.	334
Christie, Pte. M.	344
Citron, Pte. L.	153
Clements, 1st A/M. W. J.	127
Cohen, Pte.	154
Cohen, L/Cpl. A. (London Regt.)	286
Cohen, Pte. A. (Northumberland Fus.)	30
Cohen, Pte. A. (K.R.R.C.)	158
Cohen, Pte. A. (R.A.S.C.)	303
Cohen, Pte. A.	342
Cohen, S/Sgt. B.	298
Cohen, Sgt. C. W.	24
Cohen, Rfn. D. (K.R.R.C.)	53
Cohen, Rfn. D. (London Regt.)	116
Cohen, Pte. D. (R. Fus.)	124
Cohen, Pte. D.	190
Cohen, Spec. Constable Dave	226
Cohen, Pte. D.	338
Cohen, Pte. D. (Gloucester Regt.)	355
Cohen, Pte. E. (M.M.)	148
Cohen, 2nd A/M. E.	355
Cohen, Spr. H.	48
Cohen, Pte. H.	153
Cohen, Pte. H. (R.A.S.C.)	247
Cohen, Pte. H.	348
Cohen, Dvr. H. (R.A.S.C.)	351
Cohen, Pte. I.	307
Cohen, Spr. J.	162
Cohen, Gnr. J.	188
Cohen, 1st A/M. J.	246
Cohen, C/Q/M/S. J.	298
Cohen, Rfn. J.	330
Cohen, Rfn. J.	363
Cohen, Pte. J. G.	37
Cohen, Pte. L. (R.A.S.C.)	16
Cohen, Rfn. L.	310
Cohen, Pte. L. (R. Fus.)	350
Cohen, Sgt. L. C.	349
Cohen, Pte. M. (M.M.)	115
Cohen, Pte. M. (Labour Corps)	173
Cohen, Spr. M.	298
Cohen, Pte. N.	334
Cohen, Sgt. O.	188
Cohen, Sgt. P.	338
Cohen, Pte. P. (R. Fus.)	62
Cohen, P. (R.N.A.S.)	302
Cohen, Pte. P. (38th R. Fus.)	165
Cohen, Pte. P.	348
Cohen, 2nd A/M. R.	263
Cohen, Rfn. S.	140
Cohen, Pte. S. (Middlesex Regt.)	127
Cohen, Pte. S.	247
Cohen, Pte. W.	206
Coleman, Pte. H.	62
Coleman, Spr. S.	349
Collier, Tpr.	153
Collins (Shapiro), Rfn. D.	280
Collock, L/Cpl. H.	355
Collock, Pte. L.	355
Conlan, Pte. A.	318
Conley, Pte. L.	206
Constad, Pte. H.	116
Conway, Rfn. S.	251
Cooper, Pte. J.	363
Cooper, Pte. M.	271
Cornblatt, A/B. S.	302
Cornofsky, Bdr. L.	310
Cornofsky, A/M. L.	342
Cossick, Sgt. S.	140
Costa, Sgt. A.	348
Cotton, Pte.	154
Couplan, Cpl. A.	346
Couplan, Bdr. P.	346
Cowan, Cpl. M.	62
Cowen, Cpl. Ellis	86
Cowen, Sig. F.	127
Cramer, L/Cpl. A.	303
Crash, Pte. M.	162
Cremer, Pte. S.	24
Cremer, Pte. S.	62
Cristol, Pte. J.	143
Crom, Pte.	283
Cross, Pte. J.	359
Crugman, Pte.	16
Cruley, Pte. G.	318
Da Costa, Pte. J.	306
Dainow, Sgt. M.	16
Dainow, Pte. M.	181
Dalmer, Pte.	363
David, Sub/Conduc. M. S.	320
Davies, Pte. A.	312
Davies, Pte. H.	181
Davis, Pte.	71
Davis, L/Cpl. A.	350
Davis, Pte. A.	320
Davis, Pte. C. M.	108
Davis, Pte. D. G.	108
Davis, L/Cpl. H.	294
Davis, Pte. H.	344
Davis, Pte. J.	247
Davis, Pte. J. (R. Fus.)	271
Davis, Pte. J.	306
Davis, R/Q/M/S. R. G.	108
Davis, Cpl. S.	124
Davis, Pte. S.	110
Davis, Bdsmn. S.	348
Defries, L/Cpl. J.	251
Defries, Pte.	283
De Friend, Stoker I.	302
De Friend, C/S/M. M.	335
Delow, L/Cpl. L.	348
Dembofsky, Pte. H.	173
Dembofsky, Pte. J.	331
Diamond, Pte. B.	333
Diamond, L/Cpl. C.	303
Diamond, Pte. J.	124
Diamond, Gnr. L.	191
Diamond, Cyclist W.	28
Diesner, Cpl. E.	28
Dobkin, Rfn. M.	135
Doodeward, Pte. (R.A.M.C.)	30
Doodeward, Pte. S.	55
Dorfman, Cpl. M.	350
Dragovitch, Pte.	306
Drapkin, Pte. H.	306
Dresner, Sgt. J. M.	363
Driver, R/S/M.	148
Driver, Gnr. J.	346
Drukker, Cpl. J.	344
Dubens, Sgt. V.	350
Dudinsky, Rfn. J.	141
Dufresnoy, Pte. A.	173
Dyson, Pte. J.	333
Edelberg, Sgt. E.	6
Ehrlich, Sgt. M.	247
Elias, Tpr. A.	247
Ellen, Cpl. S.	344
Ellis, Dvr. A.	30
Ellis, Pte. A. M.	126
Ellis, Pte. B.	191
Ellis, R/Q/M/S. E. E.	126
Ellis, L/Cpl. W.	247
Eprile, Pte. C. J.	126
Epstein, Spr.	53
Epstein, Pte. B.	346
Epstein, L/Cpl. H. (D.C.M.)	239
Epstein, Pte. P.	334
Epstein, Pte. S.	227

	Plate		Plate		Plate
Epstein, Pte. S.	334	Frankel, Pte. I.	267	Garcia, Bdr. H.	318
Erlstein, Pte. H.	346	Franklin, 2nd A/M. A.	6	Gardner, Pte. M.	16
Esterson, 2nd A/M. E.	168	Franklin, Pte. E.	334	Garson, Pte. J.	317
Ezekiel, Spr. E. S.	28	Franklin, Cpl. H.	6	Gatoff, Pte. M.	115
Fainer, Dvr. S.	124	Franklin, Pte. H.	30	Gavson, Pte. M.	351
Fairman, Pte. W.	30	Franklin, Pte. I.	188	Gavson, Pte. M.	116
Falk, Pte. E.	333	Franklin, Pte. J.	165	Gelberg, Pte. J. L.	127
Farra, A/M. J.	154	Franks, Pte. H.	126	Gembitski, Pte. H.	48
Fay, Cpl. A.	333	Franks, Pte. H.	267	Gembitski, 2nd A/M. S. H.	48
Feigenbaum, Pte. I.	8	Franks, C/P/O/ L.	31		
Feigenbaum, Pte. J.	8	Franks, P/Officer L.	306	Gepstein, Pte. S.	330
Feldman, Pte.	71	Franks, Sgt. M.	126	Gerber, Pte. J.	331
Feldman, Pte. D.	144	Fraser, Pte. E. M.	342	Gershon, Gnr. J.	28
Feldman, Pte. E.	350	Freedland, Pte. H.	355	Gershon, Cpl. S. S.	263
Feldman, Pte. J.	240	Freedman, Pte.	71	Gershon, Pte.	331
Feldman, Pte. J.	320	Freedman, Gnr. A.	8	Gerson, Gnr. S.	307
Feldman, Senior W/O. J.	331	Freedman, Spr. A.	333	Gerson, Cpl. V.	126
Felix, Pte. A.	191	Freedman, Pte. B. J.	191	Gilbert, Pte. E.	363
Feltbrodt, Rfn. H.	338	Freedman, Dvr. C.	124	Gilbert, Pte. J.	190
Ferber, Pte. C.	344	Freedman, Spr. D.	147	Gilbert, C/S/M. J. (D.C.M.)	226
Ferber, Pte. H.	344	Freedman, Dvr. H.	136		
Ferber, Pte. M.	344	Freedman, Spr. H.	322	Gilbert, Seaman J.	235
Fern, Rfn. J.	55	Freedman, Pte. H.	359	Gilder, L/Cpl. B.	140
Fieldman, Pte. P.	306	Freedman, Gnr. H.	363	Gillis, L/Cpl. L.	86
Fine, Pte.	71	Freedman, Sig. I.	8	Gillis, Cpl. L.	298
Fine, Pte. P.	346	Freedman, L/Cpl. J.	355	Ginsberg, Dvr. L.	318
Fine, Pte. W.	248	Freedman, Pte. J. (C.M.C.)	24	Ginsberg, S/Sgt.	331
Fineberg, Pte. S.	335			Ginsberg, Trumpr.	331
Finesilver, Pte. A.	346	Freedman, Pte. J.	86	Ginsberg, Gnr. S.	22
Finkle, Pte. J.	136	Freedman, Pte. J.	127	Glass, A/M.	53
Finklestein, Rfn. H.	87	Freedman, Pte. L.	335	Glass, Spr. J.	191
Finklestone, Spr. J.	152	Freedman, 2nd A/M. L.	348	Glassen, Spr. B.	140
Finn, L/Cpl. H.	236	Freedman, Pte. R.	338	Gleek, Pte.	71
Finn, L/Cpl. J.	236	Freedman, Pte. S. (R.A.S.C.)	127	Glick, Pte. I.	148
Fischer, Pte.	306			Gluckman, Pte. B. (later Lt.)	108
Fisher, Pte. D.	16	Freedman, Pte. S.	136		
Fisher, Pte. W.	271	Freeman, Pte.	71	Gluckman, Pte. L.	108
Fishman, Pte. W.	335	Freeman, Sgt./Major B.	62	Gluckman, Pte. S.	108
Fitelson, Pte. A.	126	Freeman, Pte. J.	191	Gluckstein, Sgt. C.	166
Flack, Pte. I.	320	Freeman, Pte. L.	350	Gluckstein, Pte. R.	140
Flatow, Cpl. F. W. (M.M.)	346	Freeman, Dvr. M.	350	Glynn, L/Cpl S. (M.M.)	226
		Freshwater, Pte. N. (D.C.M.)	313	Gnessen, Pte. M.	126
Flatow, Pte. L. W.	298			Gobowsky, Pte.	71
Fleisig, L/Cpl. C. S. (R.E.)	152	Fried, Pte. H.	149	Godansky, Pte. A.	354
		Friedlander, Sgt. B.	130	Godfrey, Tpr. A.	348
Fleisig, Sig. D.	260	Friedlander, L/Cpl. R.	298	Godfrey, Pte. T.	148
Fleisig, Sgt. M. (M.M. and Bar)	260	Friedlander, Pte. R.	116	Goldberg, Pte. ("Judeans")	152
		Friedlander, Pte. R.	242		
Fleisig, Sgt. S.	260	Friedlander, Cpl. W. J.	331	Goldberg, Pte. A.	162
Fligelstone, A/M. D.	127	Frieze, Gnr. N.	355	Goldberg, Cpl. A.	264
Fligelstone, L/Cpl. J.	127	Fry, Pte. E.	22	Goldberg, Pte. G.	22
Fligelstone, Pte. P.	127	Fwyansofsky, Pte. M.	62	Goldberg, Pte. J.	338
Ford, Stoker M.	165	Galician, Pte. S. E.	351	Goldberg, C/Q/M/S. J.	144
Fordanski, Pte. J.	247	Galizer, Pte. H.	325	Goldberg, Pte. J.	330
Forstein, Tel. P.	152	Gallewski, Spr. M.	307	Goldberg, Cpl. M.	263
Forster, L/Cpl. G.	152	Gantz, Dvr. J.	162	Goldberg, Sgt. M. J.	62

INDEX TO THE ILLUSTRATIONS 625

	Plate
Goldberg, Pte. W.	140
Goldburgh, Pte. B. H.	140
Golding, L/Cpl. A.	22
Goldman, Pte. A.	116
Goldman, Pte. H.	156
Goldman, Pte. H.	317
Goldman, Pte. J.	178
Goldman, Spr. J.	227
Goldman, Pte. L.	136
Goldman, Pte. S.	355
Goldsmith, Pte. A.	162
Goldsmith, Pte. L.	190
Goldsmith, Pte. P.	340
Goldstein, Pnr. A.	136
Goldstein, Pte. D. H.	235
Goldstein, A/M. H.	191
Goldstein, Sgt. J. D.	246
Goldstein, Dvr. M.	162
Goldstein, Cpl. M.	40
Goldstein, Pte. M.	48
Goldstein, Pte. M.	166
Goldstein, Pte. S.	5
Goldstein, Pte. S.	338
Goldstein, Sig. S. M.	140
Goldstein, Sig. W.	330
Goldston, L/Cpl. D.	174
Goldstone, Pte. A.	363
Goldstone, Pte. B.	126
Goldstone, Sgt. I.	7
Goldstone, Pte. M.	310
Goldstuck, Pte. N.	116
Goldsweig, Pte. M.	353
Goldwater, Dvr. D. L.	335
Golgowsky, Pte. B.	224
Golgowsky, Pte. H.	48
Gompertz, Pte. A.	263
Good, Sgt. J.	194
Goodman, Pte. H.	162
Goodman, Rfn. H.	191
Goodman, Pte. J.	227
Goodman, Spr. J.	294
Goodman, Sgt. J. H.	87
Goodman, Pte. L.	318
Goodman, Pte. M.	156
Goodman, Pte. M. A.	7
Goodman, Sgt. R.	116
Goodman, Pte. R. (R.A.M.C.)	87
Goodman, Pte. S.	147
Goodman, Tpr. S.	190
Goodman, Cadet S. F.	87
Goodyear (Goldstein), Pte. A.	147
Gordon, Pte. A.	156
Gordon, Pte. E.	320
Gordon, Pte. M.	246
Gordon, L/Cpl. T.	335
Gordon, Pte. V.	188
Gorovitch, L/Cpl. S.	16
Gosschalk, Gnr. M.	165
Gotlob, Pte. M.	320
Gottlieb, Pte. E.	212
Gottlieb, Pte. N.	188
Gould, Pte. H.	330
Green, Pte. A.	62
Green, Pte. A.	87
Green, Pte. G.	330
Green, Pte. H.	127
Green, 2nd A/M. H.	40
Green, Pte. I.	251
Green, Bdr. J.	24
Green, L/Cpl. L.	22
Green, Pte. M.	212
Green, Dvr. M.	334
Green, Tpr. M.	348
Green, Cpl. S.	251
Green, Pte. S.	318
Greenberg, Pte. J.	330
Greenstone, Pte. A.	330
Greenwald, Pte. R.	136
Grossman, Pte. D.	162
Groszhip, Pte. L.	131
Grouchkowsky, Cpl. M. (D.C.M.)	354
Grover, Pte. R.	298
Guterman, Cpl. J.	344
Haagerman, Sgt.	283
Haft, Sgt. J.	169
Halper, Pte. I.	147
Hamani, Sig. E. E.	48
Hamani, Pte. E. E.	136
Hamani, Pte. V.	239
Hardy, Tpr. D.	191
Harman, Dvr. A.	251
Harman, Pte. R. B.	149
Harris, Rfn. D.	170
Harris, 2nd A/M. F.	110
Harris, Rfn. H. (London Regt.)	126
Harris, Pte. H.	306
Harris, Pte. H.	310
Harris, Sig. H. M.	28
Harris, Sgt. J.	116
Harris, Pte. J.	140
Harris, Pte. J. (R.A.M.C.)	263
Harris, Rfn. J.	342
Harris, Cpl. J.	333
Harris, Dvr. L.	320
Harris, Cpl. M.	31
Harris, R/S/M. M.	271
Harris, Pte. M.	318
Harris, Sgt. M.	344
Harris, Cpl. M. J. H.	16, 136
Harris, Spr. R.	6
Harris, Gnr. R.	272
Harris, Pte. S.	355
Harris, Pte. S. (1/15 London Regt.)	6
Harris, Pte. S. (R.A.M.C.)	124
Harris, Pte. S.	174
Harris, Pte. S.	189
Harris, Pte. S.	263
Harris, Pte. W.	62
Harris, Pte. W.	191
Harrison, Cadet A.	188
Hart, Pte. H.	136
Hart, Dvr. J. (R.F.A.)	69
Hart, Cpl. J.	243
Hart (Assenheim), Gnr. P.	142
Hart, Pte. S.	267
Hayman, Sgt. H. M.	263
Hayman, Sgt. H. S.	263
Hayward, Pte. E. (Abrahams)	148
Hecker, Pte. M.	124
Heilbuth, Tpr. C. F.	310
Henochsberg, Sgt. E. N.	110
Henry, Sgt. C. A.	110
Henry, Pte. J.	342
Henry, Sgt. M.	24
Hernberg, L/Cpl. D.	191
Hernberg, S/Sgt. N.	110
Hershman, Dvr. J.	116
Herwald, Pte. M.	348
Hess, Pte. A. J.	263
Hess, Pte. F. J.	263
Hess, Tpr. H.	263
Hickman, Pte. L.	174
Hillier, Pte. L.	16
Himmel, Sgt. H. (M.M.)	298
Himmel, Pte. J.	307
Himmel, Pte. L.	307
Himmel, Gnr. M.	307
Hoffmann, Pte. A.	335
Hollander, Cpl. H.	271
Holtz, L/Cpl. L. A.	126
Holzberg, Pte. S.	243
Hooten, Q/M/S.	71
Hopper, Tpr.	153
Horevitz, Pte. J.	322
Horevitz, Rfn. M.	322
Horevitz, Sig. N.	243
Horowitz, Sgt. H.	294
Horowitz, Sgt. N.	294
Hunter, Pte. A.	153

INDEX TO THE ILLUSTRATIONS

Name	Plate
Hyams, Sgt. B.	263
Hyams, Bdr. B.	283
Hyams, Spr. D.	294
Hyams, Pte. M.	55
Hyams, Sgt. M.	344
Hyamson, Dvr. S.	124
Hyman, A/Sgt. C.	87
Hyman, H. (R.N.)	239
Hyman, Pte. J.	147
Hyman, Pte. L.	30
Idels, Pte. H.	199
Ikin, Pte. J. E.	29
Isaacs, Pte. A.	246
Isaacs, Rfn. B.	15
Isaacs, S/Sgt. C. (M.S.M.)	141
Isaacs, Dvr. D.	69
Isaacs, L/Cpl. D. S.	110
Isaacs, Pte. E.	29
Isaacs, Pte. F.	28
Isaacs, Sgt. H.	86
Isaacs, Pte. H. L.	286
Isaacs, Pte. H. M.	32
Isaacs, Rfn. V. A.	141
Israel, Gnr. G.	141
Israel, Pte. H. F.	110
Israel, Tpr. L.	199
Israels, 3rd A/M. A.	6
Israels, 2nd A/M. H.	6
Izen, Gnr. H.	166
Jacks, Dvr. A.	170
Jacobi, Cpl. H.	351
Jacobs, Q/M/S. A.	5
Jacobs, Q/M/S. A.	200
Jacobs, Sgt. A.	203
Jacobs, Spr. B.	236
Jacobs, Ldg. Stoker B.	302
Jacobs, Pnr. C. H.	156
Jacobs, Gnr. C. N.	166
Jacobs, Pte. D.	190
Jacobs, Pte. F.	7
Jacobs, Dvr. F. R.	295
Jacobs, L/Cpl. G. J.	120
Jacobs, Pte. G. L.	181
Jacobs, Tpr. H.	55
Jacobs, A/C/S/M. H.	117
Jacobs, Cpl. H.	189
Jacobs, 2nd A/M. H.	211
Jacobs, Gnr. H. (R.F.A.)	272
Jacobs, Pte. I.	23
Jacobs, Flight/Sgt. J. (M.M.)	168
Jacobs, Pte. J.	236
Jacobs, Pte. J. D.	246
Jacobs, Sgt. L.	259
Jacobs, 2nd A/M. M.	236
Jacobs, Gnr. M.	236
Jacobs, Cpl. M. J. (R. Fus.)	184
Jacobs, Pte. M. J. (D.C.M.)	286
Jacobs (Pickholtz), Pte. S.	149
Jacobs, Rfn. S.	236
Jacobs, Pte. S.	307
Jacoby, L/Cpl. H.	259
Jay, Pte. A.	202
Jaye, Sgt. J. E.	307
Jeffrey, Pte. H.	248
Jeffreys, Gnr. H.	259
Jeffreys, Rfn. J.	259
Jellen, Bandsman B.	246
Jellen, S/S/M. J.	28
Jenkins, R/S/M. M.	110
Jewell, Q/M/S. Joel	28
Joels, Pte. A.	307
Joels, Pte. L.	178
Joels, Pte. S.	307
Joffe, Pte. J.	5
Johnson (Bards), Tpr. H.	147
Johnson, Sgt. V.	37
Jonas, L/Cpl. L. M. (M.M.)	178
Joseph, Pte. C. S.	272
Joseph, Dvr. E.	286
Joseph, Sgt. J.	7
Joseph, L/Cpl. L.	211
Joseph, L/Cpl. L.	322
Joseph, Pte. M.	286
Joseph, Sgt. R.	156
Joseph, Spr. S.	178
Joseph, Pte. S.	290
Joseph, Pte. V.	286
Josephs, Pte. B.	190
Josephs, Pte. B.	117
Josephs, Cpl. E.	246
Judah, Pte. S.	146
Kain, Rfn. I.	200
Kaplinsky, Pte. L.	166
Kapshut, Pte. K.	246
Karo, C/S/M. M.	203
Kass, Rfn. A.	259
Kauffmann, Rfn. C.	178
Kauffmann, Pte. J. B.	28
Kay, Rfn. M.	295
Keesing, 1st Class Stoker J.	302
Kempner, Pte. A. A.	340
Kempner, Cpl. S. A.	156
King, Pte. H. J.	156
King, Sgt. I.	298
Klein, Sgt. P.	37
Kleinfield, Pte. C.	202
Kleinfield, Cpl. D.	195
Knopf, Pte. D.	142
Koftoff, Sgt. A. S.	7
Kolasky, Pte.	71
Kollenberg, Pte. D.	195
Koopchick, Pte. J.	212
Korn, 2nd A/M. S.	351
Kosky, Pte. C.	286
Kosky, Pte. F.	322
Kosky, Sgt. M.	322
Kosky, Leading A/C. W.	322
Kosminsky, Pte. C. S.	340
Kossick, Pte. J.	188
Kramer, L/Cpl. J.	212
Krantz, Cpl. A.	340
Krebsman, Spr. B. J.	120
Kreemer, Pte. J. (M.M.)	23
Kremner, Pte. S.	166
Krisman, A/M.	53
Kroftchinsky, Pte. L.	108
Krohmlick, Pte. A.	156
Kronenberg, Pte. A.	240
Kronenberg, Pte. I.	239
Kronenberg, Cpl. N. (M.M.)	240, 165
Kurtz, Pte. D. M.	200
Kutchinsky, Pte. A.	259
Kutchinsky, Pte. S.	259
Lackmaker, W/Op. S.	62
Lance, Pte. M.	195
Lanchin, Pte. H.	153
Landanski, Pte. J.	248
Landaw, C/Q/M/S. M.	166
Landstone, Spr. A.	224
Lang, Pte. A.	311
Langdon, L/Cpl. W.	239
Lasker, Sgt. L. J.	334
Latner, Pte. B.	178
Lattner, Pte. R.	359
Lawgorse, Dvr. D.	199
Lawrence, L/Cpl. A.	80
Lawson, Pte. A.	148
Lawson, (Cohen, N.) Pte. T.	149
Lazarus, Pte.	71
Lazarus, Pte. C. M.	166
Lazarus, Pte. H. R.	286
Lazarus, Rfn. I.	194
Lazarus, Pte. M.	182
Lazarus, Cpl. M. D.	286
Lazarus, Pte. P.	190
Lazarus, Cpl. R.	80
Lazarus, Pte. S. C.	190
Lazarus, Pte. S. J.	212
Lazarus, Pte. S. J.	290

INDEX TO THE ILLUSTRATIONS

	Plate	
Leavey, Bdr. G.	- 239
Lelyveld, L/Cpl. L.	- 239
Lenbie, Pte. E.	- 295
Lennenberg, Pte. H.	- 37
Leon, Sgt. A.	- 203
Leon, Bdr. B. M.	- 203
Lerman, Pte. S.	- 211
Leslie, L/A/C. A.	- 7
Leslie, Tpr. L. A.	- 323
Leslie, L/Cpl. M.	- 7
Leslie, Bdr. R.	- 323
Lesnie, L/Cpl. J. H.	202
Lessar, Pte. H.	- 181
Lessman, Pte. S.	- 116
Levene, Pte. I.	- 40
Levene, Pte. J.	- 230
Levene, Pte. M.	- 173
Levene, Rfn. M.	- 178
Levene, Pte. S.	- 149
Leveson, Pte.	- 283
Levey, Pte. H.	- 294
Levi, Pte. B.	- 340
Levi, Gnr. M. H.	- 349
Levin, Pte. L.	- 23
Levine, Pte. A.	- 173
Levine, Pte. A.	- 243
Levine, Pte. B.	- 59
Levine, Pte. H.	- 189
Levine, Pte. H.	- 340
Levine, A/C/I. H.	- 351
Levine, Pte. J.	- 59
Levine, Dvr. J.	- 351
Levine, Pte. L.	- 59
Levine, Pte. M.	- 325
Levine, Gnr. S.	- 315
Levinger, Pte. J.	- 50
Levinson, Cpl. D.	- 312
Levinson, Sgt. H.	- 55
Levison, Gnr. A.	- 40
Levison, Pte. S.	- 40
Levitski, Pte. M.	- 349
Levy, Pte.	- 283
Levy, Pte.	- 71
Levy, Pte.	- 71
Levy, A/M. A.	- 59
Levy, Pte. A.	- 134
Levy, Gnr. A. N.	- 340
Levy, L/Cpl. A. S.	- 50
Levy, S/M. B.	- 117
Levy, Cpl. B.	- 282
Levy, Cpl. B. H.	- 108
Levy, Pte. C.	- 143
Levy, C/Q/M/S. E.	- 169
Levy, Pte. E.	- 178
Levy, Pte. H. E.	- 115
Levy, Pte. I.	- 55
	Plate
Levy, Pte. I.	- 153
Levy, Cpl. I. J.	- 108
Levy, Pte. I. J.	- 212
Levy, Cpl. I. J.	- 264
Levy, Pte. J.	- 24
Levy, Pte. J. (23rd Middlesex Regt.)	- 50
Levy, Rfn. J.	- 170
Levy, Pte. J. (R. Fus.)	- 182
Levy, Pte. J.	- 243
Levy, Pte. J.	- 311
Levy, Gnr. J. A.	- 29
Levy, Pte. L. (Witwatersrand Rfls.)	- 7
Levy, Rfn. L.	- 80
Levy, Pte. L.	- 116
Levy, Pte. L.	- 243
Levy, Pte. M.	- 357
Levy, Rfn. M.(K.R.R.C.)	37
Levy, Pte. M.	- 116
Levy, 3rd Writer M.	- 306
Levy, Pte. M.	- 230
Levy, Pte. M.(R.A.M.C.)	280
Levy, Pte. M.	- 336
Levy, Pte. N.(R.A.M.C.)	317
Levy, Gnr. P.	- 190
Levy, Dvr. Raphael	- 267
Levy, Dvr. R.	- 199
Levy, Pte. R.	- 349
Levy, Dvr. S. (R.A.S.C.)	24
Levy, Pte. S.	- 282
Levy, A/B. S. R.	- 174
Lewbitz, L/Cpl. A.	- 80
Lewin, Cpl. W. (M.M.)	53
Lewis, Pte. A.	- 351
Lewis, 2nd A/M. A.	- 212
Lewis, L/Cpl. A.	- 206
Lewis, 1st A/M. A.	- 272
Lewis, Pte. A. A.	- 242
Lewis, Pte. B.	- 235
Lewis, Stoker B.	- 239
Lewis, Pte. B. (R. Fus.)	247
Lewis, A/Cpl. B.	- 318
Lewis, Sgt. H. (D.C.M.)	37
Lewis, Pte. H.	- 152
Lewis, Pte. I.	- 195
Lewis, Pte. I.	- 240
Lewis (R. Lapidoth), Pte. J.	- 147
Lewis, L/Cpl. M. (M.M.)	130
Lewis, A/B. N.	- 240
Libstein, Pte. H. S.	- 181
Libstein, Rfn. M.	- 243
Lightstone, Pte. G.	- 30
Lion, S/Sgt. H. M.	- 194
Lion, Cpl. O. S.	- 158
	Plate
Lipman, Rfn.	- 251
Lipman, Pte. A. E.	- 178
Lipman, Pte. J.	- 165
Lipowsky, Des. Rider L.	158
Lippman, Pte. T. M.	- 295
Lipton, Cyclist B.	- 280
Lipton, Pte. S.	- 307
List, Pte. S.	- 115
Littman, Pte.	- 283
Littman, Pte. J.	- 110
Littman, Pte. S.	- 80
Lizar, Pte. L.	- 206
London, Pte. M.	- 37
Loveguard, Gnr. A.	- 280
Loveguard, Pte. N.	- 29
Loverman, Sgt. D.	- 246
Lowne, Dvr. A.	- 165
Lubel, L/Cpl. J.	- 168
Lubrinsky, Pte. M.	32, 88
Lunzer, Pte. A.	- 242
Lunzer, L/Cpl. F.	- 242
Lunzer, Pte. R.	- 242
Lupinsky, Tpr. W.	- 28
Lyons, L/Cpl. B.	- 116
Lyons, Pte. B.	- 153
Lyons, S/S/M. B.	- 272
Lyons, Pte. L.	- 351
Lyons, Pte. L. S.	- 202
Lyons, L/Cpl. M.	- 154
Lyons, L/Cpl. P.	- 298
Lyons, Pte. S.	- 115
Magnus, Pte. J.	- 23
Malinsky, Pte.	- 211
Malinsky, 1st A/M. E.	- 286
Malles, Pte. J.	- 230
Mallin, Pte. M.	- 141
Mander, Gnr. S.	- 202
Mann, L/Cpl. A.	- 5
Marchant, A/M. M.	- 272
Marchinski, Gnr. I.	- 152
Marcus, Pte. B.	- 294
Marks, Pte.	- 71
Marks, Pte. C. M.	- 120
Marks, L/Cpl. D.	- 153
Marks, Pte. H.	- 141
Marks, Sgt. J. (M.M.)	148
Marks, Stoker J.	- 168
Marks, L/Cpl. J.	- 231
Marks, Cadet L. C.	- 298
Marks, Pte. M.	- 131
Marks, Pte. N.	- 29
Marks, Pte. S. (R.A.M.C.)	- 15
Marks (Levitski), Seaman S. J.	- 149
Markson, Rfn. B.	- 267

	Plate	
Markson, Cpl.-Dr. D.	- 267
Markson, Sig. L.	- 267
Marsden, S/Sgt. F. M.	- 298
Martin, Pte. D. A.	- 15
Martin, Cpl. J.	- 50
Martyn, Pte. H.	- 152
Martyn, Pte. J.	- 152
Marvin, D.	- 239
Mason, Pte. P.	- 312
Mason, L/Cpl. S.	- 311
Matofsky, Pte.	- 71
Matthews, Pte. A.	- 264
Matthews, Pte. S.	- 117
Matz, Sgt. A.	- 182
Matz, Pte. P.	- 7
Mazarkoff, Gdsman. A.	- 6
Mazarkoff, Gdsman. S. H.	188
Mazarskoff, Cpl. M.	- 6
Medwediner, Pte.	- 71
Melnick, Spr.	- 53
Melnik, Pte. A.	- 317
Mendelsohn, Gnr. M.	- 264
Mendes, Tpr. H. J.	- 142
Mendes, Pte. M.	- 181
Mendoza, Cpl. E.	- 251
Menkin, Spr. C. S.	- 53
Menkin, S/Sgt. H. (D.C.M.)	- 53
Mentel, Pte. E.	- 286
Meropolsky, Gnr. A.	- 351
Mersky, Pte.	- 230
Mervish, Sgt. G.	- 243
Meyer, Pte. R. V.	- 141
Meza, Pte. A. de	- 226
Michael, Rfn. G.	- 144
Michael, Pte. H. (Manchester Regt.)	- 271
Michael, Sgt. J.	- 144
Michael, 1st A/M. J.	- 144
Michael, Cpl. M.	- 144
Michaels, Pte. H. (R. Fus.)	- 86
Michaels, Sgt. H.	- 144
Michaels, L/Cpl. J.	- 190
Michaelson, 1st A/M. A.	168
Michaelson, Sgt. H.	- 294
Mickler, W/T. L.	- 140
Middleman, L/Cpl. H.	- 325
Middleman, Pte. S.	- 203
Millem, Pte. M.	- 7
Miller, Pte. A.	- 246
Miller, Pte. B.	- 295
Miller, Seaman E.	- 149
Miller, A/B. E.	- 320
Miller, Pte. H.	- 50
Miller, Pte. H.	- 181
Miller, Pte. H.	- 211
Miller, Pte. I.	- 37
Miller, Dvr. J.	- 194
Miller, Pte. L.	- 181
Miller, Pte. T.	- 325
Millingen, Sgt. C. P.	- 231
Milman, L/Cpl. B.	- 156
Miron, L/Cpl. G. (M.M.)	199
Mistofsky, Senior W/O. J.	- 331
Mistofsky, Senior W/O. M.	- 331
Mivansky, Pte. J.	- 86
Molin, Pte. A.	- 353
Mordecai, Tpr. A.	- 264
Mordecai, Pte. A. B.	- 267
Mordecai, Pte. B.	- 50
Mordecai, Pte. R.	- 357
Moreberg, Pte. A.	- 231
Morris, Pte. A.	- 231
Morris, Bdr. A.	- 280
Morris, Pte. A.	- 311
Morris, Rfn. A. B.	- 53
Morris, Gnr. B.	- 134
Morris, Pte. C. L.	- 243
Morris, Pte. G.	- 226
Morris, Cpl. H.	- 286
Morris, Tpr. H. I.	- 37
Morris, Pte. J. (London Regt.)	- 87
Morris, 2nd A/C. J.	- 202
Morris, Pte. J.	- 212
Morris, Sgt. J.	- 260
Morris, Sgt. J. L. (M.M.)	340
Morris, Pte. L. G.	- 130
Morris, Rfn. M.	- 170
Morris, Pte. M.	- 226
Morris, Ldg. A/M. N. G. M.	- 29
Morris, Pte. S.	- 88
Morris, Pte. S.	- 271
Moscovitch, Pte. S. (R. Fus.)	- 259
Moscovitch, Pte. S. (N'land Fus.)	- 259
Moscow, C/Q/M/S. H.	- 175
Moses, A/M. C. S.	- 59
Moses, Cpl. E.	- 53
Moses, Cpl. H. N.	- 174
Moses, Pte. J.	- 40
Moses, Pte. J. (Queen's)	159
Moses, Pte. L.	- 152
Moss, Rfn. C.	- 325
Moss, Rfn. D.	- 325
Moss, Sgt. L.	- 130
Moss, Sgt. M.	- 30
Moss, Pte. S.	- 307
Moss, Sgt. S. D.	- 37
Most, Sig. A.	- 168
Musikansky, Ldg. A/C. A.	- 291
Myers, Bglr.	- 130
Myers, Tpr. A.	- 134
Myers, Tpr. A.	- 194
Myers, Arm./Sgt. E.	- 88
Myers, Pte. I.	- 231
Myers, Cpl. J.	- 134
Myers, Sig. J. L.	- 15
Myers, Gdsman. L.	- 134
Myers, Pte. L.	- 259
Myers, Pte. N.	- 148
Myers, L/Cpl. R.	- 248
Myers, A/B. S.	- 62
Myerson, Sig. A.	- 156
Nathan, Pte. A.	- 267
Nathan, Sgt./Major A. J.	203
Nathan, A. L.	- 55
Nathan, Pte. B. (R. Welsh Fus.)	- 23
Nathan, Pte. E.	- 340
Nathan, Sgt. (later Lt.) G.	- 23
Nathan, Bdr. G.	- 23
Nathan, Pte. J. B.	- 23
Nathan, Sgt. L. (M.M.)	116, 295
Nathan, S/Major M.	23, 313
Nathan, Pte. R.	- 130
Nathan, Bdr. V. J.	- 203
Needle, Pte. M.	- 7
Needle, Pte. M.	- 116
Nelson, 1st A/M. R.	- 178
Newman, Pte. M. (Middlesex Regt.)	203, 294
Nieberg, L/Cpl. A.	- 295
Nigon, Pte. B.	- 23
Nordwind, Gnr. R.	- 248
Norton, Rfn M.	- 170
Norton, Pte. M.	- 295
Novinski, Sig. S.	- 202
Ognall, Pte. H. H.	- 202
Olswang, Pte. M.	- 295
Onwood, Pte. L.	- 30
Opitz, Gnr. H.	- 203
Ossofsky, Pte. H.	- 203
Palley, Pte. S.	- 357
Pam, Pte.	- 357
Park, Pte. H.	- 272
Park, Pte. L.	- 188
Park, L/Cpl. S.	- 188
Parkes, Pte.	- 71
Pasch, Sig. W/O. A. H.	31

INDEX TO THE ILLUSTRATIONS

Name	Plate
Pearlman, A/M. A.	165
Pearlman, Pte. H. E.	294
Pearlman, Pte. R.	259
Pemzeck, Pte. M.	295
Penn, Gnr. Jacob	322
Perkoff, Rfn. B.	174
Perlmutter, Pte. H.	174
Perlmutter, Cpl. M.	174
Perlmutter, 2nd Cpl. N.	174
Perlstone, Pte. J.	247
Pescoff, Pte. A.	141
Pezaro, Tpr. B.	203
Pezaro, Rfn. S. A.	340
Pezim, Spr. S.	280
Phillips, Spr.	315
Phillips, L/Cpl. A.	88
Phillips, Sgt. A.	236
Phillips, Pte. A.	295
Phillips, Bdr. B. G. (M.M.)	184
Phillips, Pte. E.	236
Phillips, Pte. H.	182
Phillips, Pte. I.	195
Phillips, 1st A/M. J. T.	162
Phillips, Pte. L.	184
Phillips, Pte. M.	182
Phillips, Seaman M.	338
Phillips, A/M. N.	235
Phillips, L/Cpl. S. F.	202
Phillips, Cadet S. S.	236
Pick, Pte. M.	231
Pickles, Cpl. M.	184
Pieters, Rfn. J.	170
Pinner, Sgt. M.	15
Pinto, L/Cpl. C.	280
Pinto, Pte. R.	260
Pitch, Pte. J.	340
Plotsky, Pte. M.	178
Podgus, A/M. W.	259
Polack, Sgt. M. M.	116
Pollack, Rfn. S.	170
Porter, 1st Class Clerk E.	318
Porter, Rfn. P.	203
Portrait, Pte. S.	271
Posner, L/Cpl. G.	184
Potock, Pte. M.	315
Press, Tpr. A.	15
Pressman, 1st Cl. Stoker J.	302
Price, Pnr. P.	141
Prooth, C/S/M. J. (D.C.M.)	200
Pyser, Rfn. L.	323
Quesky, Pte. H.	108
Quesky, Pte. J. N.	108
Quesky, Scout S.	108
Rae, L/Cpl. J.	32
Raekind, Pte. S.	117
Raisman, Bdr. M.	271
Raitiff, Pte. J.	184
Rapaport, Pte. A.	282
Rapaport, L/Cpl. E.	173
Rapaport, Pte. J.	315
Rapaport, Pte. L.	189
Rapp, Tpr. L.	311
Rapp, Cpl. S.	311
Raymon, Cpl. M.	224
Reece, Pte. H. J.	230
Reece, Pte. S.	336
Reed, Pte. R.	115
Rees, Sgt. T.	282
Reuben, O/R/Sgt. D. B.	86
Reuben, Pte. S. I.	146
Rich, Pte.	134
Rich, Dvr. C. J.	336
Richman, Pte. M.	143
Roberts, Pte. H. I.	231
Roberts, L/Cpl. J.	194
Robin, Pte. A.	143
Robinson, Sgt. E. H.	115
Robinson, Pte. H.	226
Robinson, A/M. L.	235
Rome, C/S/M. S. and friend	74
Rosansky, Spr. A. J.	230
Rose, Pte.	71
Rose, Rfn.	251
Rose, Pte. A.	349
Rose, Gnr. H.	115
Rose, A/B. J.	235
Rose, Pte. S.	120
Roseberg, Spr. M.	117
Roseberg, Pte. M.	264
Rosen, Gnr. M. L.	325
Rosenbaum, Sgt. M.	231
Rosenberg, Pte. A.	315
Rosenberg, Tpr. C.	311
Rosenberg, Pte. D.	295
Rosenberg, Pte. H.	80
Rosenberg, Pte. I.	357
Rosenberg, Pte. L. (R. Welsh Fus.)	15
Rosenberg, Pte. L.	141
Rosenberg, Drm. S.	32
Rosenberg, Pte. S.	200
Rosenbloom, Pte. A.	184
Rosenbloom, Pte. I.	184
Rosenbloom, Pte. J.	184
Rosenbloom, Pte. L.	184
Rosenbloom, Pte. L.	311
Rosenbloom, Bdr. S.	168
Rosenfield Pte. D.	200
Rosenfield, Fitter L.	88
Rosenheim, Pte. J.	117
Rosenstern, Pte. M.	282
Rosenthal, Pte. H.	336
Rosenthal, Pte. I.	29
Rosenthal, Pte. S.	340
Roskin, 1st A/M. E.	264
Ross, Pte. B.	336
Rothberg, Pte. H.	130
Rothstein, Gnr.	211
Rubens, Pte. S.	134
Rubenstein, Pte. H.	59
Rubenstein, Pte. J.	194
Rubenstein, Pte. L.	134
Rubenstein, Pte. N.	15
Rubin, Pte. H.	349
Rubinski, Pte. M.	134
Rubinstein, Sig. L.	314
Rubinstein, Pte. Myer	314
Rudolf, Rfn. L. J.	224
Rudolf, Rfn. M. E.	224
Rutner, Cpl.	282
Safferty, C/Q/M/S. A.	120
Sagman, L/Cpl. J.	242
Sagman, Pte. J.	290
Sakovitch, Pte. P.	143
Salberg, Pte. S. G.	88
Salmon, Pte. B.	116
Salmon, Dvr. B.	231
Salmon, Pte. D.	224
Salmon, Sig./Cpl. J.	182
Salmon, Sig./Cpl. J.	325
Salmon, Rfn. S.	170
Salom, Cpl. B.	15
Salomons, Arm./S/Sgt. A. G.	29
Saltiel, Sig. J. F.	143
Sams, Sgt. S. L.	117
Samson, Cpl. J. E. R.	211
Samson, Pte. S.	53
Samson, A/M. S.	264
Samuel, Pnr. D. L.	264
Samuel, C/S/M. Inst. of Mus. J. M.	182
Samuel, Pte. L. M.	264
Samuel, Pte. M.	59
Samuel, Sgt. M.	141
Samuel, Pte. M. R.	120
Samuel, L/Cpl. S.	243
Samuels, Pte. A.	211
Samuels, Pte. B.	55
Samuels, Cpl. D.	323
Samuels, Pte. E.	323
Samuels, Pte. H. E.	311
Samuels, Pte. J.	224

INDEX TO THE ILLUSTRATIONS

Name	Plate
Samuels, Pte. M. (London Regt.)	32
Samuels, Rfn. S.	15
Samuels, Pte. S.	131
Sandall, Pte. R.	165
Sanders, Pte. J.	311
Sandown, Pte. M. L.	53
Sankerwitz, Pte. A.	120
Sankerwitz, Pte. J.	282
Sankerwitz, L/Cpl. P.	120
Sapper, Cpl. M.	357
Sarna, Pte. E.	158
Sasieni, Cpl. D.	230
Sasofsky, Pte. L.	134
Saul, Pte. I.	88
Saunders, Pte. A.	153
Saunders, Pte. H.	322
Saville, Sig. A.	134
Saxton, L/Cpl. L. H.	194
Scalnick, Pte. B.	173
Scareff, Cpl. L.	199
Scarminsky, Pte.	71
Scharff, Pte. S.	227
Schatz, Pte. C.	315
Schatz, Pte. H.	282
Schein, L/Cpl. A.	195
Schein, Pte. S.	336
Schiff, Cpl. A.	282
Schneider, A/M. A.	154
Schneider, Tpr. E.	325
Schneiderman, Pte. H.	80
Scholefield, Cpl.	23
Schonberg, Pte. M.	117
Schonfield, Cpl. L.	271
Schottlander, S/M. S. (M.M.)	272
Schwartz, Pte. J. L.	317
Schwartz, Pte. S.	206
Schweitzer, Dvr. S.	116
Scott, Tpr. A.	144
Seeley, Pte. A.	242
Seftor, Pte. B.	206
Segal, Pte. L.	30
Seigar, Gnr. H.	115
Selby, Bdr. M.	224
Seltzer, Pte. L.	271
Serano, Pte. M.	282
Shane, Pte. S.	168
Shanthall, Pte. G.	130
Shapero, Pte. D.	184
Shapero, Pte. L. (M.M.)	184
Shapero (W. Dixon), Pte. M.	149
Shapero, Pte. S.	184
Shapiro, Pte. S.	206
Shapiro, Pte. S.	317
Sharp, Pte. L.	324
Sharp, Cpl. L. M.	31
Sherek, Rfn. H.	80
Sherman, Gnr.	283
Sherman, Pte. A.	206
Shern, Rfn. J.	170
Sherwin, L/Cpl. M. (M.M.)	294
Shiers, Tpr. A.	248
Shiers, Pte. H.	248
Shiers, Pte. J.	248
Shilony, Pte. J.	130
Shinberg, Pte. W.	59
Shinburg, L/Cpl. N. A.	59
Shindler, Cpl. E.	200
Shindler, Cpl. P.	200
Shinegold, Asst./Vict.	324
Shneerson, Sgt. M.	227
Shneiders, A/M. H.	29
Shorts, Pte. A.	211
Shtitzer, Pte. B.	291
Shtitzer, Sgt./Instr. D.	291
Shtitzer, Sgt./Instr. P.	291
Sidney, Pte. R.	290
Silver, Cpl. E.	59
Silverfield, Pte. H.	131
Silverman, Pte.	71
Silverman, Pte. B.	147
Silverman, Dvr. H.	115
Silverman, Pte. L.	231
Silverman, Pte. L.	336
Silverman, Pte. M.	182
Silverman, Cpl. M.	200
Silverman, Pte. P.	182
Silverman, Bdmn. S. S.	80
Silverstone, Sgt. H.	80
Silverstone, 1st. Cl. Stoker H.	302
Simler, Dvr. J.	317
Simmons, Pte.	331
Simmons, Pte. I.	195
Simmons, Stoker J.	302
Simmons, Pte. R.	116
Simnock, L/Cpl. A.	230
Simon, Pte. S.	55
Simons, A/B. P.	314
Simons, Pte. S. (M.M.)	314
Simons, L/Cpl. W.	50
Simpson, Sig. A. E.	282
Singer, Dvr. A.	248
Singer, Rfn. H.	251
Singer, Pte. J.	158
Singer, Pte. J.	272
Singer, Gnr. L.	143
Sloman, Pte. W.	48
Slomovitch, Pte. S.	80
Smith, Sgt. Issy (V.C.)	1
Smith, Pte. H. S.	282
Smole, Sgt. B.	59
Snell, L/Cpl. A.	144
Snell, Pte. J.	144
Snider (Kushneider), Pte. N.	147
Sniders, Pte. P.	88
Snipper, Pte. A.	227
Snipper, Pte. I.	227
Snipper, Dvr. S.	227
Solet, Pte. I.	87
Solomon, Pnr. A. (R.E.)	29
Solomon, Cpl. A.	235
Solomon, Tpr. A.	349
Solomon, Pte. A. H.	211
Solomon, Dvr. J.	230
Solomon, Pte. S.	149
Solomon, Pte. S. (R. Fus.)	242
Solomon, Sgt. S. N.	130
Solomons, Pte. C.	359
Solomons, Pte. F.	173
Solomons, Bdr. G.	206
Solomons, Pte. H.	239
Solomons, Pte. I.	239
Solomons, Pte. J.	23
Solomons, Pte. J. (R. Fus.)	86
Solomons, Gnr. J. (R.F.A.)	280
Solomons, Pte. M. (Lab. Coy.)	325
Solomons, Gnr. M.	349
Solomons, Pte. S.	149
Solomons, A/B. S.	235
Somers, Pte. B.	322
Somers, Pte. M. R.	322
Spector, Pte. N.	240
Speigel, Cpl. D.	357
Spero, Pte. J.	116
Spevack, Pte.	71
Spevack, Rfn. J.	53
Spicker, Pte. F.	116
Spiegal, Pte. M.	134
Spielman, Sgt. I.	158
Spielmann, Sgt. F. I.	199
Spiers, Pte. H.	206
Spiers, Pte. H. W.	202
Spilg, Pte. G. (M.M. and Bar)	283
Spilg, Pte. R.	283
Spiro, Pte. I.	6
Spurling, Pte. S. R.	280
Spyer, R/S/M. S. M.	86
Stahl, Cpl. F.	315
Stahl, Cpl. M. E.	315
Stall, Sgt. M.	230

INDEX TO THE ILLUSTRATIONS

	Plate
Stanley, Cpl. H. (M.M.)	202
Stomachien, 1st A/M. M.	158
Stone, Pte. M.	336
Stringer, A/M. A.	158
Stroom, Pte.	71
Strump, Sgt. R.	158
Strump, 2nd Clerk S. M.	158
Stungo, Cpl. S.	158
Suchard, Pte. S.	174
Sugarman, Pte. D.	88
Sugarman, A/B. H.	8
Sugarman, Sig. H.	162
Sugarman, Pte. L. (Queen's)	8
Sugarman, Pte. L.	147
Sugarman, Pte. L.	226
Sugarman, Sgt. S.	143
Sultag, Pte. P.	50
Swatski, Pte. L.	315
Symons, Rfn. L.	32
Symons, Pte. L.	158
Symons, Pte. M. H. V. (M.M.)	320
Tabatsky, Bugler S.	182
Tannenbaum, Pte. S.	357
Tarnopolsky, Pte. A.	15
Tasch, Pte. E. E.	210
Tasch, Pte. M. A.	210
Taube, Dvr. S. de	23
Taylor, Pte. D. I.	146
Taylor, Gnr. J.	200
Taylor, Gnr. M. (R.G.A.)	120
Taylor, Pte. M.	195
Taylor, Cpl. S.	6
Taylor, Pte. S.	182
Teacher, Drmr. A.	357
Terry, P.	239
Terry, P. (R.N.A.S.)	302
Theomin, Sgt. E. M.	120
Thomas, Cpl. C.	334
Timbler, Pte. J.	55
Tobias, Sig. N.	141
Toff, Seaman A.	40
Toff, S/Sgt. E. J.	40
Toff, L/Cpl. G.	189
Toff, Cpl. J. (M.M.)	40
Toff, Special Con. J.	40
Toomin, Tpr. M.	195
Tragen, Pte. I.	312
Travis, A/Cpl. H.	165
Turitz, Pte. J.	195
Tytz, Pte. J.	23
Ullman, 2nd A/M. L.	31
Umlauf, C/S/M. S.	40

	Plate
Valentyne, Pte. P.	5
Valinsky, Pte. A.	303
Valinsky, Pte. B.	303
Valinsky, Pte. I.	303
Valinsky, Pte. M.	303
Valinsky, Pte. Percy	303
Valinsky, Pte. Phil.	303
Valinsky, Pte. S.	303
Vallentine, Sgt. P.	117
Vallentine, Pte. P. (R.A.M.C.)	117
Vallentine, Flight/Cadet P. (R.A.F.)	117
Van Cleff, Pte.	71
Vancliffe, Pte. L.	211
Vellemun, Pte. H.	189
Verblowki, Pte. I.	227
Verblowky, Pte. H.	142
Verblowsky, Sgt. D.	87
Vitofsky, Sig. B.	195
Vos, Cpl. S. J.	32
Voss, Pte. A.	199
Vyner, Pte. G.	211
Wacholder, Cpl. H. M.	334
Walters, Pte. S.	264
Wansker, Sgt. H.	248
Wansker, Cpl. R.	248
Warchawski, Cpl. W.	280
Ward, Pte. G.	224
Warshawsky, Sgt. J. H.	194
Watson, S/Major R. M.	5
Wattsman, Pte. J.	349
Waxman, Pte. M.	148
Wedell, Pte. F.	311
Weinberg, L/Cpl. A.	32
Weinberg, Gnr. D.	88
Weinberg, 2nd A/M. G.	88
Weinberg, Pte. L.	15
Weinberg, C/P/O. L.	302
Weinberg, Pte. M.	50
Weinberg, Cpl. R.	88
Weinberg, Pte. W.	336
Weiner, Rfn. S.	194
Weinrich, Pte. E.	148
Weinstein, S/Sgt. A.	168
Weisbloom, L/Cpl. P. D.	199
Weitzenfeld, Pte. M.	206
Wender, Pte. I.	315
Wender, Pte. L.	240
Werbeloff, Cpl. L.	199
Wesansky, Cpl. M.	349
White (Weiss), Pte. J. (V.C.)	1
White, Cpl. L. (M.M.)	280

	Plate
Whyl, A/M. J.	334
Wilkins, Pte. J.	141
Williams, Cpl. J.	182
Wilson, Gnr. F.	108
Wise, Pte. C.	325
Witonski, Sgt. A. N.	317
Witowsky, Pte.	71
Wolf, Pte. S.	322
Wolfensohn, Sgt. M. J.	152
Wolfson, Pte. J.	357
Wolfson, Pte. M. (R. Scots)	40
Wolfson, Gnr. M.	267
Wolfyansky, Pte. H.	23
Wood, Tpr. H.	8
Wood, Tpr. I.	8
Wood, Tpr. M.	8
Wood, Tpr. S.	8
Woodburn, Sgt. L.	144
Wooler, Dvr. L.	317
Woolf, Pte.	71
Woolf, Pte. A.	317
Woolf, Pte. D.	248
Woolf, Bdr. E.	50
Woolf, Pte. F. A.	224
Woolf, Dvr. H.	336
Woolf, Pte. J. (Welch Regt.)	336
Woolf, Pte. J. (King's Liverpool Regt.)	336
Woolf, Sgt. M.	194
Woolf, Pte. R.	32
Woolf, Pte. S.	349
Woolfe, Pte. D. L.	224
Woolfe, L/Cpl. E.	55
Woolfe, Pte. E.	181
Woolfish, Pte. M.	315
Wurms, Pte. A.	32
Wurms, Pte. J.	29
Zang, Pte. C.	231
Zealander, Sig. J.	120
Zeitlin, L/Cpl. J.	200
Zeitlin, Ldg.-Seaman S. W.	37
Zeitlin, Pte. W. S.	200
Zeizeran, Gnr. D.	29
Zimmerman, L/Cpl. P.	231
Zimmerman, Pte. W.	32
Zissman, Cpl. G. G. (D.C.M.)	120
Zucker, Pte. H.	23
Zucker, C/P/O. S. E.	330
Zuckerman, Pte. D.	5
Zussman, Pte.	71

INDEX TO THE ILLUSTRATIONS

CHAPLAINS, OFFICIATING CLERGYMEN, NURSES, ETC.

Name	Plate
Abrahams, Mrs.(R.R.C.)	68
Abrahams, Rabbi M.	201
Altman, Mrs. O. A.	328
Alvarez, Mrs. B.	326
Alvarez, Miss Betty	70
Alvarez, Miss R.	327
Aschman, Nurse B.	326
Ashberry (Annenberg), Staff Sister E.	326
Baker, Sister Bessie	326
Baker, Miss C.	326
Bamberger, Miss Muriel	328
Barnett, The Rev. A. (S.C.F.)	129, 146, 215, 216, 249, 319, 321
Barnett, Mrs.	68
Barnett, Mrs.	71
Bischoffsheim, Mrs.	70
Bolton, Mrs. Madge	328
Borgzinner, Miss	68
Brodie, The Rev. I. (C.F.)	43
Cohen, Rev. A.	201
Cohen, Rabbi B. I.	201
Cohen, Rev. E. M. D.	253
Cohen, Mrs.	71
Cohen, Miss Esther	328
Colman, Mrs.	68
Dangton, Rev. J. (C.F)	177, 215, 265
Davidson, Mrs. F. (M.B.E.)	68, 108
Davidson, Mrs. F.	108
Davis, Miss E.	71
De Bear, Miss	71
Falk, Rev. L. A. (C.F.)	337
Frampton, Rev. S.	201, 296
Frankenthal, Rev. I. (C.F.)	234, 312
Franks, Mr. Henry	352
Franks, Mrs. Queenie	326
Franks, Miss Rosie	326
Freedman, Rev. D. I.	258
Froomberg, Nursing Sister	326
Gaster, Dr. A. (M.D.)	70
Geffen, Rev. L. (C.F.)	146, 161, 167, 223
Goldston, Rev. N. (S.C.F.)	201
Gollop, Rev. M. (C.F.)	258
Grajewsky, Rev. S. (C.F.)	31, 234, 312
Greenberg, Mrs. L. J.	327
Greisbach, Miss	68
Halford, Miss Hilda	328
Harris, Miss	68
Harris, Miss Hetty	328
Henry, Miss	68
Herring, Orderley L.	327
Hertz, Dr. J. H. (Very Rev. the Chief Rabbi)	Page ix, 249
Hess, Mrs. F.	70
Hess, Miss M.	327
Hirsch, Rev. D.	64, 160, 345
Hirschland, Miss	68
Hirschland, Miss D.	327
Hudson, Miss K.	327
Hyams, Mr.	68
Isaac, Mrs. H. (Miss A. Woolf)	153
Isaacs, Miss	68
Jacobs, Mr. A. J.	108
Jacobs, Miss C.	108
Jacobs, Mr. H. H.	108
Jacobs, Mr. J. D.	108
Jacobs, Miss R. R.	108
Jerevitch, Rev. H.	201
Jonas, Mrs. M. J.	326
Joseph, Miss	68
Joseph, Miss J. (O.B.E.)	68, 71
Kerman, Miss	71
Kopenhagen, Miss	71
Kreemer, Miss Rose	23, 326
Lazarus, Miss H.	68
Lazarus, Miss L.	68
Lazarus, Miss M.	68
Leveson, Rev. Capt.	5
Levin, Rev. W. (C.F.)	201
Levine, Rev. N. (C.F.)	160, 161
Levy, Mrs.	68
Levy, Rev. E. M. (C.F.)	31, 159
Lieberman, Rev. B. B. (C.F.)	108
Lipman, Miss	71
Lipson, Rev. S.	56, 64, 201, 257
London, Miss C.	327
Lowenthal, Mrs.	71
Lowenthal, Dr. L.	71
Lubin, Miss,	71
Ludlow, Miss A.	70
Lyons, Mrs. Julia	70
Magnus, Miss Katz	70
Marks, Miss A.	68
Marks, Miss G.	68
Marks, Mrs. Julian S.	326
Marsden, Mrs. (R.R.C.)	68, 108
Marsden, Mr.	108
Marx, Mrs. M.	327
Mendel, Miss	71
Middleton, Miss	71
Morris, Chaplain L.	53
Myers, Mrs. J. W.	326
Nahon, Miss Jamilla	328
Nathan, Miss Jeanette	70
Oppenheimer, Sister F.	327
Phillips, Mrs. B.	70
Phillips, Rev. J.	201
Phillips, Mrs. Rosa	328
Pinto, Miss Rosie	260
Pinto, Miss Sophie	260
Platnauer, Mrs. Rose	328
Price, Rev. N. L. (C.F.)	290, 337
Prince, Lady	71
Rains, Miss	68
Rains, Miss Rose	70
Rapaport, Adolph	327
Regensburg, Miss	68
Ritch, Miss	71
Ritch, Miss S.	71
Robinson, Mrs.	71
Roe, Miss Nita	328
Rose, Miss Ella	70
Rosenthal, Miss	68
Rosenstein, Miss Irene	327
Salom, Miss	68
Samuels, Miss	68
Samuels, Miss H.	71
Selby, Miss Rose	328
Shandel, Rev. H.	109, 167, 201, 242, 266, 299
Simmons, Mrs.	68
Simmons, Rev. V. G. (C.F.)	329, 249, 198, 201
Singer, Mrs.	68
Speelman, Miss Violet	70
Stember, Mrs.	68
Tayer, Mr. A. J.	30
Trenner, Miss F. J.	272
Van Gelder, Miss G.	327
Wasserzug, Rev. D.	201
Weil, Rabbi C.	223
Weiner, Sister S.	71, 326
Weizman, Dr. C.	97
Woolf, Miss	71
Woolf, Miss K. A.	326
Woolfe, Rev. L.	201

INDEX TO THE ILLUSTRATIONS

JEWISH WAR MEMORIALS ABROAD

	Plate
Specimen of the Jewish Headstone to be erected by the Imperial War Graves Commission	49

GRAVES

	Plate
Bamberger, Capt. C. W., R.E., Bethune Cemetery	65
Bender, L/Cpl. J., 8th Roy. Fus., Houplines, nr. Armentieres	209
Benjamin, Sub/Lieut. N. H., R.N.D., Aubigny	41
Brown, Pte. H., 2nd Roy. Sussex Regt., St. Omer Cemetery	209
Danziger, 2nd/Lt. C. W. J., 21st Manchester Regt., Achiet Le Grand	9
Davis, Capt. L. J., 1/19th London Regt., High Wood, nr. Albert	273
Davis, Pte. N., 10th Roy. Fus., Berles-au-Bois	9
de Pass, Lt. F. A., the first Jewish V.C., Bethune Cemetery	65
Fine, Lt. S., R.A.F., Belgium	41
Ginsburg, Pte. D., 13th London Regt., Estaires	41
Goldberg, L/Cpl. H., 21st K.R.R.C., Ploegstreet	9
Hart, Capt. C. L., 2nd West Riding Regt., Colincamps	41
Herman, 2nd/Lt. R., 1st Canterbury Regt., New Zealanders, Armentieres	273
Isaacs, Pte. L., 1st King's Liverpool Regt., Cambrin	41
Levy, Pte. H. M., 8th Australian Inft., Estaires Cemetery	273
Lewis, Rfn. H. R., 1/12th London Regt., Poperinghe Cemetery	65
Lurie, Pte. I., 4th S. African Inft., Ploegstreet Cemetery	273
Markus, Pte. H., 19th Canadian Inft., Vormezeele, nr. Ypres	273
Simon, Capt. E. C., Lancashire Fus., Millencourt Cemetery, nr. Albert	209
Smith, Pte. H., 2nd S. Staffs. Regt., Cambrin	41
Stander, Spr. B., R.E., Lillers	41

JEWISH WAR MEMORIALS AND ROLLS OF HONOUR

SYNAGOGUES, CLUBS, SCHOOLS, ETC.

Achei Brith and Shield of Abraham Friendly Societies	21
Brighton Synagogue	217
Cape Town Synagogue, South Africa	145
Edinburgh Congregation	25
Edinburgh Synagogue, Memorial in the Cemetery	121
Glasgow Synagogue	57
Liverpool Hebrew School	121
Liverpool Old Hebrew Congregation	185
Liverpool Synagogue, Princes Road	121
London:	
Bayswater Synagogue, W.	121
Central Synagogue, W., Memorial Candelabrum	358
Central Synagogue, W., Roll of Honour	360
Hampstead Synagogue, N.W.	33
Liberal Jewish Synagogue, Willesden, N.W.	113
New West End Synagogue	2
St. John's Wood Synagogue, N.W.	361
Stepney Jewish Lads' Club, E.	217
West London Synagogue, Upper Berkeley Street, W.	13
Manchester, Higher Broughton Synagogue	105
Sydney, Australia, Great Synagogue	17

MEMORIALS

Comor, L/Cpl. M., 1st Newfoundland Regt., Blackpool	289
Ezra, Capt. D., R.G.A., Calcutta	39
Franks, 2nd/Lt. B. A., Central Synagogue	47
Jacobs, 2nd/Lt. D., Willesden Cemetery, London	25
Jacobs, Sub/Lt. T., Willesden Cemetery, London	25
Langdon, Capt. Wilfred M., 10th Cheshire Regt.	47
Mendelsohn, Tpr. F., S. African M.T.	25
Myer, 2nd/Lt. Denzil A., East London Synagogue	121
Samuel, Lt. Gerald George, East London Synagogue	121
Stern, 2nd/Lt. L. H., East London Synagogue	39

INDEX TO THE ILLUSTRATIONS

"JUDEANS," 38th–40th ROYAL FUSILIERS, PALESTINIANS, ZION MULE CORPS, ETC.

AT HOME

	Plate
Royal Fusiliers, 38th Battalion:	
In Saltash Depôt	23
Q.M.Staff, Saltash Camp	74
Group of Men from Liverpool	75
N.C.O.s of, Plymouth, 1918	77
Band of, Plymouth, 1918	77
Concert Party at Plymouth	78
Football Team, Plymouth, 1918	78
Three Sergeants of	85
Group of	85, 95
Officers of, Plymouth, 1918	89
At Plymouth, 1917	91, 92, 93
Lt.-Col. J. H. Patterson, D.S.O., and Recruits, Plymouth, 1917	94
In Camp	96
Royal Fusiliers, 38th and 40th Battalions:	
Group at Saltash Depôt	95
Private at Saltash Depôt	291
Royal Fusiliers, 40th Battalion:	
Depôt	79
Group at Saltash Depôt	95, 277
Zion Mule Corps:	
Soldiers from, transferred to 3/20th London Regt.	353, 354

ABROAD

	Plate
Royal Fusiliers, 38th Battalion:	
Musketry Staff, Palestine, 1918	76
At dinner, Egypt	82
Group of, in Palestine	83
Group of Scouts in Palestine	83
Entraining at Cairo for Palestine Front, 1918	84
Regimental Military Police	84

	Plate
Royal Fusiliers, 39th Battalion:	
Officers of, Helmieh Camp, Cairo, August, 1918	90
Royal Fusiliers, 40th Battalion:	
Group in Palestine	74
Open-Air Service, Sgt. Ruben officiating	81
Signalling Section	82
Recruiting Officers, Tel-Aviv, 1918	97
Dr. C. Weizmann presenting Scroll of Law and Flag to Recruits of, Tel-Aviv, 1918	97
Recruits of:	
(1 and 2) The raw material at Kantara, Egypt; (3) A month later in Camp, at Tel-Aviv, Jaffa	98
(1) After two weeks; (2) The Guard; (3) Lesson in Bayonet Fighting	99
On Shore of Mediterranean, nr. Jaffa	100
At the Sports	100
Musketry Staff, Palestine	101
Medal presented to Recruits of, designed at the Belazel School of Art, Jerusalem	102
Badge of	102
Earliest Routine Orders issued in Palestine to Recruits of	103, 104
Recruits for (Palestine Colonists), Palestine, 1918	123
On Active Service	169
Sgt. J. Morris at Pyramids, Egypt	260

PHOTOGRAPHS TAKEN IN FRANCE AND BELGIUM

	Plate
Very Revd. The Chief Rabbi (Dr. J. H. Hertz) on visit to G.H.Q., France, 1915	249
Adler, Revd. M., D.S.O., and Group, Rouen, May, 1915	116
and Revd. V. G. Simmons, C.F., nr. Arras	249
Barnett, Revd. A., S.C.F., and 1st Inft. Labour Coy., Middlesex Regt., France	146
and Group of Soldiers, Lille Synagogue, 1918	216
and Revd. V. G. Simmons, C.F., on Active Service	249

	Plate
Barnett, Revd. A., S.C.F., and Jewish Soldiers in Douai, 1919	319
and Jewish Soldiers in Synagogue, Lille, 1919	321
Geffen, Revd. L., C.F., and Jewish Soldiers in France	146
and Group of R.A.F., with Major J. Kemper	161
and Group of Royal Engineers, Calais	167
and Rabbi C. Neil, with Soldiers at Boulogne, 1919	223
Group in France	161

INDEX TO THE ILLUSTRATIONS

	Plate
Jewish Soldiers in Lille	129
in Belgium	283
Jewish Soldiers, Middlesex Regt., in France	274
Labour Company in France	283
Levy, Revd. E. M., C.F., and Jewish Soldiers in France	159
Levine, Revd. N., C.F., and R.A.F. men, France	161
Price, Revd. H. L., C.F., and Group in France	290
Silverman, Revd. H., C.F., and Jewish Soldiers in France, 1918	304

PHOTOGRAPHS TAKEN IN INDIA, MESOPOTAMIA, PALESTINE, ITALY, SALONICA, MALTA, GIBRALTAR, ETC.

	Plate
Baghdad, Group of Soldiers, New Year, 1918	219
Bangalore, Group of Soldiers, Passover, 1920	46
Bombay, Jewish Division, St. John's Ambulance Brigade, four members of	146
Group of Soldiers, Passover, 1918	216
Calcutta, Group of Soldiers, New Year, 1918	14
Group of Soldiers, Passover, 1918, at House of Mr. D. Ezra	253
Egypt, Group of Royal Welch Fus. in	283
India:	
Jewish Soldiers, 9th Middlesex Regt., 1914	181
Jewish Soldiers in	208
Leeds Jewish Soldiers in	208
Italy, Jewish Soldiers, 1/7th Roy. Warwick Regt. in	167
Jerusalem:	
Anzac and British Regts., Jewish Soldiers of, in, Pentecost, 1918	81
British Units, Passover, 1918	101
Outside Walls of, Jewish Soldiers, Passover, 1918	233
In, Jewish Soldiers, Passover, 1918	234
Malta:	
Group, 1915	30
1/4th London Regt., December, 1914	225
Presentation of Medals of the O.B.E. to Lt. L. Shneerson and Lt. J. Davidesco, Palestine Jews, by Major-General Hodgson	73
Salonika, Jewish Soldiers in	159
Sialkot, Punjab, Jewish Officers and Men, Passover, 1917	278

PHOTOGRAPHS TAKEN AT HOME

	Plate
Cpl. D. Miller, M.M., 19th Manchester Regt., receiving the M.M. from Field-Marshal Lord French	138
Revd. H. Shandel and Group of Soldiers	167
Revd. H. Shandel with Jewish Soldiers of the K.R.R.C. and Rifle Brigade	299
Aldershot:	
Group of Officers and Men, 1915	64
Group outside Synagogue, September, 1914 (showing replica of S. African War Roll of Honour)	232
Group at Hut of Jewish and Military Association, 1918	329
Canterbury, Group at	177, 208
Chatham, Group at, 1917, with Revd. H. Shandel	14
Clacton, Group at	290
Colchester, 11th Roy. Fus. at, 1914	274
Curragh Camp, Group of Soldiers, 1915	193
Deal, Group of Officers, Jewish Lads' Brigade Camp, 1911	297
England, Chaplains and Officiating Clergymen in, 1917	201
Hatfield, 17th London Regt. in training, 1914	170
Liverpool Regt., Group of Soldiers with Revd. S. Frampton	296
London:	
Officers and Men, Hammersmith Synagogue, in training, November, 1914	56
Staff of Beech House Military Hospital	68
Tudor House Military Hospital, Hampstead	71, 72

London:
   Sailors, Regulars, and Reservists at the Central Synagogue prior to the War - 137
   Capt. and Mrs. H. Isaac (Miss A. Woolf) at Buckingham Palace - 153
   Managers and Members of Notting Hill Jewish Club who served during the War - 161
   Soldiers of Victoria Working Lads' Club - 281
   Jewish Australian Y.M.C.A. Hut, Strand, 1919 - 287
   Seder Service, Australian Y.M.C.A. Hut, Passover, 1919 - 288
   Sgt. Issy Smith, V.C., placing wreath on Cenotaph, November 11th, 1920, in honour of Jewish dead - 289
   Group of Jewish Soldiers, London, Passover, 1915 - 312

London:
   Group at Feast of Chanucah, December 13th, 1914 - 313

Manchester:
   Jewish Soldiers outside a Synagogue, September, 1914 - 35
   Jewish Soldiers in Pembroke Yeomanry - 75

Northampton, Group of Soldiers at Synagogue - 266

Plymouth, Revd. S. Lipson, S.C.F., and Group, at - 364

Ramsgate, Chanucah Service held by Revd. H. Shandel, 1918 - 242

Reading, R.A.F. and 30th Middlesex Regt. at - 241

Salisbury Plain, Australian Jewish Service on - 177

Westgate, Group with the Revd. H. Shandel, 1917 - 266

THE JEWISH "V.C.'s"

1. The late Lieut. F. A. de Pass, Poona Horse; 2. Sergt. Issy Smith, 1st Manchester Regt.; 3. Capt. R. Gee, M.C., 2nd Royal Fusiliers; 4. Pte. (later Lieut.) Leonard Keysor, 1st Australian Infantry; 5. Pte. J. White (Weiss), 6th King's Own Royal Lancaster Regt.

ROLL OF HONOUR
New West End Synagogue, London
UNVEILED BY SIR ISIDORE SPIELMANN, C.M.G.
19th September, 1920 — 7th Tishri, 5681

In Memoriam

1. Pte. S. Woolfson, 1st Royal Warwick Regt.; 2. Pte. L. Reckler, 6th Northampton Regt.; 3. Pte. C. Norman, 1st Grenadier Guards; 4. Pte. L. Levy, 51st Welsh Regt.; 5. Pte. L. Glatt, 2nd Loyal North Lancs Regt.; 6. Pte. N. Gordon, 2nd Royal Berkshire Regt.; 7. Pte. E. B. Ludski, 7th London Regt.; 8. S.-Sergt. J. Canton-Cohen, 46th Field Ambulance, R.A.M.C.; 9. Pte. J. Woolf, 9th Royal Irish Fusiliers; 19. Pte. H. Welt, 1/8th Worcester Regt.; 11. Pte. B. Cohen, 2/3rd London Regt.; 12. Pte. W. Greenbury, 2nd Northampton Regt.

1. Pte. A. Woolman, 15th D.L.I.; 2. Pte. S. Van Engle, 10th Essex Regt.; 3. Pte. W. Weinberg, 38th Royal Fusiliers; 4. Pte. P. Louis (Sugar), 2nd London Regt.; 5. L.-Cpl. J. Levy, 16th Northumberland Fusiliers; 6. Sergt. R. B. Jacobs, 12th Manchester Regt.; 7. Spr. I. Levene, 210 Field Coy. R.E.; 8. Pte. H. Weinberg, 1st Manchester Regt.; 9. Pte. J. Tennenbaum, 2nd London Regt.; 10. Pte. H. Friedlander, R.A.M.C.; 11. Sig. M. Jackoff, 2nd Royal Scots; 12. Rfn. J. Tennens, 1/12th London Regt.

A JEWISH GUARD OF THE CAPE PENINSULA GARRISON REGIMENT.

Back Row.   A. MANN, L.-Cpl.   M. B. BERNSTEIN   D. ZUCKERMANN   J. JOFFE   Q.M.S. A. JACOBS
Front Row.   R. M. WATSON   L. BERNSTEIN   P VALENTINE   S. GOLDSTEIN   L. W. NOAH   Rev. Capt. LEVESON
(Jewish Chaplain)

1. Cpl. M. Mazarkoff, 3rd Canadian Infantry; 2. Pte. S. Harris, 1/15th London Regt.; 3. Sergt. E. Edelberg, R.F.A.; 4. 2nd-A.M. H. Israels, R.A.F.; 5. Cpl. S. Taylor, R.A.P.C.; 6. A.B. Leonard Bloom, Royal Naval Division; 7. 3rd-A.M. A. Israels, R.A.F.; 8. Spr. Reginald Harris, R.E.; 9. Pte. I. Spiro, King's Liverpool Regt.; 10. Guardsman A. Mazarkoff, Grenadier Guards; 11. 2nd-A.M. A. Franklin, R.A.F.; 12. Cpl. H. Franklin, R.A.P.C.

1. Pte. L. Levy, Witwatersrand Rifles; 2. Sergt. I. Goldstone, 40th Royal Fusiliers; 3. Pte. F. Jacobs, Australian Infantry; 4. Pte. P. Matz, 38th Royal Fusiliers; 5. L.A.C. A. Leslie, R.A.F.; 6. Pte. M. Millem, 16th Queen's; 7. L.-Cpl. M. Leslie, 1/12th London Regt.; 8. Pte. H. Brown, R.A.M.C.; 9. Sergt. A. S. Koftoff, R.A.M.C.; 10. Pte. M. Needle, 39th Royal Fusiliers; 11. Pte. M. A. Goodman, Labour Coy.; 12. Sergt. L. Joseph, 12th Canadian Infantry.

GROUPS OF BROTHERS.

1. Tpr. SIDNEY WOOD, Tpr. ISIDORE WOOD, Tpr. HARRY WOOD, Tpr. MARK WOOD, Royal Horse Guards.
2. Pte. J. FEIGENBAUM, Pte. I. FEIGENBAUM, Middlesex Regt.
3. Three Brothers BAKESEF.
4. Gnr. A. FREEDMAN, R.G.A.; Sig. I. FREEDMAN, 10th Scottish Rifles.
5. A.B. H. SUGARMAN, H.M.S. Submarine L12; Pte. L. SUGARMAN, 2nd Queen's.

JEWISH WAR MEMORIALS ABROAD.

Grave of L.-Cpl. H. Goldberg, 21st K.R.R.C., Ploegsteert Wood.   Grave of Pte. N. Davis, 10th R. Fusiliers, Berles-au-Bois.   Grave of 2nd-Lieut. C. W. J. Danziger, 21st Manchester Regt., Achiet-le-Grand.

In Memoriam

1. 2nd-Lieut. A. Slowe, 6th K.O.Y.L.I.; 2. Lieut. Gerald G. Samuel, 10th Royal West Kent Regt.; 3. Lieut. Moss Cohen, M.M., 2nd Durham L.I.; 4. 2nd-Lieut. N. G. Cook, 1/6th North Staffs Regt.; 5. 2nd-Lieut. P. S. Joyce, 60th Squadron, R.A.F.; 6. Lieut. Arthur S. Marks, 9th Royal Sussex Regt.; 7. Lieut. Ronald Henry Arnholz, 1st Herts Regt.; 8. 2nd-Lieut. B. Clifford Isaacs, M.G.C.; 9. 2nd-Lieut. G. A. L. Ohlmann, Northampton Regt. and 3rd Royal Fusiliers.; 10. 2nd-Lieut. G. R. Alexander, 14th Royal Sussex Regt.; 11. 2nd-Lieut. W. B. Rodney, 11th Royal West Kent Regt; 12. 2nd-Lieut. A. Rosenthal, 65th Squadron, R.A.F.

In Memoriam

1. Pte. A. G. Marienberg, 13th King's Liverpool Regt.; 2. Pte. A. Levy, 21st Manchester Regt.; 3. Pte. M. H. Lichtenstein, 2nd Lancashire Fusiliers; 4. Pte. E. Levi, 1/5th West Yorks Regt.; 5. Pte. I. M. Kay, 16th K.R.R.C.; 6. Pte. H. Marcus, 8th Royal Inniskilling Fusiliers; 7. Pte. M. Perlberg, R.A.F.; 8. Pte. A. Morris, 17th King's Liverpool Regt.; 9. Pte. A. Phillips, 32nd Royal Fusiliers; 10. Sergt. A. Solomons, 12th Middlesex Regt.; 11. Cpl. S. Karker, 1st South Staffs Regt; 12. Pte. M. W. Lipshack (Phillips), 7th London Regt.

1. Rfn. A. J. Lion, 9th Rifle Brigade; 2. Pte. J. Gans, 20th Middlesex Regt.; 3. Pte. A. Lewis, 14th Northumberland Fusiliers; 4. Rfn. B. Gordon, 8th Rifle Brigade; 5. L.-Cpl. L. V. Cats, 23rd London Regt.; 6. Pte. M. Cossack, 6th Loyal N. Lancs Regt.; 7. Pte. H. Grodzinsky, R.D.C.; 8. Pte. J. Kalminsky, R.A.S.C.; 9. Cpl. A. Cohen, 2/4th Leicester Regt.; 10. Pte. H. S. Cristole, 11th Royal Scots Fusiliers; 11. L.-Cpl. J. Cohen, 2/17th London Regt.; 12. Pte. B. Levine, 2nd Royal Warwickshire Regt.

ROLL OF HONOUR OF WEST LONDON SYNAGOGUE, UPPER BERKELEY STREET, LONDON, W.

Top.—Group at Chatham 1917, with Rev. H. SHANDEL.
Bottom.—Group of Jewish soldiers, Calcutta, New Year 1918.

1. Cpl. B. SALOM, Australian Infantry; 2. Pte. L. ROSENBERG, 4th Royal Welsh Fusiliers; 3. Pte. A. TARNOPOLSKY, Labour Coy.; 4. Sergt. M. PINNER, Middlesex Yeomanry; 5. Sig. J. L. MYERS, Australian Infantry; 6. Rfn. S. SAMUELS, Rifle Brigade; 7. Rfn. B. ISAACS, 16th K.R.R. Corps; 8. Tpr. A. PRESS, 20th Hussars; 9. Pte. N. RUBENSTEIN, 2nd Welsh Regt.; 10. Pte. D. A. MARTIN, 2/5th The Buffs; 11. Pte. S. MARKS, R.A M.C.; 12. Pte. L. WEINBERG, K.O.R. Lancaster Regt.

1. Sergt. J. Benjamin, 13th Essex Regt.; 2. Pte. M. Gardner, 38th Royal Fusiliers; 3. Pte. L. Cohen, R.A.S.C.; 4. 1st A.M. H. Appleton, R.A.F.; 5. Pte. B. Ash, 4th Yorks Regt.; 6. L.-Cpl. J. H. Harris, Black Watch; 7. Pte. D. Fisher, 1st Notts and Derby Regt.; 8. Pte. L. Hillier, Labour Battn.; 9. Sergt. M. Dainow, 1/9th Middlesex Regt.; 10. Rfn. B. Benjamin, 13th Royal Irish Rifles; 11. L.-Cpl. S. Gorovitch, 3rd Welsh Regt.; 12. Pte. Crugman, Royal Fusiliers.

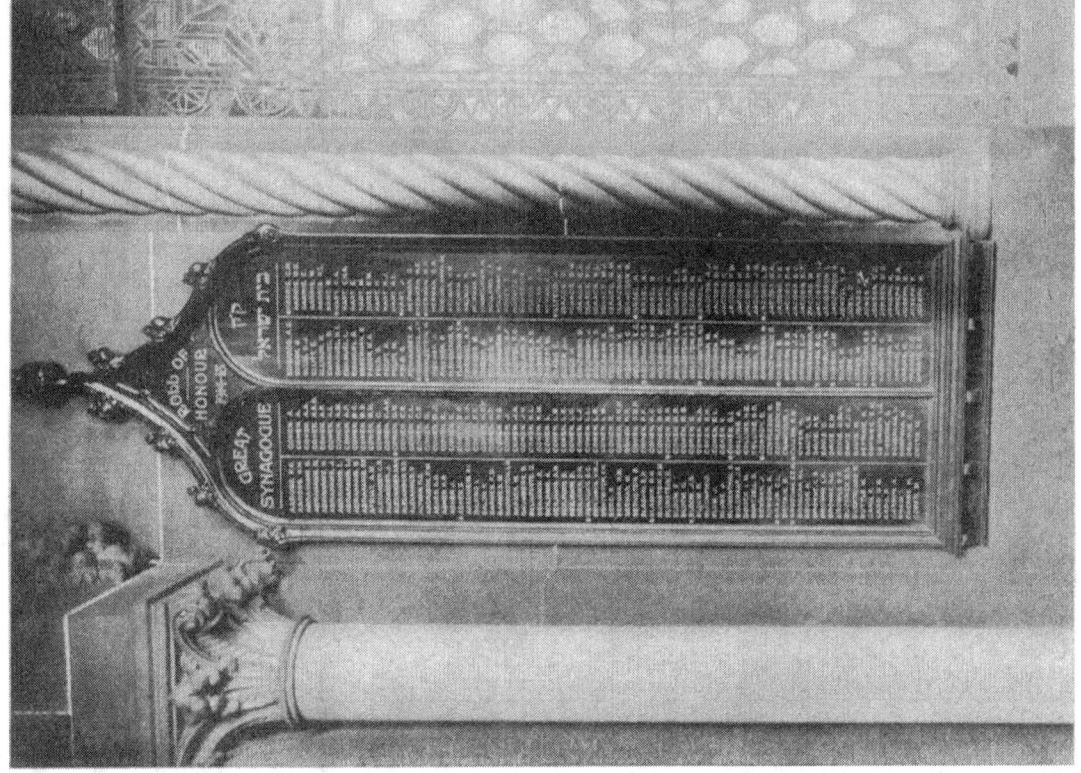

WAR MEMORIAL, GREAT SYNAGOGUE, SYDNEY, AUSTRALIA.

1. Pte. J. Tobias, 8th M.G. Battn.; 2. L.-Cpl. F. S. Levy, 1st Anzac Camel Corps; 3. L.-Cpl. J. Golding, 1/7th Manchester Regt.; 4. L.-Cpl. M. Gallewski (M.M.), R.A.M.C. 5. Sergt. A. G. Cohen, 1/6th West Yorks Regt.; 6. Sergt. R. C. Grouse, 36th Australian Inf.; 7. Pte. M. Cohen, 2nd Royal Welsh Fusiliers, 8. Gnr. E. H. Goldstein, 3rd Bgde. Canadian Field Artillery; 9. L.-Cpl. D. Rosenberg, 17th Royal Fusiliers; 10. L.-Cpl. R. A. Levy 1st H.A.C.; 11. Pte. G. N. Levy, 11th Australian Inf.; 12. Pte. L. Goldberg, 1st Essex Regt.

In Memoriam

1. Rfn. D. Hart, 10th K.R.R. Corps; 2. Pte. N. Hamburg, 2/4th London Regt.; 3. Pte. A. Rosenthal, 250th Div. Emp. Labour Coy.; 4. Pte. S. Goodman, 2nd K.O.Y.L.I.; 5. L.-Cpl. H. Levi, 2nd Lincoln Regt.; 6. Bdr. H. Gilbert, 129th Battery R.F.A.; 7. Gnr. S. Sheare, R.G.A.; 8. Pte. M. D. Raport, Scottish Canadians; 9. Pte. H. Zimmerman, 2nd Oxford and Bucks L.I.; 10. Pte. S. E. Harris, 8th S. Stafford Regt.; 11. Tpr. A. K. Rosenthal, 1st Australian Light Horse Field Ambulance; 12. Pte. S. Lewis, 9th Devon Regt.

1. Pte. H. Bernstein, 15th Cheshire Regt.; 2. Pte. S. Bishop, 5th Australian Infantry; 3. Pte. D. Sandall, 13th Durham L.I.; 4. Bdr. V. Heilbron, M.M., L/15th Bgde. R.H.A.; 5. Pte. M. Lewis (Isther), 1st Essex Regt.; 6. Pte. M. Mazerkoff, 3rd Canadian M.G.C.; 7. Stoker M. Blok, H.M.S. *Lapwing*; 8. Pte. B. E. Simmons, 16th Canadian Scottish; 9. A.B. I. Goldstein, H.M.S. *Defence*; 10. Pte. A. Anker, 3rd Auckland New Zealand Infantry; 11. Stoker W. Stern, H.M.S. *Pathfinder*; 12. Pte. G. Garrett, 4th Royal Fusiliers.

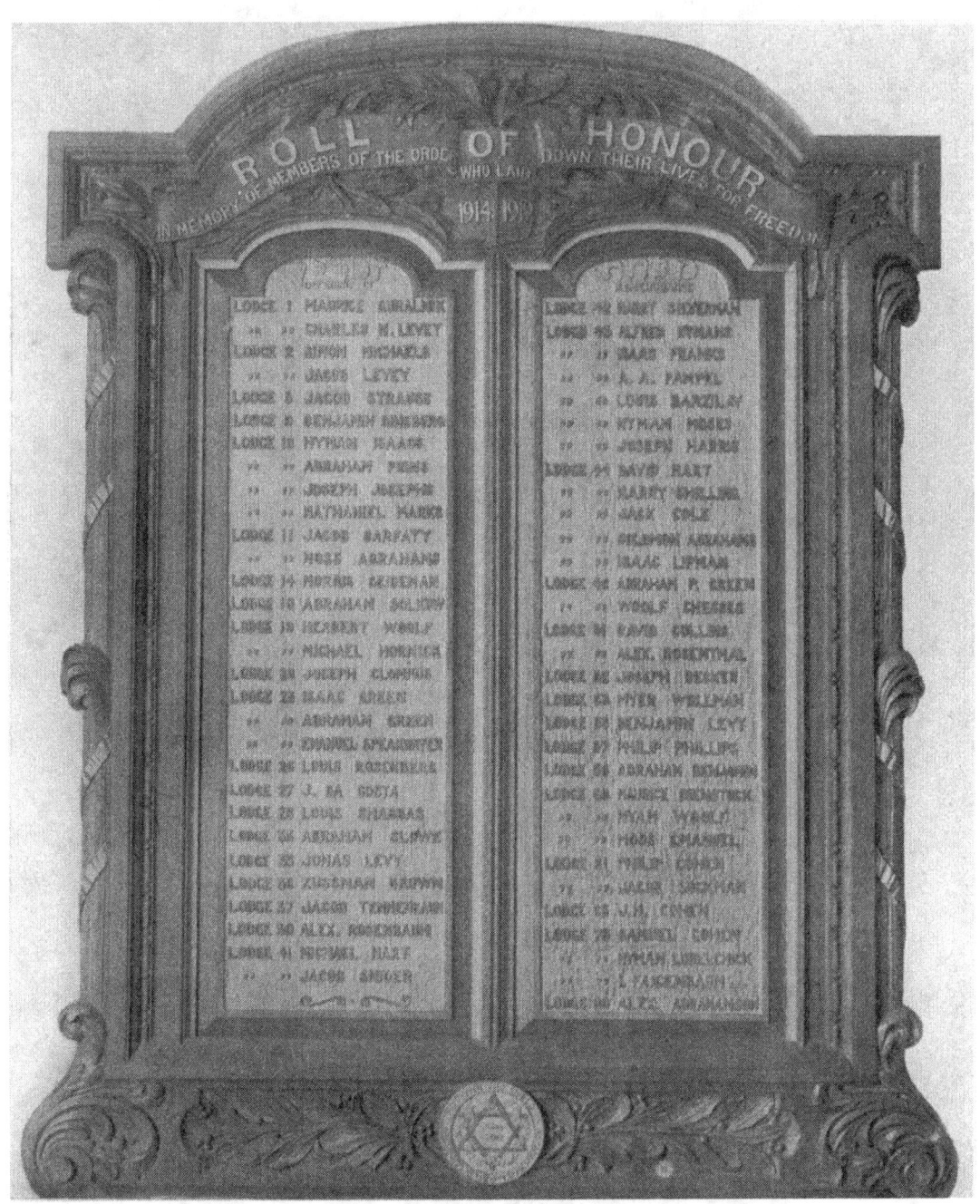

ROLL OF HONOUR OF THE MEMBERS OF THE ORDER "ACHEI BRITH" AND "SHIELD OF ABRAHAM" FRIENDLY SOCIETIES

22

1. Gnr. S. Ginsberg, R.F.A.; 2. Pte. S. Cohen, R.A.M.C.; 3. L.-Cpl. A. Golding, 38th Royal Fusiliers; 4. Pte. L. J. Bortnoski, 5th Australian Infantry; 5. Pte. P. Bergman, Middlesex Regt.; 6. Pte. A. Baker, 9th Royal Scots; 7. Pte. J. Bentata, Manchester Regt.; 8. Pte. G. Goldberg, R.A.M.C.; 9. L.-Cpl. L. Benjamin, Canadian Infantry; 10. L.-Cpl. L. Green, R.A.P.C.; 11. Pte. E. Fry, 4th Middlesex Regt.; 12. Cpl. D. Boorman, 38th Royal Fusiliers.

1. Pte. JOE BARNES, 38th Royal Fusiliers.
   Pte. J. TYTZ, 38th Royal Fusiliers.

2. Pte. B. NIGON, Royal Fusiliers.
   Pte. J. SOLOMONS, Royal Fusiliers.

3. Dvr. S. DE TAUBE, Canadian Artillery.
   Miss ROSE KREMER, V.A.D.
   Pte. J. KREMER, M.M., 1st Leinster Regt.

4. S.M. M. NATHAN, 18th London Regt.
   Bdr. G. NATHAN, " B " Bty. H.A.C.
   Pte. J. B. NATHAN, 20th Canadian Inf.
   Sergt. (later Lieut., D.L.I.) G. NATHAN, H.A.C.

5. Pte. B. NATHAN, Royal Welsh Fusiliers.
   Pte. H. WOLFYANSKY, Royal Welsh Fusiliers.
   Pte. I. JACOBS, Royal Welsh Fusiliers.

6. Pte. H. ZUCKER, 38th Royal Fusiliers.
   Pte. L. LEVIN, 38th Royal Fusiliers.
   Pte. A. BERNARD, 38th Royal Fusiliers.

7. 38th Royal Fusiliers in SALTASH Depot.

8. Cpl. SCHOLEFIELD, R.A.S.C.
   Pte. J. MAGNUS, 3rd Queen's (R.W. Surrey) Regt.

1. Pte. J. FREEDMAN, Canadian Medical Corps; 2. Sergt. C. W. COHEN, 7th Australian Inf.; 3. Pte. V. ASH, R.A.S.C.; 4. Dvr. S. LEVY, R.A.S.C.; 5. S.Sergt.-Major J. JELLEN, M.S.M., R.A.S.C.; 6. Pte. S. BOSS, M.G. Corps; 7. Pte. S. CREMER, Lancashire Fusiliers; 8. Pte. J. BLUMENTHAL, 38th Royal Fusiliers; 9. Pte. J. LEVY, N. Zealand Inf.; 10. Sergt. M. HENRY, Canadian Forces; 11. Pte. A. BLOOM, Australian Army Medical Corps; 12. Bdr. J. GREEN, R.F.A.

Memorial to Trooper F. Mendelsohn, South African Mechanical Transport.

Memorial at Willesden Cemetery, London, N.W., to Sub-Lieut. T. Jacobs and 2nd-Lieut. D. Jacobs.

Roll of Honour, Edinburgh Congregation.

1. Pte. H. Schilling, 7th London Regt.; 2. Pte. P. Rapoport, 12/13th Northumberland Fusiliers; 3. Pte. B. Schwartz, Imperial Camel Corps; 4. Dvr. C. J. Hillier, 2nd T.M.B., R.F.A.; 5. Pte. L. Harris, 10th West Yorks Regt.; 6. Pte. I. Rosenberg, 1st K.O.R. Lancaster Regt.; 7. Pte. H. Abrahams, 17th King's Liverpool Regt.; 8. Pte. J. Solomon, 1/5th R. Warwick Regt.; 9. Pte. A. Hillier, 26th Royal Fusiliers; 10. Pte. M. Freiner, 38th Royal Fusiliers; 11. Pte. L. Rosen (Rosenberg), 6th Gloucester Regt.; 12. Rfn. J. Herman, 9th London Regt.

27

In Memoriam

1. Pte. M. ROSENBERG, 1st London Regt.; 2. Rfn. J. STOTT, 1/8th London Regt.; 3. Pte. B. ANNENBERG (ASHBERRY), 1/13th London Regt.; 4. Pte. S. ABRAHAMS, 1/4th London Regt.; 5. Rfn. D. JACOBS, 2nd K.R.R.C.; 6. Pte. J. R. HEWSON, 6th Border Regt.; 7. Tpr. R. ANNENBERG (ASHBERRY) City of London Rough Riders; 8. Tpr. A. L. JACOBS, Royal Bucks Hussars and 1st R. W. Kent Regt.; 9. Pte. M. JOSEPH AARONS, London Scottish; 10. Sergt. G. JACOBS (D.C.M.), R.A.M.C.; 11. Pte. W. A. ANDRADE, 4th London Regt.; 12. Pte. S. ROSENBAUM, 1st London Regt.

1. Sig. H. M. Harris, 309th (H.A.C.) Siege Bty.; 2. Gnr. J. Gershon, 13th Mountain Bty. R.G.A.; 3. Gnr. Victor Ash, R.F.A.; 4. Pte. J. B. Kauffmann, R.A.S.C.; 5. Tpr. Woolf Lupinsky, Royal Horse Guards; 6. Cyclist W. Diamond, 19th Corps Cyclist Battn.; 7. Cpl. E. Dresner, 217th Siege Bty. Amm. Column; 8. Q.M.S. Joel Jewell, R.A.M.C.; 9. Sergt. R. Goodman, R.A.M.C.; 10. Pte. S. Braham, Bedford Regt.; 11. Spr. E. S. Ezekiel, Indian Engineers; 12. Pte. Fred Isaacs, 18th King's Liverpool Regt.

1. Armourer S.-Sergt. A. G. Salomons, R.A.O.C.; 2. A.M. H. Shneiders, R.A.F.; 3. Pte. N. Marks, R.A.O.C.; 4. Gnr. D. Zeizeran, R.G.A.; 5. Pte. N. Loveguard, Middlesex Regt.; 6. Pte. J. Wurms, Middlesex Regt.; 7. Pnr. A. Solomon, R.E.; 8. Pte. E. Isaacs, Royal Fusiliers; 9. Pte. I. Rosenthal, Middlesex Regt.; 10. Pte. J. Edison Ikin, Australian Infantry; 11. Leading A.M. N. G. M. Morris, R.A.F.; 12. Gnr. J. A. Levy, R.F.A.

GROUP: MALTA, 1915.

Top Row: Pte. Doodeward, R.A.M.C.; Pte. L. Segal, London Regt.; Pte. L. Onwood, 3rd London Regt.; Pte. A. Cohen, Northumberland Fus.; Pte. H. Benjamin, 4th London Regt.
Middle Row: Driver A. Ellis, R.H.A.; Sergt. M. Moss, West Yorks Regt.; Mr. A. J. Tayar; Pte. L. Hyman, R.A.M.C.; Pte. M. Comor, 1st Newfoundland Regt. (later died of wounds).
Front Row: Pte. H. Franklin, R.A.M.C.; Pte. G. Lightstone, Canadian Field Amb.; Pte. W. Fairman, 4th London Regt.

1. 2nd-Lieut. A. L. Wurm, Middlesex Regt.; 2. Capt. J. Afriat, Egyptian Labour Corps; 3. 2nd-Lieut. Harold Boodson, R.F.A.; 4. Rev. E. M. Levy, C.F.; 5. 2nd-Lieut. B. Cooper, R.G.A.; 6. Rev. S. Grajewsky, C.F.; 7. Cpl. L. M. Sharp, R.A.S.C.; 8. Cpl. Montague Harris, 9th H.L.I.; 9. 2nd A.M. L. Ullman, R.A.F.; 10. L.-Cpl. D. Baroque, Royal Fusiliers and American Air Force; 11. C.P.O. L. Franks, Royal Navy; 12. Sig. W.O. A. H. Pasch, H.M.S. *Benbow*.

32

1. Pte. M. Samuels, 2/13th London Regt.; 2. Sergt. M. Baker, D.C.M., M.M., R.E.; 3. Pte. A. Wurms, 1st Rifle Brigade; 4. Pte. R. Woolf, 1st East Surrey Regt.; 5. Pte. W. Zimmerman, R.A.S.C.; 6. Drummer S. Rosenberg, 26th Royal Welsh Fusiliers; 7. L.-Cpl. A. Weinberg, 1st Worcestershire Regt.; 8. Cpl. S. J. Vos, 1st Rifle Brigade; 9. Rfm. L. Symons, 2nd K.R.R.C.; 10. Pte. H. M. Isaacs, 38th Royal Fusiliers; 11. Pte. M. Lubrinsky, Labour Corps; 12. L.-Cpl. J. Rae, 9th West Riding Regt.

ROLL OF HONOUR OF THE HAMPSTEAD SYNAGOGUE, LONDON, N.W.

1. 2nd-Lieut. S. J. Dundon, 13th King's Liverpool Regt.; 2. Lieut. N. N Levene, 8th King's Liverpool Regt.; 3. 2nd-Lieut. J. P. Caro, 2/17th London Regt.; 4. Lieut. L. Barron, 7th Border Regt.; 5. 2nd-Lieut. S. Van der Linde, 6th Bedford Regt.; 6. Lieut. N. I. Lion, 1st R.M.L.I.; 7. 2nd-Lieut. W. F. G. Joseph, 2nd Royal Berks Regt.; 8. 2nd-Lieut. M. J. T. Van der Linde, 9th London Regt.; 9. 2nd-Lieut. E. H. Hyman, 11th South Lancashire Regt.; 10. 2nd-Lieut. C. Freeman-Cowen, 175th Brigade, R.F.A.; 11. 2nd-Lieut. I. D. Marks, 10th West Riding Regt.; 12. Lieut. P. J. Stuart-Smith, 74th Squadron, R.A.F.

GROUP OF JEWISH SOLDIERS OUTSIDE A MANCHESTER SYNAGOGUE, SEPTEMBER 1914.

36

In Memoriam

1. Pte. S. Hamburg, 1st Roy. Scots Fusiliers; 2. Pte. S. Abrahams, 12th Roy. Scots Fusiliers; 3. Pte. M. Rogalek, 1001st Labour Coy.; 4. Rfn. W. Abrahams, 1st Rifle Brigade; 5. Pte. S. Hyman, 9th East Surrey Regt.; 6. L.-Cpl. R. Hart, 9th K.O.R. Lancaster Regt.; 7. Pte. D. Heller, 1/28th London Regt.; 8. Pte. P. Hyams, 2nd S. African Infantry; 9. Pte. A. S. Rose, 10th Royal Fusiliers; 10. Pte. A. Harris, 26th Field Ambulance, R.A.M.C.; 11. Pte. M. Abrahams, R.A.M.C.; 12. Pte. B. Hockin, 1st East Lancs Regt.

1. Sergt. H. Lewis, D.C.M., 1/16th London Regt.; 2. C.P.O. M. J. E. Brock, H.M.S. *Eaglet*; 3. Rfn. M. Levy, K.R.R.C.; 4. Pte. I. Miller, R.A.S.C.; 5. Leading Seaman S. W. Zeitlin, H.M.S. *Victory*; 6. Sergt. V. Johnson, R.A.M.C.; 7. Pte. J. G. Cohen, London Regt.; 8. Pte. H. Lenneberg, Australian Infantry; 9. Sergt. S. D. Moss, Indian Army; 10. Pte. M. London, King's Liverpool Regt.; 11. Sergt. P. Klein, R.A.F.; 12. Tpr. H. I. Morris, Hampshire Yeomanry.

1. Pte. H. M. Novitzky, 2/10th London Regt.; 2. Pte. S. Lazoff, 3rd Canadian Infantry; 3. 2/A.M. J. Solomons, 4th Squad. R.A.F.; 4. Sgt. E. Joseph, 14th R. Warwickshire Regt.; 5. Telegraphist M. Solomon, R.N.V.R.; 6. Pte. J. Lipman, 84th Labour Coy.; 7. Gnr. P. Schweitzer, R.G.A.; 8. Gnr. J. Sultan, 90th M.G.C.; 9. Steward D. Gold, H.M.S. "Dido"; 10. Gnr. S. Morris, R.G.A.; 11. Pte. A. Jacobs, 4th East Yorks Regt.; 12. L/Cpl. B. Selman (Solomons), 1/17th London Regt.

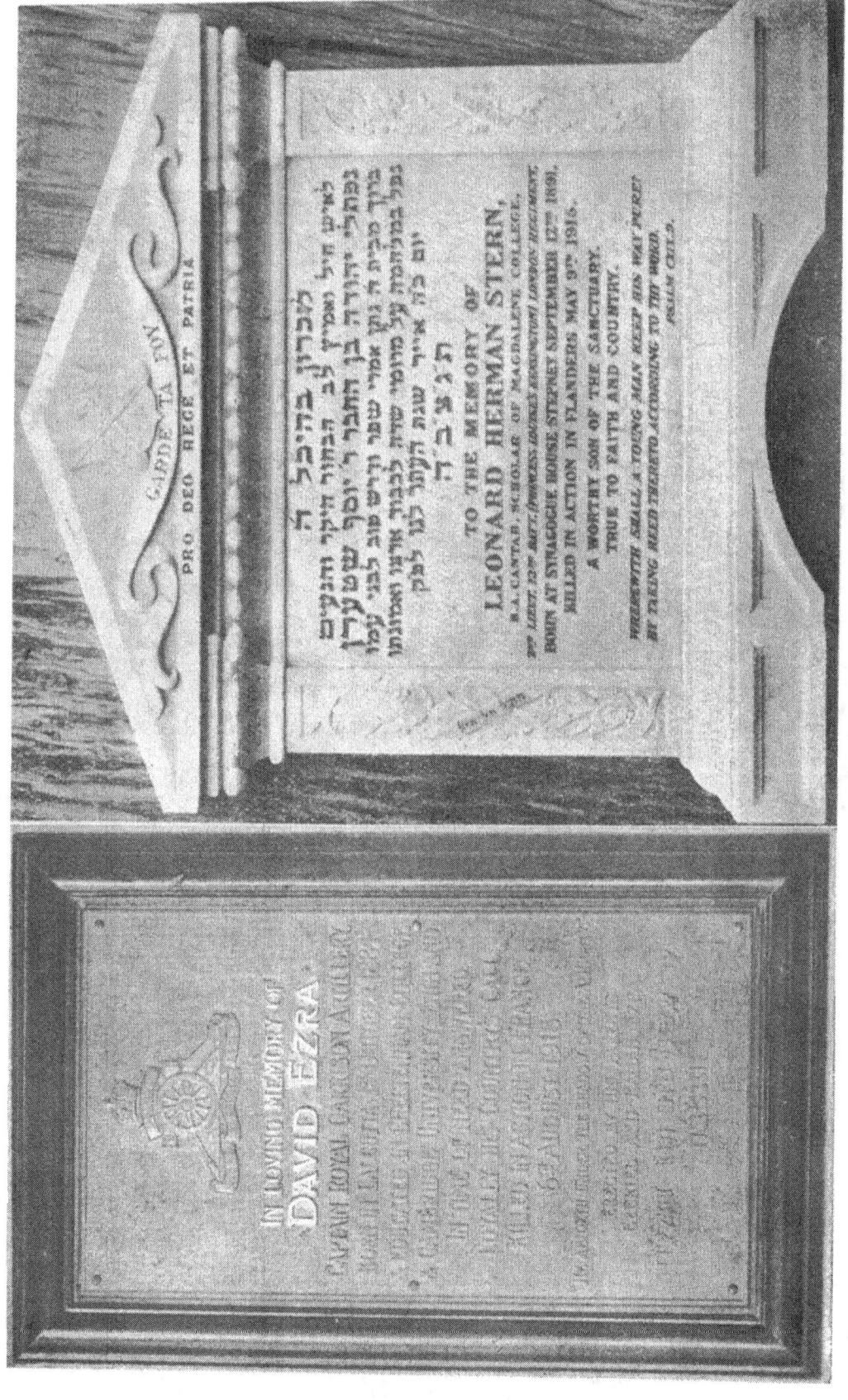

MEMORIAL TO CAPT. D. EZRA, R.G.A., MEMORIAL TO 2ND-LIEUT. L. H. STERN, EAST LONDON CALCUTTA. SYNAGOGUE.

1. Pte. M. Wolfson, Royal Scots; 2. 2nd A.M. H. Green, R.A.F.; 3. Cpl. M. Goldstein, R.A.F.; 4. Cpl. J. Toff, M.M., 2nd Middlesex Regt.; 5. Seaman A. Toff, H.M.T.B.D.; 6. C.S.M. S. Umlauf, 5th Middlesex Regt.; 7. Pte. J. Moses, 14th R. W. Surrey Regt.; 8. Pte. I. Levene, 8th Labour Battn. Royal Fusiliers; 9. Gnr. A. Levison, R.H.A., and 3rd City of London Yeomanry; 10. Special Constable J. Toff; 11. Pte. S. Levison, 13th Suffolk Regt.; 12. S.-Sergt. E. J. Toff, Army Gymnastic Staff.

JEWISH WAR MEMORIALS ABROAD.

1. Grave of Spr. B. STANDER, R.E., Lillers.
2. Grave of Lieut. S. FINE, R.A.F., Belgium.
3. Graves of Pte. L. ISAACS, 1st King's, and Pte. H. SMITH, 2nd South Staffs Regt., Cambrin.
4. Grave of Sub-Lieut. N. H. BENJAMIN, Royal Naval Division, Aubigny.
5. Grave of Pte. D. GINSBURG, 13th London Regt., Estaires.
6. Grave of Capt. C. L. HART, 2nd West Riding Regt., Colincamps.

In Memoriam

1. Lieut. E. M. Gosschalk, 2nd K.O.Y.L.I.; 2. Capt. L. M. Tobias, 25th Royal Welch Fusiliers; 3. 2nd-Lieut. W. H. Hurstbourne (Hirschbein), 4th Wessex Brigade R.F.A.; 4. 2nd-Lieut. H. L. A. Keyzor, 25th Welch Fusiliers; 5. Lieut. C. A. M. Bingen, 5th (Cinque Ports) Battn. Royal Sussex Regt.; 6. Lieut. A. L. Arnold, 9th London Regt.; 7. Capt. A. G. Lezard, 13th Rifle Brigade; 8. 2nd-Lieut. E. Salaman, R.F.A.; 9. 2nd-Lieut. S. M. Cohen, 1/12th London Regt.; 10. 2nd-Lieut. M. G. Klean, 16th Northumberland Fusiliers; 11. 2nd-Lieut. S. J. Fink, 2/5th South Lancs Regt.; 12. 2nd-Lieut. W. S. Nathan, 12th Royal Fusiliers.

1. Lieut. EDWARD MARKS, 5th Royal Fusiliers; 2. Col. D. DE LARA COHEN, V.D., 10th London Regt.; 3. Lieut. E. HARRIS, H.L.I. and Royal Fusiliers (Jewish); 4. 2nd-Lieut. SIDNEY M. SAMUELS, M.C. and Bar, 26th Royal Fusiliers; 5. Rev. I. BRODIE, C.F.; 6. 2nd-Lieut. A. BESSO, Manchester Regt. (attd. Camel Corps); 7. Capt. DESMOND TUCK, R.A.F and French Flying Corps; 8. Rev. L. GEFFEN, C.F.; 9. 2nd-Lieut. H. SOLOMON, 21st Middlesex Regt,; 10. Lieut. R. E. WHITE, Norfolk Yeomanry; 11. Lieut. SYDNEY HARRIS, King's Liverpool Regt.; 12. Capt. SYDNEY FRANKENBURG, 1/8th Manchester Regt.

44

In Memoriam

1. Capt. CLEMENT J. B. DAVIS, R.E.; 2. 2nd-Lieut. LEONARD H. STERN, 13th London Regt.; 3. Lieut. OLIVER EMANUEL, 1st Wilts Regt.; 4. Major LESSER SAMUEL, R.F.A.; 5. 2nd-Lieut. VICTOR D. GROSSMANN, 24th Northumberland Fusiliers; 6. 2nd-Lieut. E. COHEN, M.C., 12th Royal Fusiliers; 7. 2nd-Lieut. J. H. CANSINO, 22nd Manchester Regt.; 8. Lieut. V. V. JACOB, 2nd Oxford & Bucks L.I.; 9. Lieut. C. W. TELFER, 1st K.O.Y.L.I.; 10. Lieut. H. A. TELFER, 9th K.O.Y.L.I. att. 64th T.M.B.; 11. Capt. WILFRED M. LANGDON, 10th Cheshire Regt.; 12. Capt. EDGAR B. GOLLIN, 13th King's Liverpool Regt.

45

1. 2nd-Lieut. OSCAR R. FRANKENSTEIN, 5th Welsh Regt.; 2. Capt. S. A. LIEBSON, M.C., S. African Medical Corps; 3. Lieut. LAURENCE B. ROSENBAUM, 1/2nd Monmouthshire Regt.; 4. 2nd-Lieut. CLAUDE H. BOWMAN, 1st Oxford & Bucks L.I.; 5. 2nd-Lieut. J. FRIEND, 20th Northumberland Fusiliers; 6. 2nd-Lieut. BRAHAM A. FRANKS, 8th West Riding Regt.; 7. Lieut. HARRY HARRIS, 10th West Riding Regt.; 8. 2nd-Lieut. HERBERT PINDER DAVIS, 12th Essex Regt.; 9. 2nd-Lieut. F. J. LEVI, 2/5th Lincolnshire Regt.; 10. Lieut. HERBERT N. DAVIS, R.E.; 11. Capt. LEON SIMONS, M.C., 22nd Royal Fusiliers; 12. 2nd-Lieut. MARCUS SEGAL, 13th King's Liverpool Regt.

INDIA: GROUP OF JEWISH SOLDIERS, BANGALORE, PASSOVER, 1920.

Top.—Memorial to the late Capt. WILFRID M. LANGDON, 10th Cheshire Regt.
Bottom.—Memorial at the Central Synagogue, London, W., to the late 2nd-Lieut. B. A. FRANKS.

1. Pte. M. Goldstein, Middlesex Regt.; 2. Pte. J. Berlinsky, Australian Infantry; 3. Cpl. R. Berg, R.A.S.C.; 4. Pte. S. C. Barnett, 2/2nd Scottish Horse; 5. A.M. D. Blatkin, R.A.F.; 6. Pte. W. Sloman, Cameron Hrs.; 7. Pte. H. Gembitski, Suffolk Regt.; 8. Tpr. H. Brilliant, Middlesex Yeomanry; 9. Spr. H. Cohen, R.E.; 10. Pte. H. Golgowsky, R.A.S.C.; 11. 2nd A.M. S. H. Gembitski, R.A.F.; 12. Sig. E. E. Hamaui, 2/7th Manchester Regt.

JEWISH WAR MEMORIALS ABROAD.

Grave and Memorial of Sergt. D. Goodman, R.F.A. Specimen of the Jewish Headstone to be erected by the Imperial War Graves Commission. Grave and Memorial of Pte. B. Goldsmith, 6th Canadian Field Ambulance.

1. Pte. J. Levy, 23rd Middlesex Regt.; 2. Bdr. E. Woolf, R.F.A.; 3. L.-Cpl. A. S. Levy, 40th Royal Fusiliers; 4. Cpl. J. Martin, Grenadier Guards; 5. Pte. M. Weinberg, Tank Corps; 6. L.-Cpl. W. Simons, R.A.S.C.; 7. Pte. J. Levinger, Royal Fusiliers; 8. Cpl. F. Bernstein, 10th Northumberland Fusiliers; 9. Pte. B. Mordecai, Royal West Kent Regt.; 10. Pte. P. Sultag, 38th Royal Fusiliers; 11. Pte. H. Miller, R.A.O.C.; 12. L.-Cpl. M. Braham, R.A.M.C.

In Memoriam

1. 2nd-Lieut. DARYL JACOBS, 2/4th S. Lancs Regt.; 2. 2nd-Lieut. G. H. COHEN, 5th King's Liverpool Regt.; 3. Sub-Lieut. TREVOR JACOBS, Hood Battn. R. Naval Div.; 4. 2nd-Lieut. L. A. KLEMANTASKI, 8th Royal Berkshire Regt.; 5. 2nd-Lieut. A. R. HENRY, 1st Middlesex Regt.; 6. 2nd-Lieut. GEORGE H. LURY, 15th Auckland Battn. New Zealand Inf.; 7. Capt. R. SEBAG-MONTEFIORE, Royal East Kent Yeomanry; 8. Flight-Lieut. C. F. LAN-DAVIS, Royal Naval Air Service; 9. Capt. HAROLD L. I. SPIELMANN, 10th Manchester Regt.; 10. 2nd-Lieut. J. JOSEPHS, 12th London Regt.; 11. Capt. S. L. ROZELAAR, 8th Royal Berkshire Regt.; 12. Lieut. G. M. MICHAELIS, East Anglia R.E.

1. 2nd-Lieut. B. Bloom, 3rd King's Liverpool Regt.; 2. Capt. N. L. Harris, M.C., 9th Royal Welch Fus.; 3. Lieut. J. Marks, 15th Durham L.I.; 4. 2nd-Lieut. C. J. Frankenstein, 13th Battn. Tank Corps; 5. Nurse E. Hartman, V.A.D.; 6. 2nd-Lieut. J. Jacobs, 5th Yorks Regt.; 7. 2nd-Lieut. R. Hyman, 6th Duke of Cornwall's L.I.; 8. Capt. A. Jeffreys, 20th Northumberland Fusiliers; 9. 2nd-Lieut. M. Cohen, 21st London Regt.; 10. Capt. E. M. Green, 14th Hampshire Regt.; 11. Lieut. R. L. Q. Henriques, 2nd Royal West Surrey Regt.; 12. Capt. M. E. H. Schiff, 12th Suffolk Regt.

1. Cpl. E. Moses, India Defence Force.
   Pte. S. Samson, India Defence Force.

2. Rfn. J. Spevack, 18th K.R.R.C.
   Rfn. D. Cohen, 18th K.R.R.C.

3. Chaplain L. Morris.
   Rfn. A. B. Morris, 1/12th London Regt

4. A.M. Berstein, R.A.F.
   A.M. Krisman, R.A.F.
   A.M. Glass, R.A.F.

5. Three Jewish R.E.'s.

6. Sapper Epstein, I.W. & D.R.E.
   Sapper Melnick, I.W. & D.R.E

7. Pte. M. L. Sandown, R.A.S.C.
   Cpl. W. Lewin, M.M., M.G.Corps.

8. S.-Sergt. H. Menkin, D.C.M., R.F.A.
   Sapper C. S. Menkin, R.E.

54

In Memoriam

1. Pte. D. J. Goldberg, 8th Middlesex Regt.; 2. Pte. E. M. Cave, 6th East Kent Regt.; 3. Rfn. S. Samuel, 3rd Rifle Brigade; 4. Pte. H. F. Racionzier, R.F.A. and 27th Northumberland Fusiliers; 5. Pte. A. J. Jacobs, R.A.S.C.; 6. Pte. H. Shatcofsky, 8th M.G.C.; 7. Pte. M. Stibbe, 2nd Northumberland Fusiliers; 8. Rfn. M. Abrahams, 18th K.R.R. Corps; 9. Pte. A. A. Cohen, 1st Northampton Regt.; 10. Pte. J. Jacobs, 2/2nd London Regt.; 11. Pte. W. Rose (Rosenbaum), 15th Notts and Derby Regt.; 12. Rfn. H. Hart, 1/18th London Regt.

1. Pte. B. Samuels, 1/6th Highland L.I.; 2. Sergt. H. Levinson, 1st Cheshire Regt.; 3. Pte. Isaac Levy, 1st Border Regt.; 4. L.-Cpl. E. Woolfe, R.E.; 5. Pte. S. Simon, 13th Australian Infantry; 6. Pte. M. Hyams, London Rifle Brigade; 7. Pte. L. Barnett, R.A.S.C.; 8. Pte. S. Doodeward, R.A.M.C.; 9. Rfn. J. Fern, 17th London Regt.; 10. A. L. Nathan, 5th Seaforth Highlanders; 11. Pte. J. Timbler, R.F.A.; 12. Tpr. H. Jacobs, 15th Hussars.

Capt. A. Lesser. Rev. M. Adler. Rev. S. Lipson.

JEWISH OFFICERS AND MEN, HAMMERSMITH SYNAGOGUE—IN TRAINING—NOVEMBER 1914.

ROLL OF HONOUR, GLASGOW SYNAGOGUE.

In Memoriam

1. Rfn. DAVID DAVIS, 11th Rifle Brigade; 2. 1st-A.M. A. M. SCHNEIDERS, R.A.F.; 3. Tpr. M. PHILLIPS, Household Battn.; 4. Pte. J. COHEN, 18th King's Liverpool Regt.; 5. Pte. L. ALLONOWITZ, 38th Royal Fusiliers; 6. Pte. I. COHEN, 24th Cheshire Regt.; 7. Pte. S. MELTZER, 108th Labour Coy.; 8. Cpl. S. M. ISAACS, 1st Gordon Highlanders; 9. Pte. L. BARONOVICH, 1st Worcester Regt.; 10. Pte P. BLOSTEIN, M.M., 2nd Royal Dublin Fusiliers; 11. Pte. D. SMOLLEN, 7th Training Reserve Battn.; 12. Pte. R. WISE (COHEN), 2nd Lancashire Fusiliers

1. Sergt.-Major M. B. Beards, D.C.M., Canadian Artillery; 2. Pte. J. Levine, 10th Royal Warwick Regt.; 3. Pte. B. Levine, Lincoln Regt.; 4. A.M. A. Levy, R.A.F.; 5. Pte. L. Levine, 2nd Worcester Regt.; 6. A.M. C. S. Moses, R.A.F.; 7. Cpl. E. Silver, 1st K.R.R. Corps; 8. Sergt. B. Smole, Durham L.I.; 9. Pte. H. Rubenstein, 1st London Regt.; 10. Pte. M. Samuel, Canadian A.S.C.; 11. L.-Cpl. N. A. Shinberg, York and Lancaster Regt.; 12. Pte. W. Shinberg, London Regt.

1. Pte. I. ABRAHAMS, 2/10th London Regt.; 2. Pte. H. WISE (M. SIMCOVITCH), 40th Royal Fusiliers; 3. Pte. M. WOOLF, Royal Fusiliers and 5th South Wales Borderers; 4. Dvr. W. CHESSES, 31st Div. Signals R.E.; 5. Rfn. J. COHEN, 13th Rifle Brigade; 6. L.-Cpl. M. PHILLIPS, 1st East Lancs Regt.; 7. Pte. S. GINSBERG, 22nd Royal Fusiliers; 8. Pte. H. NYMAN, 1st West Yorks Regt.; 9. Pte. G. ROSENTHAL, 16th Northumberland Fusiliers; 10. Pte. M. GOLDSTEIN, 2nd Middlesex Regt.; 11. Pte. S. ROBINSON-MOLIVER, 2nd Royal Fusiliers; 12. L.-Cpl. J. I. COHEN, 2nd Wiltshire Regt.

1. Lieut. I. L. Bernstine, S. African Forces; 2. Lieut. M. G. Epstein, R.A.F.; 3. Lieut. M. L. Pool, 5th Dorset Regt.; 4. Capt. H. Davis, R.A.M.C.; 5. Capt. I. M. Gluckstein, 2/10th London Regt.; 6. Lieut. L. C. Marks, R.A.F.; 7. Major C. M. Spielman, M.C., R.E.; 8. 2nd-Lieut. H. C. Mendes, R.G.A.; 9. 2nd-Lieut. J. Shortt, R.A.F.; 10. Major W. Schonfield, T.D., 19th London Regt. and Royal Fusiliers Depot; 11. Sub-Assist.-Surgeon A. Ezekiel, I.S.M.C.; 12. Lieut. P. W. Davis, R.E.

1. Sergt. M. J. Goldberg, R.A.M.C.; 2. Pte. S. Cremer, 4th Lancashire Fusiliers; 3. Pte. H. Coleman, 18th York and Lancaster Regt.; 4. Sergt.-Major B. Freeman, R.A.S.C.; 5. Pte. M. Fwyansofsky, 9th Royal Irish Rifles; 6. Cpl. M. Cowan, R.A.F.; 7. Pte. A. Green, 3rd D.C.L.I.; 8. Wireless-Operator S. Lackmaker, R.N.; 9. Pte. W. Harris, R.A.F.; 10. L.-Cpl. C. Abrahams, 3rd Essex Regt.; 11. A.B. S. Myers, H.M.S. *Devonshire*; 12. Pte. P. Cohen, 5th Royal Fusiliers.

In Memoriam

1. Rfn. S. Sherman, 2/8th West Yorks Regt.; 2. Rfn. L. L. Levy, 9th Scottish Rifles; 3. Pte. H. Moscovsky, 1st East Kent Regt.; 4. Gnr. J. Isaacs, A/92nd Brigade, R.F.A.; 5. Pte. L. Levy, 1st Hants Regt; 6. Pte. L. E. Franks, 1/6th Northumberland Fusiliers; 7. Cpl. J. Page (Rosenthal), 18th Canadian Infantry; 8. Pte. C. Levine, 112th M.G.C.; 9. Rfn. J. Polakoff, 2nd K.R.R.C.; 10. Pte. N. Morris, 19th Manchester Regt.; 11. Rfn. D. Fox, 15th London Regt.; 12. Pte. I. Schwartz, 4th Royal Fusiliers.

GROUP OF JEWISH OFFICERS AND MEN, ALDERSHOT, 1915.

Lieut. G. G. Samuel (later killed in action); Rev. D. Hirsch; Rev. S. Lipson, S.C.F.; Lieut. De S. Lewis-Barned.

JEWISH WAR MEMORIALS ABROAD.

Top.—Grave of Rfn. H. R. LEWIS, 1/12th London Regt., Poperinghe Cemetery.
Bottom.—Graves of the first Jewish V.C., Lieut. F. A. DE PASS, Poona Horse, and Capt. C. W. BAMBERGER, R.E., Cethune Cemetery.

1. Pte. I. Mason, 14th Gloucester Regt.; 2. Pte. Dan Glassman, 1st Duke of Cornwall's L.I.; 3. Tpr. David Cohen, 4th Hussars; 4. Rfn. P. P. Singer, 2nd Rifle Brigade; 5. Pte. M. Bluestone, 1001st Labour Coy.; 6. Pte. M. Newhouse, 14th Highland L.I.; 7. Gnr. H. Bloom, R.H.A.; 8. Pte. H. Lubel, 8th North Staffs Regt.; 9. Sergt. L. Cohen, 1st Royal Welch Fusiliers; 10. Q.M.S. J. S. Conquy, R.A.M.C.; 11. Pte. I. Bomberg, 2nd Yorks Regt.; 12. Rfn. R. Barnett, 1st Rifle Brigade.

In Memoriam

1. Rfn. L. E. Goldston, 21st London Regt.; 2. Sergt. Martin Sobel, Locker Lampson Armoured Car; 3. Pte. J. Glassberg, 12th Manchester Regt.; 4. Pte. M. S. Vanderlind, R.A.M.C.; 5. Pte. J. Gold, 1st King's Liverpool Regt.; 6. C.Q.M.S. S. Schonewald, 2nd L.R. Bgde.; 7. Pte. L. Gerlisky, 4th Royal Sussex Regt.; 8. Pte. P. Cohen, 7th Royal Fusiliers; 9. Pte. J. Tubb, R.A.S.C.; 10. Pte. R. Claff, 1st Somerset L.I.; 11. Pte. M. Carmel, 302nd Labour Coy.; 12. Pte. A. Woodrow, 4th Canadian Inf.

STAFF OF BEECH HOUSE MILITARY HOSPITAL

Back Row: Miss Regensburg; Miss Greisbach; Miss Samuels; Miss Harris; Mr. Hyams; Mr. Joseph; Miss Hirschland; Miss A. Marks.
Second Row: Miss Rosenthal; Miss Salom; Mrs. Colman; Mrs. Stember; Miss Henry; Mrs. Levy; Mrs. Singer; Mrs. Simmons; Miss G. Marks; Miss Rains.
Third Row: Miss Isaacs; Miss Janie Joseph; Mrs. Marsden, R.R.C.; Mrs. Davidson, M.B.E.; Mrs. Abrahams, R.R.C.
Fourth Row: Miss L. Lazarus; Miss H. Lazarus; Miss M. Lazarus; Mrs. Barnett; Miss Borgzinner.
Miss J. Joseph became Commandant of Tudor House.

1. Dvr. D. Isaacs, R.F.A.; 2. Capt.-Qr.-Mr. C. Goodman, 14th King's Liverpool Regt.; 3. Dvr. J. Hart, R.F.A.; 4. Lieut. J. Hart, 2/4th Hampshire Regt.; 5. Pte. P. Bernstock, Somerset Light Infantry; 6. Pte. H. C. Bernstock, Canadian A.S.C.; 7. Lieut.-Col. C. Waley. Cohen, C.M.G., R.A.S.C.; 8. 2nd-Lieut. J. A. Drapkin, M.M., Royal Fusiliers and 2nd K.R.R.C.; 9. Lieut. T. H. Fligelstone, M.C., 38th Royal Fusiliers; 10. Capt. and Adjt. I. Jaffe, 38th Royal Fusiliers; 11. 2nd-Lieut. L. Stone, 39th Royal Fusiliers; 12. Lieut. G. John Jacobs, R.A.S.C.; 13. Lieut. H. Wolfensohn, 38th Royal Fusiliers.

1. Miss KATE MAGNUS, V.A.D.; 2. Mrs. BISCHOFFSHEIM, who gave Tudor House, Hampstead, as a Military Hospital; 3. Mrs. JULIA LYONS, V.A.D.; 4. Miss JEANETTE NATHAN, V.A.D.; 5. Mrs. F. HESS, V.A.D.; 6. Miss VOILET SPEELMAN, V.A.D; 7. Miss AUGUSTA LUDLOW, V.A.D.; 8. Dr. A. GASTER, M.D., attached to Tudor House; 9. Miss BETTY ALVAREZ, V.A.D.; 10. Miss ELLA ROSE, V.A.D.; 11. Mrs. BERTHA PHILLIPS, V.A.D.; 12. Miss ROSE RAINS, V.A.D.

TUDOR HOUSE MILITARY HOSPITAL, HAMPSTEAD.

Back Row: Ptes. Witowsky, Medwediner, Scarminsky, Woolf, Levy, Stroom, Matofsky, Feldman, Freedman, Freeman, Davis, Lazarus, Kolasky.
Second Row: Pte. Gleek, Miss E. Davis, Mrs. Cohen, Miss S. Ritch, Miss Kopenhagen, Miss Ritch, Miss Lubin, Mrs. Lowenthal, Pte. Fine, Q.M.S. Hooten.
Sitting: Miss Woolf, Miss de Bear, Lady Prince, Sister Weiner, Dr. Lowenthal, Miss J. Joseph, O.B.E. (Commandant), Miss H. Samuels, Miss Mendel, Miss Lipman, Mrs. Robinson, Mrs. Barnett, Miss Kerman.
Front Row: Ptes. Levy, Parkes, Spevack, Abrahams.

Back Row: Ptes. Levy, Van Cleff, Zussman.
Second Row: Ptes. Gobowsky, Scarminsky, Feldman, Marks, Rose, Miss E. Davis, Ptes. Woolf, Gleek, Levy.
Centre Row (sitting): Pte. Silverman, Miss De Bear, Miss Middleton, Mrs. Lowenthal, Miss J. Joseph, O.B.E. (Commandant), Dr. L. Lowenthal, Sister S. Weiner, Miss Lubin, Mrs. Barnett.
In Front: Ptes. Parkes, Spevack, Barnett.

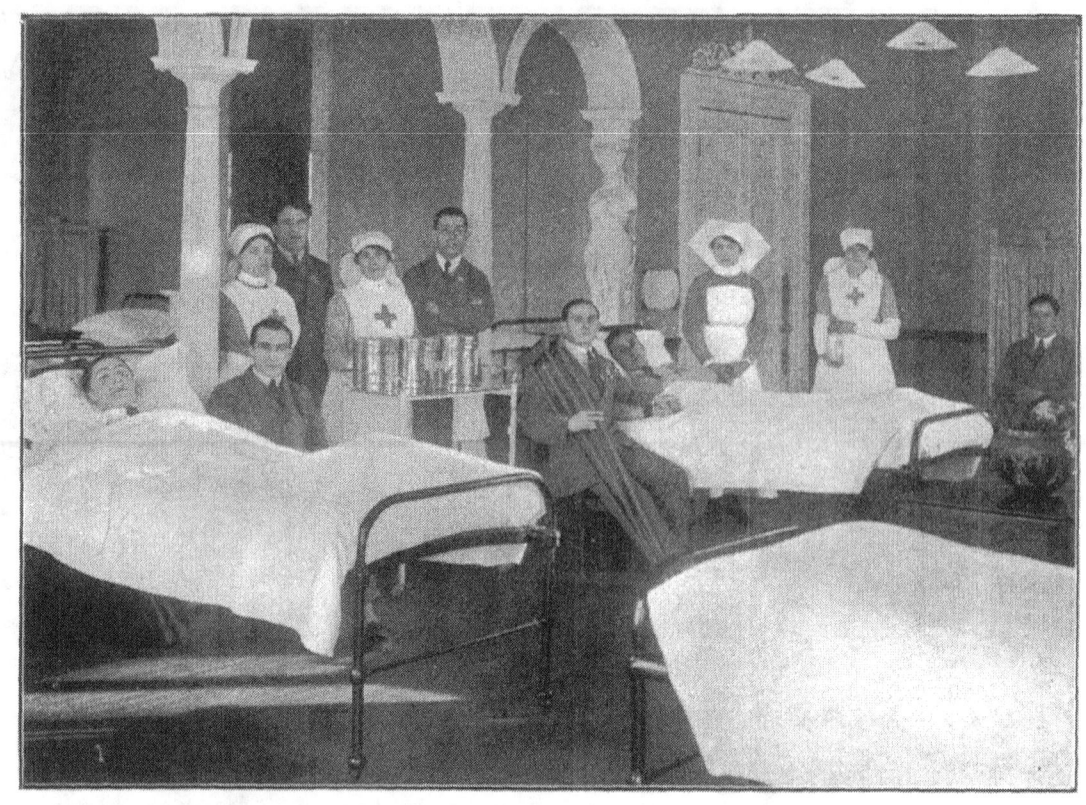

TUDOR HOUSE MILITARY HOSPITAL.

Presentation of the Medals of the O.B.E. to Lieut. LIOVA SHNEERSON (1) and Lieut. JUSSEF DAVIDESCO (2), Palestine Jews, by Major-General HODGSON, (3), at Haifa, Palestine, on September 10th, 1919; (4) Colonel STANTON; (5) Capt. A. AARONSON, D.S.O., Intelligence Dept., E.E.F.

1. C.S.M. S. ROME AND FRIEND, 39TH ROYAL FUSILIERS.
2. GROUP OF 40TH ROYAL FUSILIERS IN PALESTINE.
3. Q.M. STAFF, 38TH ROYAL FUSILIERS, SALTASH CAMP.

Top.—Group of Manchester Jewish soldiers in the Pembroke Yeomanry.
Bottom.— 38th Royal Fusiliers (Jewish). Group of men from Liverpool.

38TH ROYAL FUSILIERS (JEWISH) MUSKETRY STAFF, PALESTINE, 1918.

Top.—Band of the 38th Royal Fusiliers, Plymouth, 1918.
Bottom.—N.C.O.'s of 38th Royal Fusiliers, Plymouth, February 1918.

Top.—38th Royal Fusiliers' Football Team, Plymouth, 1918.
Bottom.—Concert Party, Royal Fusiliers, Plymouth.

DEPOT: 38TH—40TH ROYAL FUSILIERS (JEWISH), 1918.
Major W. Schonfield, T.D., in command.

1. Pte. E. Berg, Royal Fusiliers; 2. Cpl. R. Lazarus, 2nd Queen's (R.W. Surrey Regt.) and Royal Fusiliers; 3. Pte. S. Slomovitch, 38th Royal Fusiliers; 4. Sergt. H. Silverstone, 2nd K.O.R. Lancaster Regt.; 5. Rfn. H. Sherek, 9th London Regt.; 6. Bdmn. S. S. Silverman, 3rd Canadian Infantry; 7. L.-Cpl. A. Lewbitz, 2nd Gloucester Regt.; 8. Rfn. L. Levy, 13th K.R.R. Corps; 9. Pte. H. Schneiderman, Middlesex Regt.; 10. Pte. S. Littman, 3rd Essex Regt.; 11. L.-Cpl. A. Lawrence, K.O.R. Lancaster Regt.; 12. Pte. H. Rosenberg, R.A.M.C.

Top.—Open-air Service, 40th Palestinian Royal Fusiliers, Sergt. RUBEN officiating.
Bottom.—Jewish soldiers of Anzac and British Regiments in Jerusalem, Pentecost, 1918.

Top.—38th Royal Fusiliers (Jewish) at dinner, Egypt.
Bottom.—Signalling Section, 40th Royal Fusiliers.

Top.—Group of 38th Royal Fusiliers (Scouts), Palestine, with Lieut. S. ABRAHAMS.
Bottom.—Group of Royal Fusiliers, Palestine, with Lieut. S. LIPSEY.

Top.—38th Royal Fusiliers entraining at Cairo for Palestine Front, 1918.
Bottom.—38th Royal Fusiliers : Regimental Military Police.

1. THREE SERGEANTS 38TH ROYAL FUSILIERS.
2. GROUP OF 38TH ROYAL FUSILIERS.
3. GROUP OF 38TH ROYAL FUSILIERS.

1. Sergt. BILLY BLOCK, 38th Royal Fusiliers; 2. Pte. J. SOLOMONS, 38th Royal Fusiliers; 3. Sergt. H. ISAACS, 39th Royal Fusiliers; 4. O.R. Sergt. D. B. REUBEN, 40th Royal Fusiliers (Palestinians); 5 and 6. Pte. H. MICHAELS and Friend, 40th Royal Fusiliers; 7. R.S.M. J. CARMEL, 38th Royal Fusiliers; 8. R.S.M. S. M. SPYER, 40th Royal Fusiliers (Palestinians); 9. L.-Cpl. L. GILLIS, 38th Royal Fusiliers; 10. Pte. J. FREEDMAN, 40th Royal Fusiliers; 11. Cpl. ELLIS COWEN, 39th Royal Fusiliers; 12. Pte. J. MIVANSKY, 40th Royal Fusiliers; 13. L.-Cpl. LO BAGOLA (native of Dahomey), 39th Royal Fusiliers.

1. Pte. I. Solet, 11th Queen's (R.W. Surrey Regt.); 2. Pte. S. Bernstein, Labour Corps; 3. Sergt. D. Verblowsky, Canadian Infantry; 4. Rfn. H. Finklestein, K.R.R.C.; 5. Pte. J. Morris, 2/19th London Regt.; 6. Pte. A. Green, 38th Royal Fusiliers; 7. Pte. S. Blendis, 26th Royal Fusiliers; 8. Pte. R. Goodman, R.A.M.C.; 9. Pte. A. Blendis, R.A.F.; 10. A/Sergt. C. Hyman, 38th Royal Fusiliers; 11. Sergt. J. H. Goodman, King's Liverpool and 5th West Riding Regt.; 12. Spr. S. Blendis, R.E.; 13. Cadet Sydney F. Goodman, R.A.M.C.

1. Pte. S. Morris, 3rd R.W. Kent Regt.; 2. Armourer-Sergt. E. Myers, Canadian Infantry; 3. Cpl. R. Weinberg, Australian A.M.C.; 4. L.-Cpl. A. Phillips, 11th Welsh Regt.; 5. Pte. P. Sniders, R.M.L.I.; 6. 2nd A.M. G. Weinberg, R.A.F.; 7. Pte. D. Sugarman, R.A.M.C.; 8. Pte. S. G. Salberg, D.C.M., 9th Royal Scots.; 9. Fitter L. Rosenfeld, R.F.A.; 10. Pte. I. Saul, 18th York and Lancs Regt.; 11. Gnr. D. Weinberg, R.F.A.; 12. Gnr. M. Lubrinsky, R.F.A.

OFFICERS OF 38TH ROYAL FUSILIERS (JEWISH), PLYMOUTH, FEBRUARY 1918.

Lieuts. Cross, Evans, H. Morris, E. M. Daltroff, I. Jaffe, H. Wolfensohn, Harris, M. Symonds, Nevill, B. M. Wolffe (died from an accident).
Sitting.—Capt. Julian, Capt. Hyams, Capt. Neill, Lieut.-Col. J. H. Patterson (D.S.O), Capt. Ripley, Lieut. Smythe, Capt. Harris.

OFFICERS OF 39TH ROYAL FUSILIERS (JEWISH), HELMIEH CAMP, CAIRO, AUGUST, 1918.

Row 1.—2nd-Lieut. SALMON, 2nd-Lieut. COWEN, 2nd-Lieut. MYERS, 2nd-Lieut. KEYZER, ———, 2nd-Lieut. STONE, 2nd-Lieut. PHILLIPS.
Row 2.—Lieut. GILMAN, Lieut. NEWPORT, Lieut. MURPHY, Capt. BEATTY, Capt. BARNETT, Lieut. H. DE V. RUBIN, 2nd-Lieut. MURPHY, 2nd-Lieut. BARNETT.
Row 3.—Capt. SAMUELSON, Capt. CATHER, Capt. J. L. RACIONZER, Dr. R. N. SALAMAN, Lieut.-Col. E. MARGOLIN, D.S.O., Major D. HOPKIN, M.C., Capt. WHITWORTH, D.S.O., Capt. SMALLEY, Capt. REID.
Row 4.—Lieuts. RICH, LEVY, JACOBS, HARRIS, H. WOLFENSOHN, COUSSIN, ARNOLD, BROWN.

38TH BATTN. ROYAL FUSILIERS ("JUDEANS"), PLYMOUTH, 1917.

38TH BATTN. ROYAL FUSILIERS ("JUDEANS"), PLYMOUTH, 1917.

38TH BATTN. ROYAL FUSILIERS ("JUDEANS"), PLYMOUTH, 1917.

LIEUT.-COL. J. H. PATTERSON, D.S.O., AND 38TH BATTN. ROYAL FUSILIERS RECRUITS.

Top.—Group of 38/40th Royal Fusiliers, Depôt, Saltash Camp.
Bottom.—Group of 40th Royal Fusiliers

Top.—Group of 38th Royal Fusiliers.
Bottom.—Group of 38th Royal Fusiliers in camp

Top.—Recruiting Officers, 40th Royal Fusiliers (Palestinians), Tel-Aviv, 1918: Major E. WALEY, O.B.E., Staff, Egyptian Expeditionary Force; Major JAMES DE ROTHSCHILD, D.C.M., O.C. *(centre)*; Lieut. H. WOLFENSOHN, Adjutant.

Bottom.—Dr. C. WEIZMANN presenting a Scroll of the Law and a Flag to the Recruits of the 40th Royal Fusiliers (Palestinians), Tel-Aviv, 1918: 1. Dr. WEIZMANN; 2. Major J. DE ROTHSCHILD; 3. Major E. WALEY.

RECRUITS OF 40TH ROYAL FUSILIERS (PALESTINIANS)

1 & 2. The raw material at Kantara, Egypt
3. A month later in camp at Tel Aviv, Jaffa.

RECRUITS OF 40TH ROYAL FUSILIERS (PALESTINIANS).

1. After two weeks.
2. The guard.
3. Lesson in bayonet fighting.

Top.—Recruits of 40th Royal Fusiliers on the shores of the Mediterranean near Jaffa.
Bottom.—Recruits of 40th Royal Fusiliers at the Sports.

Top.—Musketry Staff, 40th Palestinian Royal Fusiliers, Palestine.
Bottom.—British Units, Passover, Jerusalem, 1918.

Top.—Medal presented to Recruits of 40th (Palestine) Royal Fusiliers, 1st Judeans, 1918, designed at the Belazel School of Art, Jerusalem.

Bottom.—Badge of the 40th (Palestine) Royal Fusiliers, 1st Judeans.

The design of the medal on the left is based on the coin struck by the Emperor Vespasian in A.D. 70, on the downfall of Jerusalem. This coin showed a weeping Jewess seated on the ground and a Roman soldier standing triumphant. The inscription was *Judæa Capta.* (See Madden's *Jewish Coinage*, p. 183, etc.) In the modern medal the Jewess has thrown off her chains and the soldier is fleeing, the Hebrew inscription being *Judæa Liberated.*

On the reverse the Hebrew reads: "To those who willingly offered themselves among the people." The Land of Israel, Year 1849 (i.e. from the year A.D. 70. to 1919).

The Hebrew on the badge is "Eastward."

No. 1.

Fortieth Jewish Battalion.   Tel Aviv.
Routine Orders.   January 25th June 1918.

1. Parades:- N.C.O's Classes:-
   Physical training (under Sgt Palgar D.L.) 10 am
   daily   (under Sgt Ernst S.M.) 11 am
   daily

   Recruits will parade at Bn. Hdqrs Cherush at 5 pm.
   All must attend.

   All men not yet medically examined parade
   before the Medical Officer at 2.0 pm. 26/6/18
   All men not yet addressed by Colonel Ferguson. Comdg.
   unit, parade outside the Recruiting Office at 4.0 pm 26/6/18

   Sick Parade:- 8.45 am. outside Hospital under
   Corporal Cowen.

2. General Routine:-
   Passes:- Passes will be issued between the hours of
   2 pm + 3 pm daily
   Officers:- will be attended to between 2 pm
   + 3 pm daily
   Discipline:- All men must be about daily
   hair must be worn short.
   Meals:- The time for meals will be as under:-
   Breakfast:-   7 am.
   Lunch:-   12.30 pm.
   Dinner:-   6.30 pm.

   [signature]
   Major,
   39th Royal Fusiliers.

EARLIEST ROUTINE ORDERS ISSUED IN PALESTINE TO RECRUITS OF THE 40TH
(PALESTINIAN) ROYAL FUSILIERS.

No 2.

DETACHMENT JEWISH BATTALION.

Routine Orders.

1/ PARADES:-

N.C.O's Classes. Physical Training (Under Sgt. Salzedo, S.L.) 10 a.m.
Drill (" " Spuer, S.M.) 11 a.m.

Recruits will parade at 4.30 p.m. at Beth Sepher Lebanoth. All must attend.

All men not yet medically examined will parade before the Medical Officer at 9 a.m. 27th inst.,

All men not yet approved by Colonel Fergusson, C.M.G. will parade outside the Recruiting Office at 4 p.m. 27th inst.,

Sick Parade. at 8.45 a.m. under L/Cpl. Gillis, L.

2/ GENERAL ROUTINE:-

Discipline. It is observed that Recruits attend parades unshaven. Routine Order No.2 of the 25th inst., must be strictly adhered to.

Meal Hours. Recruits must attend meals punctually; those parading late will not be served.

Tel-Aviv, Wednesday,
26th June, 1918.

EARLIEST ROUTINE ORDERS ISSUED IN PALESTINE TO RECRUITS OF THE 40TH (PALESTINIAN) ROYAL FUSILIERS.

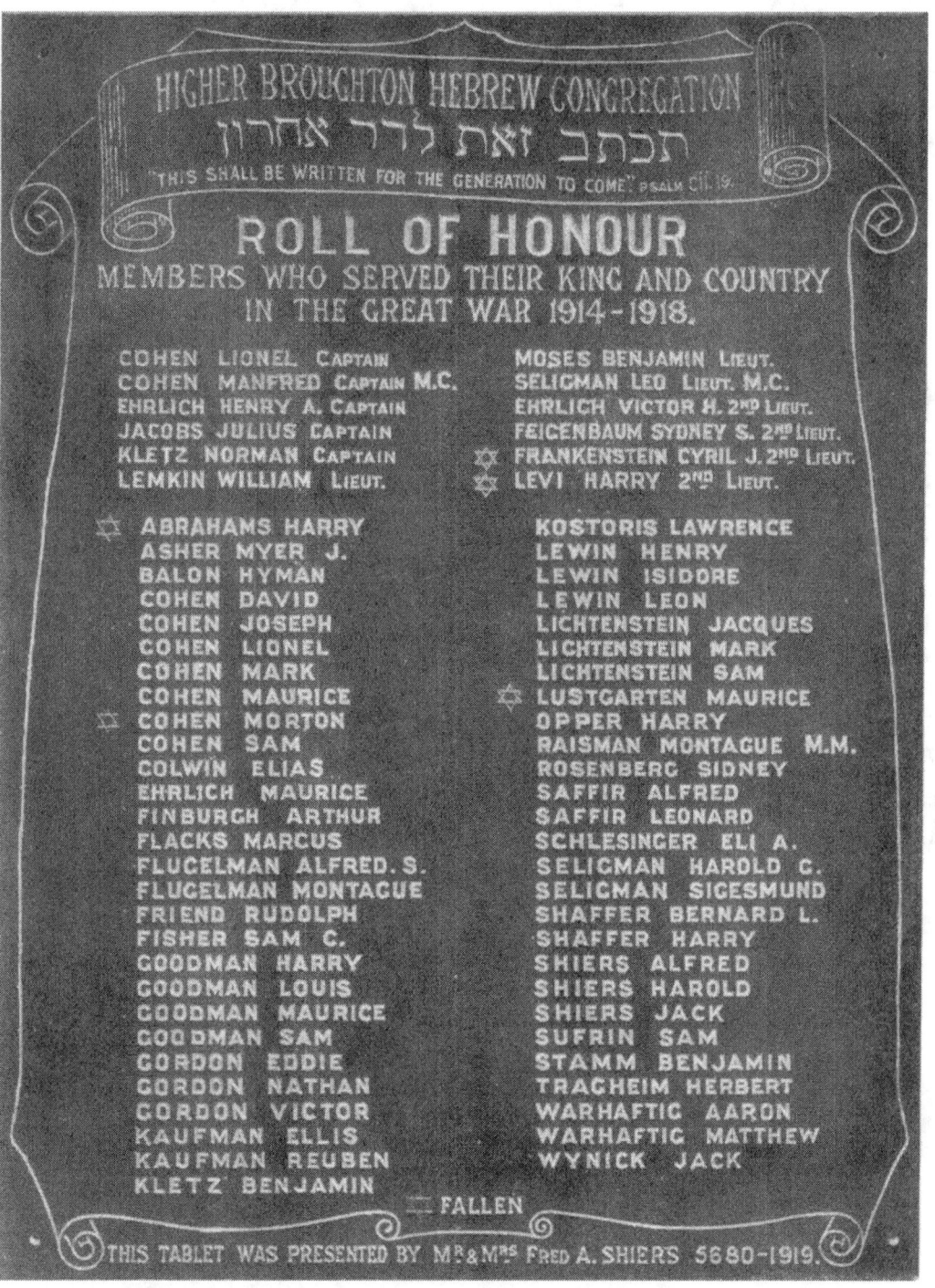

WAR MEMORIAL, HIGH BROUGHTON SYNAGOGUE, MANCHESTER.

1. Capt. R. Heumann, 2nd London Regt.; 2. Capt. H. S. Benjamin, 1/8th Worcestershire Regt.; 3. Capt. J. de Meza, M.C., 19th London Regt.; 4. Lieut. L. D. Goldseller, 2/5th West Riding Regt.; 5. 2nd-Lieut. W. E. W. Bamberger, 1/5th Gloucester Regt.; 6. 2nd-Lieut. A. Reese, M.C., 2nd W. Yorks Regt.; 7. Capt. Leigh J. Davis, 1/19th London Regt.; 8. Capt. C. D. W. Bamberger, Royal Engineers; 9. Lieut. E. J. A. Paiba, 2nd Royal Fusiliers; 10. 2nd-Lieut. S. Fine, 15th Squad. R.A.F.; 11. Lieut. B. Wolffe, 38th Royal Fusiliers; 12. Lieut. P. Sherek, Westminster Dragoons and R.A.F.

1. Pte. LIONEL ALTMAN, 1st Bedford Regt.; 2. Cpl. SYDNEY ASHER, 20th Durham L.I. att. 9th Yorks & Lancs Regt.; 3. Pte. J. BLACKMAN, 56th M.G. Corps; 4. Pte. W. BECKER, 9th Royal Fusiliers; 5. Pte. L. BARZOLOI, 1/19th London Regt.; 6. L.-Cpl. H. R. BAKER, 1st S. African Inf.; 7. Pte. M. BARNETT, 2/11th London Regt.; 8. Tpr. S. A. BERNSTEIN, Middlesex Imperial Yeomanry; 9. Pte. D. CHESNEY, 1st Coldstream Guards; 10. Pte. A. BERNHARD, 9th Lancers; 11. Pte. PHIL BLACKER, 2/6th Royal Sussex Regt.; 12. Pte. B. BRICK, 38th Royal Fusiliers.

1. Cpl. B. H. Levy, R.A.O.C.
   Cpl. I. J. Levy, West Somerset Yeomanry.

2. Gnr. F. Wilson, R.F.A.
   Pte. L. Kroftchinscky, 39th Royal Fusiliers.

3. Mrs. Marsden, R.R.C.
   Mr. Marsden, Special Constable.
   2nd-Lieut. Claude Marsden, R.A.F.
   Lieut. Chas. Marsden, R.N.

4. Lieut. P. Gluckman, 1/3rd London Regt.
   Pte. S. Gluckman, 3rd S. African Inf.
   Pte. L. Gluckman, S. African Inf.
   Pte. (later Lieut.) B. Gluckman, 3rd S. African Inf. and Royal Fusiliers.

5. Pte. M. Barnett, 1st Middlesex Regt.
   Pte. A. Barnett, 1st Middlesex Regt.
   Pte. S. Barnett, 1st Middlesex Regt.
   Pte. N. Barnett, 1st Middlesex Regt.

6. Pte. J. N. Quesky, 14th E. Yorks Regt.
   Scout S. Quesky.
   Pte. H. Quesky, 14th E. Yorks Regt.

7. A family group of Red Cross Workers:
   Back Row. Mr. F. Davidson, Mrs. F. Davidson, M.B.E., Mr. Hyam H. Jacobs.
   Front Row. Mr. John D. Jacobs, Miss Rhoda R. Jacobs, Miss Charlotte Jacobs, Mr. Albert J. Jacobs.

8. R.Q.M.S. R. G. Davis, L.R. Bgde.
   2nd-Lieut. K. Davis, L.R. Bgde.
   Pte. D. G. Davis, L.R. Bgde. (now R.A.F.).
   Pte. C. M. Davis, L.R. Bgde.

1. 2nd-Lieut. R. STRUMP, Indian Army; 2. 2nd-Lieut. JULIUS JACOBS, Manchester Regt.; 3. 2nd-Lieut. NATHAN ROBINSON, R.A.F.; 4. Rev. H. SHANDEL (Officiating Clergyman); 5. Lieut. E. E. GROSSMANN, 12th London Regt.; 6. Lieut. M. C. CASSELL, 1st K.O.R. Lancaster Regt.; 7. Capt. C. STANLEY KERIN, 7th Seaforth Hrs.; 8. Rev. B. B. LIEBERMAN, C.F.; 9. 2nd-Lieut. M. DREYFUS, South Staffs Regt.; 10. 2nd-Lieut. ARTHUR A. WHITE, 29th Battn. M.G.C.; 11. Lieut. ERIC A. BINGEN, 5th Royal Sussex Regt., attd. R.A.F.; 12. Lieut. H. L. V. BEDDINGTON, R.F.A.

1. Pte. S. Davis, Royal Welsh Regt.; 2. Sergt. E. M. Henochsberg, Intelligence Corps, S. African Forces; 3. L.-Cpl. B. Black, 1st G.B. West Yorks Regt.; 4. Cpl. H. Blom, 1/17th London Regt.; 5. Pte. S. Abrahams, Welsh Regt.; 6. Pte. D. S. Isaacs, 11th Middlesex Regt.; 7. Pte. H. F. Israel (M.T.), R.A.S.C.; 8. Sergt. C. A. Henry, R.A.S.C.; 9. R.S.M. M. Jenkins, 13th Bgde. R.F.A.; 10. S.-Sergt. H. Hernberg, Army Gymnastic Staff; 11. Pte. J. Littman, R.A.O.C.; 12. 2nd-A.M. F. Harris, R.A.F.

1. Pte. C. Rosenthal, 4th London Regt.; 2. Rfn. P. Goldstone, 9th K.R.R.C.; 3. Pte. D. Ginsberg, 13th London Regt.; 4. Tpr. C. J. Truefitt, Essex Yeomanry; 5. Rfn. N. Woolf, 17th London Regt.; 6. Pte. G. Marquis, 13th Australian Infantry; 7. Pte. R. R. Lehmann, 6th Seaforth Highlanders; 8. Pte. I. Solomons, 4th Royal Fusiliers; 9. Sergt. D. Black, 1st Highland L.I.; 10. Sergt. M. Saxon, 12th Highland L.I.; 11. Pte. C. Letzky, 2nd Durham L.I.; 12. Rfn. S. Fox, 2nd Rifle Brigade.

1. Pte. A. Caminer, 2nd Middlesex Regt.; 2. Pte. B. Berman, 4th S. African Inf.; 3. Pte. Jack Dion, M.M., 5th Northampton Regt.; 4. Pte. D. G. Collins, 1st Grenadier Guards; 5. Rfn. S. Abrahams, 16th London Regt. (Q.W.R.); 6. Pte. S. Davison, 1st Essex Regt.; 7. Rfn. J. Da Costa, 2nd Rifle Brigade; 8. Pte. D. Barnett, 39th Royal Fusiliers; 9. Pnr. S. Abrahams, R.E.; 10. Pte. C. Braham, 1/1st London Regt.; 11. Cpl. M. Crook, R.A.F.; 12. Pte. J. Diamondstone, 23rd Middlesex Regt.

WAR MEMORIAL, LIBERAL JEWISH SYNAGOGUE, WILLESDEN, N.W.

In Memoriam

1. Capt. F. W. Haldenstein, R.E.; 2. 2nd-Lieut. Edgar B. Samuel, 16th Middlesex Regt.; 3. 2nd-Lieut. P. J. Posener, 2nd Wilts Regt.; 4. 2nd-Lieut. James A. Marks, 10th North Staffs Regt.; 5. Major Montague Abrahams, 16th Rifle Brigade; 6. Capt. E. Schonfield, 2/19th London Regt.; 7. 2nd-Lieut. F. H. Isaacs, 11th Royal Scots Fusiliers; 8. 2nd-Lieut. G. B. Samuel, Durham L.I. and R.A.F.; 9. Capt. Alfred Baswitz, M.C., 1/22nd London Regt.; 10. 2nd-Lieut. Denzil G. A. Myer, 9th Worcester Regt. att. 7th N. Staffs Regt.; 11. Capt. E. R. Capper, M.C., 9th Essex Regt.; 12. Capt. J. E. Rothband, 23rd Manchester Regt.

1. Dvr. H. Silverman, R.A.S.C.; 2. L.-Cpl. A. Behrman, R.A.S.C.; 3. Gnr. H. Seigar, R.G.A.; 4. Pte. R. Reed, Welsh Regt.; 5. Pte. S. Lyons, R.A.M.C.; 6. Pte. S. List, 1/8th Worcester Regt.; 7. Pte. M. Cohen, M.M., 2nd Oxford and Bucks L.I.; 8. Sergt. E. H. Robinson, R.E.; 9. Pte. M. Gatoff, 1st Gn. Battn. North Staffords; 10. Pte. M. H. Benoliel, 8th M.G.C.; 11. Gnr. H. Rose, R.F.A.; 12. Pte. H. E. Levy, R.A.S.C.

ON ACTIVE SERVICE: Rev. MICHAEL ADLER, S.C.F., AND GROUP, ROUEN, MAY 19, 1915.

Back Row: Dvr. S. Schweitzer, A.S.C.; Pte. L. Levy, 2nd Manchester Regt.; Pte. J. Spero, A.S.C.; Sgt. L. Nathan (M.M.), Q.V.R.; Pte. J. Hepstone (killed in action), 1st K.O.R. Lancs Regt.; Pte. I. Abrahams, Indian Veterinary Corps; Pte. A. Goldman, 2nd W. Riding Regt.; Rfn. D. Cohen, 12th London Regt.; Pte. A. Carlish, A.S.C.
Second Row: Dvr. J. Hershman, A.S.C.; Pte. S. Lessman, 3rd London Regt.; Pte. F. Spicker, A.S.C.; Pte. R. Friedlander, 7th London Regt.; Pte. M. Needle, A.S.C.; Pte. R. Goodman, R.A.M.C.; Pte. M. Gavson, A.S.C.; Pte. M. Althusen (killed in action), 1st K.O.R. Lancs Regt.; Pte. M. Levy, A.S.C.; L.-Cpl. B. Lyons, 1st West Yorks Regt.
Third Row: Pte. L. Blush, A.S.C.; Pte. J. H. Bernstock, 4th London Regt.; Sergt. J. Harris, A. Cyclist Corps.; Sergt. M. M. Polack, A.S.C.; Rev. Michael Adler, S.C.F.; Capt. M. Joseph, Indian Pay Corps; Pte. B. Salmon, A.S.C.; Pte. R. Simmons, R.A.M.C.; Pte. N. Goldstuck, R.A.M.C.
At Foot: Pte. H. Constad, A.S.C.

1. Sergt. P. VALLENTINE, King Edward's Horse; 2. Sergt.-Major B. LEVY, South African Pay Corps; 3. Pte. B. JOSEPHS, R.A.M.C.; 4. Pte. M. SCHONBERG, 2nd South African Infantry Brigade; 5. Spr. M. ROSEBERG, Australian Engineers; 6. Pte. P. VALLENTINE, R.A.M.C.; 7. Pte. J. ROSENHEIM, 4th K.O.S.B.; 8. Sergt. S. L. SAMS, B.R.C.S.; 9. Pte. S. RACKIND, Army Cyclist Corps; 10. A/C.S.M. H. JACOBS, 2/16th London Regt.; 11. Flight-Cadet P. VALLENTINE, R.A.F.; 12. Pte. S. MATTHEWS, 38th Royal Fusiliers.

1. Pte. J. Levy, 16th Tank Corps; 2. Pte. E. B. Barnett, 24th London Regt.; 3. Pte. A. Reinfleisch, 19th Middlesex Regt.; 4. Pte. H. Brown, 2nd Royal Sussex Regt.; 5. Pte. J. Pearlman, R.E.; 6. Rfn. H. Jacobs, 1st K.R.R.C.; 7. Pte. A. Bankofsky, 258th Area Employment Coy.; 8. Pte. P. Rubinstein, 6/7th Royal Scots Fusiliers; 9. Pte. A. Pivansky, 2nd Middlesex Regt.; 10. Pte. W. J. Latsky, M.T., R.A.S.C.; 11. Pte. Hymon Falk, Middlesex Regt. attached 1st London Rifle Brigade; 12. Pte. A. Rosenbaum, 8th East Surrey Regt.

In Memoriam

1. Pte. N. JACOBS, 3rd Worcester Regt.; 2. Sergt. B. VAN PRAAG, 15th Durham L.I.; 3. Pte. E. E. ISAACS, 2nd Worcester Regt.; 4. Pte. M. S. C. MOSELY, 7th Border Regt.; 5. Pte. J. SUSMAN, 1st Oxford and Bucks L.I.; 6. Pte. M. PRIMACK, 49th Canadian Infantry; 7. Pte. M. MORACK, 10th East Yorks Regt.; 8. L.-Cpl. J. B. LAZARUS, 2nd South African Infantry; 9. Pte. J. LEVY, 11th R.W. Surrey Regt.; 10. L.-Cpl. W. SHENOW, 5th Royal Berks Regt.; 11. Rfn. J. WOOLF, 16th K.R.R.C.; 12. Pte. J. G. BARNEY, 2nd Honourable Artillery Company.

1. Pte. C. M. Marks, Australian Inf.; 2. Pte. A. Sankerwitz, 51st M.G.C.; 3. Spr. B. J. Krebsman, R.E.; 4. C.Q.M.S. A. Safferty, 13th Middlesex Regt.; 5. L.-Cpl. G. J. Jacobs, 3rd Royal Fusiliers; 6. Pte. M. R. Samuel, India Defence Force; 7. Sergt. E. M. Theomin, Wellington New Zealand Regt.; 8. Pte. S. Rose, 8th South Wales Borderers; 9. Sig. J. Zealander, R.F.A.; 10. Cpl. G. G. Zissman, D.C.M., R.A.M.C.; 11. Gnr. M. Taylor, R.G.A.; 12. L.-Cpl. P. Sankerwitz, 12th London Regt.

JEWISH WAR MEMORIALS AT HOME.

1. Edinburgh Synagogue: Memorial in the Cemetery.
2. Liverpool Synagogue, Prince's Road.
3. Memorial to 2nd-Lieut. DENZIL A. MYER, East London Synagogue.
4. Liverpool Hebrew School.
5. Bayswater Synagogue, London, W.

1. Sergt. MAURICE COUPLAN, 1/7th West Riding Regt.; 2. L.-Cpl. H. DREEBIN, 1st K.O.S.B.; 3. Pte. S. L. KAISSER, 1/1st London Regt.; 4. Sergt. D. TAYLOR (SCHNEIDER), 1/6th London Regt.; 5. Spr. JOE COUPLAN, 461st Field Coy. R.E.; 6. Gnr. A. ROSENBAUM, R.G.A.; 7. L.-Cpl. M. I. TRACHTENBERG, 39th Royal Fusiliers; 8. Pte. M. LAPPIN, 7th King's Liverpool Regt.; 9. Pte. S. GINSBERG, 2/7th London Regt.; 10. Pte. MAX ROTHKUGEL, 1st South African Infantry; 11. Pte. W. KITOFSKI, 2/7th Manchester Regt.; 12. Pte. G. DAINOW, 2/4th London Regt.

PALESTINE COLONISTS: RECRUITS FOR THE 40TH ROYAL FUSILIERS (JEWISH), PALESTINE, 1918.

1. Pte. M. Hecker, Army Cyclist Corps; 2. Dvr. C. Freedman, R.F.A.; 3. Pte. N. Becker, Middlesex Regt.; 4. Pte. D. Cohen, Royal Fusiliers; 5. Dvr. S. Fainer, Canadian A.S.C.; 6. Pte. J. Abraham, Indian Veterinary Corps; 7. Cpl. S. Davis, R.A.S.C.; 8. Dvr. S. Hyamson, R.F.A.; 9. Orderly J. C. Baker, British Red Cross (Scottish); 10. Tpr. K. Brown, Pembroke Yeomanry; 11. Pte. S. Harris, R.A.M.C.; 12. Pte. J. Diamond, Royal Fusiliers.

1. Pte. Oswald Baron, 24th Royal Fusiliers; 2. Pte. R. Simlo, 11th King's Liverpool Regt.; 3. Pte. M. Isaacs (Field), 4th Canadian Infantry; 4. Pte. J. Levy, 1/20th London Regt.; 5. Pte. H. C. Raphael, 1st South African Infantry; 6. Sergt. S. F. Raphael, 1st South African Infantry; 7. Gnr. H. Lewis, A/177th Brigade, R.F.A.; 8. Pte. M. Freedman, 22nd Northumberland Fusiliers; 9. Rfn. B. J. Woolf, 13th K.R.R.C.; 10. Pte. R. Sykes, 2nd London Regt.; 11. Pte. S. Fineberg, 7th Worcester Regt.; 12. Pte. S. Baumgard, 22nd Lancashire Fusiliers; 13. Pte. S. Vander-Molen, 1/8th Royal Scots.

126

1. Cpl. V. Gerson, King's Liverpool Regt.; 2. Pte. A. M. Ellis, R.A.M.C.; 3. R.Q.M.S. F. E. Ellis, R.A.S.C.; 4. Pte. M. Gnessen, 40th Royal Fusiliers; 5. Pte. C. J. Eprile, 1st London Scottish; 6. Rfn. A. Harris, 17th London Regt.; 7. Gnr. H. Franks, R.F.A.; 8. Sergt. M. Franks, R.A.M.C.; 9. Sergt. L. G. Ansell, New Zealand Inf.; 10. Pte. B. Goldstone, 12th Battn. M.G.C.; 11. L.-Cpl. L. A. Holtz, L.R. Brigade; 12. Pte. A. Fitelson, M.G.C.

1. Sig. F. Cowen, R.H.A. 2. L.-Cpl. J. Fligelstone, 85th Labour Battn.; 3. Pte. S. Cohen, Middlesex Regt.; 4. 2nd A.M. R. Breckman, R.A.F.; 5. Pte. J. L. Gelberg, 30th Middlesex Regt.; 6. 1st A.M. W. J. Clements, R.A.F.; 7. Pte. S. Freedman, R.A.S.C.; 8. Pte. P. Fligelstone, R.A.S.C.; 9. Pte. H. Green, 1st Manchester Regt.; 10. A.M. D. Fligelstone, R.A.F.; 11. Pte. J. Freedman, R.F.A.; 12. Sergt. L. L. Aarons, 1st South African Infantry.

In Memoriam

1. Sergt. I. Shall, 1st South African Infantry; 2. Pte. J. Kavarsky, 1/5th K.O.R. Lancs Regt.; 3. Sergt. G. J. Sanders, 9th Royal Fusiliers; 4. Pte. J. Spero, 1st Dorset Regt.; 5. Cpl. I. Moses, 257th Area Employment Coy.; 6. Rfn. B. Mazerkoff, 5th King's Liverpool Regt.; 7. L.-Cpl. P. M. Levy, 9th Yorks Regt.; 8. L.-Cpl. I. Jacobs, 12th Royal Scots; 9. Pte. H. Marks, 1st Scots Guards; 10. Pte. J. Bernstein, 10th West Riding Regt.; 11. Pte. G. Malnick, 2nd East Kent Regt.; 12. L.-Cpl. A. Vinefsky, 70th Labour Coy.

JEWISH SOLDIERS IN LILLE, 1919.

Rev. A. Barnett, S.C.F.

1. Pte. J. SHILONY, Australian A.M.C.; 2. Bglr. MYERS, Australian Inf.; 3. Pte. L. G. MORRIS, Australian Inf.; 4. Pte. H. ROTHBERG, Australian Inf.; 5. Sergt. B. FRIEDLANDER, Australian Inf.; 6. Sergt. LEWIS MOSS, A.F.C.; 7. Pte. R. NATHAN, Australian Inf.; 8. Pte. G. SHANTHALL, Australian Inf.; 9. Pte. CAPLIN, Australian Inf.; 10. Sergt. S. N. SOLOMON, Australian Inf.; 11. L.-Cpl. MARK LEWIS, M.M., Australian Inf.; 12. Pte. A. CARSON, Australian A.M.C.

5. Group, with American Jewish soldiers.
6. Group of London soldiers.
7. Group, Middlesex Regt.: (*from top*) Pte. S. SAMUELS, Cpl. J. BROWN, Pte. C. BROWN, Pte. M. MARKS, Pte. H. SILVERFIELD, Pte. L. GROSZHIP.
8. Labour group.

1. Pte. A. Steinberg, 17th West Yorks Regt.; 2. Pte. H. Krohn, 10th Royal Fusiliers; 3. Pte. L. Phillips (Koninsky), 10th Suffolk Regt.; 4. Pte. A. A. Isaacs, 2nd Middlesex Regt.; 5. Pte. A. Kutchinsky, 9th K.R.R.C.; 6. Pte. S. Pomerance, 1/13th London Regt.; 7. Pte. M. Solomons, 3rd Worcester Regt.; 8. Pte. J. N. Van Locken, 2/1st London Regt.; 9. Pte. C. Nathan, 1/1st London Regt.; 10. Pte. S. S. Levison, 8th Oxford and Bucks L.I.; 11. Sergt. B. M. Levy, 3rd Connaught Rangers; 12. Sig. H. E. Pinto, 1st Cameron Highlanders.

1. A/B. Michael C. Lewis, H.M.S. *Bulwark*; 2. Rfn. H. R. Lewis, 12th London Regt.; 3. Pte. M. Fuchsbalg, 1st H.A.C.; 4. Pte. J. Forstein (Foster), 1st Norfolk Regt.; 5. L.-Cpl. P. Cohen (King), 1st Lincoln Regt.; 6. Rfn. Saul Lyons, 9th Rifle Brigade and 21st Lancers; 7. Pte. J. Sandys, 3rd Cameron Highlanders; 8. Pte. L. Leventhal, 1st Seaforth Highlanders; 9. Cpl. P. Seigar, 1st Dorset Regt.; 10. Pte. P. S. Ellison, 3rd Royal Fusiliers; 11. Pte. D. Eckstein, 1st Devonshire Regt.; 12. Rfn. Morris Van Thal, 2nd Rifle Brigade.

1. Cpl. J. Myers, M.M.P.; 2. Gnr. B. Morris, R.G.A.; 3. Pte. Rich, 38th Royal Fusiliers; 4. Tpr. A. Myers, M.G.C. Cavalry; 5. Pte. L. Rubenstein, 3rd Northumberland Fusiliers; 6. Pte. A. Levy, 1st Seaforth Hrs.; 7. Pte. M. Rubinski, 1/5th East Lancs Regt.; 8. Sig. A. Saville, R.E.; 9. Pte. M. Spiegal, R.A.S.C.; 10. Guardsman L. Myers, Grenadier Guards; 11. Pte. S. Rubens, D.H. Yeomanry; 12. Pte. L. Sasofsky, Labour Coy.

1. Pte. COLIN BENJAMIN (*left*), 2nd Devon Regt. (killed in action) ; and Brother.
2. L.-Cpl. L. GOODMAN (*left*) (killed in action), and Jewish soldier, 12th Rifle Brigade.
3. Rfn. JOSEPH DOBKIN, 11th London Regt. (*sitting*) (killed in action) ; Rfn. MYER DOBKIN, 16th Royal Irish Rifles.
4. Jews in 1/1st Bucks Battn. ; Pte. J. NATHAN (*on left*) (killed in action).

1. Dvr. H. Freedman, R.A.S.C.; 2. Cpl. M. J. H. Harris, 72nd Canadian Seaforth Hrs.; 3. Pnr. A. Goldstein, R.E.; 4. Pte. M. Annenberg, 2nd Border Regt.; 5. Pte. R. Greenwald, 16th Queen's (R. West Surrey Regt.); 6. Pte. L. Goldman, Australian A.S.C.; 7. L.-Cpl. M. Annenberg, 42nd Royal Fusiliers; 8. Pte. J. Finkle, 9th East Surrey Regt.; 9. Pte. E. E. Hamaui, R.A.M.C.; 10. Pte. S. Freedman, R.A.S.C.; 11. Cpl. A. Abrahams, Royal Fusiliers; 12. Pte. H. Hart, R.A.M.C.

GROUP OF SAILORS, REGULARS, AND RESERVISTS AT THE CENTRAL SYNAGOGUE, LONDON, W., PRIOR TO THE WAR.

All were on active service in August 1914.

Top Group.—Group of Royal Welch Fusiliers.
Lower Group.—Cpl. D. MILLER, M.M., 19th Manchester Regt., receiving the M.M. from Field-Marshal Lord FRENCH.

1. Pte. T. Dreezer, 1st Royal Dublin Fusiliers; 2. Pte. H. Bober, 11th Royal Fusiliers; 3. Pte. H. Clarke, 1st Canadian Inf.; 4. Pte. A. Abrahams, 2nd Northampton Regt.; 5. Pte. J. Abelson, 1st S. African Inf.; 6. Pte. P. Berman, 1/22nd London Regt.; 7. Pte. H. Cossonman, 1st Dorset Regt.; 8. Pte. S. Cornblatt, 20th Royal Fusiliers; 9. Pte. B. Davies, 1/4th London Regt.; 10. Gnr. C. Belcher, 1st Siege Bty. R.G.A.; 11. Pte. I. Cohen, 1st Middlesex Regt.; 12. Rfn. L. Cohen, 2/9th London Regt.

1. Sig. S. M. Goldstein, R.N.V.R.; 2. Spr. B. Glassen, R.E.; 3. Wireless Telegraphist L. Mickler, H.M.S. *Europe*; 4. Sergt. S. Cossick, 20th Lancashire Fusiliers; 5. Pte. R. Gluckstein, R.M.L.I.; 6. Pte. W. Goldberg, 2/4th West Lancs R.F.A.; 7. Pte. B. H. Goldburgh, R.A.F.; 8. Rfn. S. Cohen, K.R.R.C.; 9. L.-Cpl. S. D. Barnard, Military Foot Police; 10. L.-Cpl. B. Gilder, 2nd Yorks Regt.; 11. Pte. J. Abrahams, 1st Northampton Regt.; 12. Pte. J. Harris, Labour Corps.

1. Pte. A. Pescoff, London Regt.; 2. Gnr. G. Israel, Australian Artillery; 3. Sig. N. Tobias, 1st King Edward's Horse; 4. Pte. L. Rosenberg, 2/6th Durham L.I.; 5. Pte. M. Mallin, 14th Canadian Infantry; 6. Pnr. P. Price, R.E.; 7. Pte. J. Wilkins, 10th Queen's; 8. Pte. R. V. Meyer, Australian Forces; 9. Pte. V. Besso, Middlesex Regt.; 10. Sergt. M. Samuel, R.G.A.; 11. Pte. H. Marks, 3rd Loyal North Lancs Regt.; 12. S.-Sergt. C. Isaacs, M.S.M., R.A.O.C.

KILLED IN ACTION

1. Pte. H. Verblowsky, 2/1st London Regt.; 2. Gnr. P. Hart (Assenheim), D/290 Brigade R.F.A.; 3. Pte. D. Knopf, 4th South African Infantry; 4. Rfn. V. A. Isaacs, 12th London Regt.; 5. Tpr. H. J. Mendes, 2nd Life Guards; 6. Rfn. Joe Dudinsky, 2nd Rifle Brigade.

1. Gnr. L. SINGER, R.F.A.; 2. Pte. P. SAKOVITCH, Labour Coy.; 3. Pte. J. CRISTOL, 1st London Regt. 4. Pte. C. LEVY, 38th Royal Fusiliers; 5. Sergt. S. SUGARMAN, 38th Royal Fusiliers; 6. Pte. A. ROBIN 2nd Lancashire Fusiliers; 7. Sig. J. F. SALTIEL, Essex Regt.; 8. Sergt. J. BASWITZ, R.A.M.C.; 9. Dvr L. CARPEL, R.F.A.; 10. Pte. W. S. BERNSTEIN, 1st Canadian Field Ambulance; 11. Pte. M. RICHMAN, Labour Coy.; 12. Pte. J. BROWN, 6th Royal Berks Regt.

1. Tpr. A. Scott, 19th Hussars; 2. C.Q.M.S. J. Goldberg, 5th Loyal North Lancs Regt.; 3. Rfn. G. Michael, 10th London Regt.; 4. Pte. J. Snell, Middlesex Regt.; 5. 1st-A.M. J. Michael, R.A.F.; 6. Sergt. J. Michael, R.A.S.C.; 7. Pte. D. Feldman, R.A.M.C.; 8. Cpl. H. Cassal, Middlesex Regt.: 9. Sergt. L. Woodburn, 10th Worcester Regt.; 10. Cpl. M. Michael, King's Liverpool Regt. and R.A.P.C.; 11. Sergt. H. Michaels, 40th Royal Fusiliers; 12. L.-Cpl. A. Snell, Middlesex Regt.

ROLL OF HONOUR, CAPE TOWN SYNAGOGUE, S. AFRICA.

1. Group; 2. Four members of the Bombay Jewish Division, St. John's Ambulance Brigade: (*standing, from left*) Pte. SOLOMON JUDAH, Pte. SASSOON BENJAMIN; (*sitting*) Pte. S. I. REUBEN, Pte. D. I. TAYLOR; 3. Rev. L. GEFFEN, C.F., and Jewish soldiers in France; 4. Rev. A. BARNETT, S.C.F., and 1st Infantry Labour Coy., Middlesex Regt., France.

HAYES INDUSTRIAL SCHOOL.

1. Pte. A. Abrahams, R.M.L.I.; 2. Pte. D. Chapin, 90th Winnipeg Rifles; 3. Pte. S. Cohen, Middlesex Regt.; 4. Spr. D. Freedman, R.E.; 5. Pte. S. Goodman, 16th Royal Fusiliers; 6. Pte. A. Goodyer (Goldstein), 16th Royal Fusiliers; 7. Tpr. H. Johnson (Bards), 77th Canadian A.V.C.; 8. Pte. J. Hyman, Australian Infantry; 9. Pte. I. Halper, 21st Manchester Regt.; 10. Pte. J. Lewis (R. Lapidoth), Canadian A.M.C.; 11. Gnr. B. Silverman, R.F.A.; 12. Pte. N. Snider (Kuschneider), Canadian Infantry; 13. Pte. L. Sugarman, 11th E. Surrey Regt.

HAYES INDUSTRIAL SCHOOL

1. Cpl. S. Beck, 23rd Royal Fusiliers; 2. Dvr. J. Berman (Lieberman), R.F.A.; 3. Pte. E. Cohen, M.M., 2/6th City of London Rifles; 4. R.S.M. Driver, East Surrey Regt., attached R.F.A.; 5. Pte. I. Glick, 4th Royal Fusiliers; 6. Pte. T. Godfrey, 1st M.G.C.; 7. Pte. E. Hayward (Abrahams), 1st Middlesex Regt.; 8. Pte. A. Lawson, Canadian Medical Corps; 9. Sergt. J. Marks, M.M., 12th Canadian Infantry; 10. Pte. N. Myers, South African Rifles; 11. Pte. M. Waxman, Canadian Medical Corps; 12. Pte. E. Weinrich, 53rd Royal Sussex Regt.

HAYES INDUSTRIAL SCHOOL

1. Sergt. T. Abrahams, Welch Regt.; 2. Pte. L. Brandt, 2nd Essex Regt.; 3. Pte. H. Fried, 116th Canadian Infantry; 4. Pte. R. B. Harman, 17th Canadian M.G.C.; 5. Pte. S. Jacobs (Pickholtz), R.F.A.; 6. Pte. T. Lawson (N. Cohen), Royal Canadian Dragoons; 7. Pte. S. Levene, 51st West Yorks Regt.; 8. Seaman S. J. Marks (Levitski), H.M.S. *Courageous*; 9. Seaman E. Miller, H.M.S. *New Zealand*; 10. Pte. M. Shapiro (Walter Dixon), 33rd Canadian Infantry; 11. Pte. S. Solomon, Australian Infantry; 12. Pte. S. Solomons, Royal Canadian Dragoons.

1. Pte. H. Cohen, 1st Cheshire Regt.; 2. Rfn. A. Diamond, 16th K.R.R.C.; 3. Gnr. G. H. Balchin, R.F.A.; 4. Pte. C. A. Cassell, 2/1st Norfolk Yeomanry; 5. Pte. A. Annenberg, 2nd Devon Regt.; 6. Pte. H. A. Abrahams, 13th London Regt.; 7. Cpl. M. Blackman, 1/4th London Regt.; 8. Pte. H. Cohen, 19th Battn. Australian Inf.; 9. Rfn. J. Bogard, 8th Rifle Brigade; 10. Pte. A. J. Benzimra, 3rd Hampshire Regt.; 11. L.-Cpl. J. Bender, 8th Royal Fusiliers; 12. Pte. B. Collins, 1st Grenadier Guards.

151

1. Rfn. J. David, 1/16th London Regt.; 2. Pte. M. Blint, 13th Royal Scots; 3. Pte. H. Berliner, 148th Labour Coy.; 4. Pte. M. Collock, 19th King's Liverpool Regt.; 5. Pte. A. Cooper, 6th Dorset Regt.; 6. Pte. M. Althusen, 1st K.O.R. Lancs Regt.; 7. Pte. J. Dion, 6th Royal Munster Fusiliers; 8. Pte. M. Burns, 38th Royal Fusiliers; 9. Pte. D. Abrahams, 9th Royal Fusiliers; 10. Gnr. D. Barnes, 11th Brigade Australian Artillery; 11. Cpl. H. Barnett, 2/4th London Regt.; 12. 2nd-A.M. J. Collinsky, R.A.F.

1. L.-Cpl. C. S. Fleisig, R.E.; 2. Pte. H. Lewis, 3rd Essex Regt.; 3. Pte. J. Martyn, R.A.S.C.; 4. Gnr. I. Marchinski, R.G.A.; 5. Telegraphist P. Forstein, R.N.V.R.; 6. Pte. L. Moses, Royal Fusiliers and 12th Suffolk Regt.; 7. Spr. J. Finklestone, R.E.; 8. Sergt. M. J. Wolfensohn, 30th Middlesex Regt.; 9. L.-Cpl. G. Forster, R.A.M.C.; 10. Cpl. M. Barnett, 2/5th Northumberland Fusiliers; 11. Pte. H. Martyn, R.A.S.C.; 12. Pte. Goldberg, "Judeans."

1. Capt. and Mrs. H. ISAAC (Miss A. WOOLF) at Buckingham Palace, when Mrs. Isaac was invested with the R.R.C. by H.M. the King.
2. Tpr. HOPPER, Royal Horse Guards.
3. Pte. A. COHEN, Royal Fusiliers.
4. Tpr. COLLIER, Royal Horse Guards.
5. Pte. H. LANCHIN, R.A.O.C.; Pte. LEWIS CITRON, R.A.O.C.
6. *Back.*—(*Left to right*) Pte. A. HUNTER, 1st West Yorks Regt.; Pte. A. SAUNDERS, 1st West Yorks Regt.; Pte. (later 2nd-Lieut.) H. PEARCE, 1st West Yorks Regt.
   Sitting.—Pte. I. LEVY, 1st West Yorks Regt.; Cpl. D. FALLON, 2nd Northumberland Fusiliers (later Lieut., M.C.); L.-Cpl. D. MARKS, 1st West Yorks Regt.
   On ground.—Pte. B. LYONS, 1st West Yorks Regt.

1. *Left to right.*—Pte. COTTON, 2nd South Lancs. Regt.; Pte. A. BYE, Labour Coy.; Pte. COHEN, Labour Coy.; Cpl. R. BREST, 19th Coy., C.L.C.
2. A.M. A. SCHNEIDER, A.M. J. FARRA, R.A.F.
3. 2nd-A.M. M. BLOOM, R.A.F.; L.-Cpl. M. LYONS, R.A.S.C.
4. Pte. A. BASS, Pte. L. BERMAN, 1st Manchester Regt.

1. Lieut. ARTHUR H. BEER, M.C., West Lancs R.F.A.; 2. Capt. W. G. SAMUEL, 2nd Bedford Regt.; 3. Lieut. W. R. MORTIMER WOOLF, 2nd Border Regt.; 4. 2nd-Lieut. C. W. J. DANZIGER, 22nd Manchester Regt.; 5. Lieut. S. BENZECRY, 17th Royal Fusiliers; 6. Lieut. A. C. L. ABRAHAMS, 3rd Coldstream Guards; 7. Lieut. BERT SOLOMONS, R.A.F.; 8. Lieut. FRED A. ARON, 2nd South Lancs Regt.; 9. 2nd Lieut. L. E. DAVIS, 5th Manchester Regt.; 10. Lieut. C. C. HENRY, Hussars and 2nd Worcester Regt.; 11. Lieut. ARTHUR F. MYERS, 4th Hussars; 12. Lieut. L. B. SOLOMONS, 2nd Royal Fusiliers and R.A.F.

1. Pte. M. Goodman, 2/23rd London Regt.; 2. Cpl. S. A. Kempner, 38th Royal Fusiliers; 3. Pte. P. Bowick, Labour Coy.; 4. Pte. A. Gordon, R.A.O.C.; 5. Pnr. C. H. Jacobs, R.E.; 6. Pte. H. Goldman, 5th Northants Regt.; 7. Pte. A. Krohmlick, Labour Coy.; 8. Pte. H. J. King, Australian Infantry; 9. L.-Cpl. B. Milman, 39th Royal Fusiliers; 10. Sig. A. Myerson, R.F.A.; 11. Pte. H. Brotman, Middlesex Regt.; 12. Sergt. R. Joseph, R.G.A.

In Memoriam

1. Lieut. S. G. Katz, 8th K.O.R. Lancaster Regt.; 2. Lieut. R. M. Leveson, 10th Durham L.I.; 3. 2nd-Lieut. Maurice L. Bernstein, M.C., 11th Lancashire Fusiliers; 4. Cpl. M. Gabrielson, 1st King Edward's Horse; 5. Cpl. B. Elias, R.A.S.C.; 6. Rfn. Noah Boss, 16th Queen's Westminsters; 7. Cpl. Bernard Greenbaum, 9th Buffs; 8. Cpl. Laurence Boodson, 6th Manchester Regt.; 9. Pte. M. Solomons, 13th London Regt.; 10. Pte. A. Russell (Rosenbaum), 7th Royal Sussex Regt.; 11. Pte. N. Lisbona, 20th Royal Fusiliers; 12. Rfn. A. I. Buck, 12th London Regt.

1. Pte. L. Symons, R.A.M.C.; 2. 2nd-Clerk S. M. Strump, R.A.F.; 3. Pte. J. Singer, 38th Royal Fusiliers; 4. Sergt. I. Spielman, 1/15th London Regt.; 5. A.M. A. Stringer, R.A.F.; 6. Despatch-Rider L. Lipowsky, R.A.S.C.; 7. Pte. E. Sarna, 38th Royal Fusiliers; 8. Cpl. S. Stungo, R.A.S.C.; 9. Sergt. R. Strump, 39th Royal Fusiliers (Judeans); 10. Cpl. O. S. Lion, 1st Canadian Infantry; 11. 1st A.M. M. Stomachien, R.A.F.; 12. Pte. A. Cohen, K.R.R.C.

Rev. E. M. Levy, C.F., and group of Jewish soldiers in France. Group of Jewish soldiers in Salonika. In front, Pte. J. Moses, 14th Queen's. Brothers: (standing) Capt. E. M. Wolf, M.C., Tank Corps; Capt. G. M. D. Wolf; (sitting) Lieut. C. M. Wolf. R. Irish Regt.

1. 2nd-Lieut. G. E. Kaum, West Lancs R.F.A.; 2. Lieut. Selig Levy, M.G.C.; 3. Lieut. H. Brown, M.G.C.; 4. Rev. David Hirsch, C.F.; 5. Lieut. W. Hurwitz, South Lancs Regt.; 6. 2nd-Lieut. D. Caminer, R.A.F.; 7. Major G. P. Oppenheim, Royal Marines; 8. 2nd-Lieut. Frank Vyner, R.G.A.; 9. 2nd-Lieut. L. B. Seligman, M.C., M.G.C. and Royal Fusiliers (Jewish); 10. Rev. H. P. Silverman, C.F.; 11. Rev. N. Levine, C.F.; 12. 2nd-Lieut. Samuel Friend, R.F.A.

1. Group of R.A.F. with Major J. KEMPER, O.B.E., and Rev. L. GEFFEN, C.F., France
2. Group in France, 1916.
3. Rev. N. LEVINE, C.F., and R.A.F. men, France.
4. Managers and members of the Notting Hill Jewish Club who have served during the War.

1. Spr. J. Cohen, R.E.; 2. Sig. H. Sugarman, R.N.; 3. 1st A.M. J. T. Phillips, R.N.A.S.; 4. Pte. M. Brookstone, South African Scottish; 5. Pte. H. Goodman, 2nd Gloucester Regt.; 6. Pte. A. Goldberg, 25th Northumberland Fusiliers; 7. Dvr. M. Goldstein, R.A.S.C.; 8. Pte. A. Goldsmith, 4th K.R.R.C.; 9. Dvr. J. Gantz, R.F.A.; 10. Pte. M. Crash, 3rd Worcester Regt.; 11. Pte. D. Grossman, Labour Coy.; 12. Dvr. L. Bloom, R.A.S.C.

1. Pte. C. Lewis (Grodner), 4th Royal Fusiliers; 2. Gnr. I. Green, A/121st R.F.A.; 3. Rfn. L. B. Gosschalk, 2/5th London Regt.; 4. Pte. A. Grouse, 1st London Regt.; 5. Pte. I. E. Jacobs, 15th Royal Warwick Regt.; 6. Pte. L. Greenwald, 22nd London Regt.; 7. Pte. M. Davis, 2/10th London Regt.; 8. Pte. H. M. Gabriel, 14th Royal Warwick Regt.; 9. Cpl. A. Goldman, 2nd Royal Warwick Regt.; 10. Rfn. I. Solomons, 1st Rifle Brigade; 11. Pte. I. Gordon, 1st Cheshire Regt.; 12. Pte. S. E. Isaacs, 2/20th London Regt.

1. Pte. J. Gardner, 8th M.G.C.; 2. S/Sergt. L. Bernard (B. Levy), 15th Canadian Highlanders; 3. Pte. I. Franks, 2/4th London Regt.; 4. Pte. W. Kitchenoff, 13th Royal Fusiliers; 5. Cpl. A. Ferner, D.C.M., 6th Yorks Regt.; 6. L.-Cpl. H. D. Selman, 19th London Regt.; 7. Pte. J. Ginsberg, 58th Machine Gun Battn.; 8. Rfn. M. Tompofsky, M.M., 1/8th West Yorks Regt.; 9. Pte. P. D. Benjamin, 3/5th Lancashire Fusiliers; 10. Rfn. J. Tobias, 1st Rifle Brigade; 11. Pte. M. I. Freeman, 17th H.L.I.; 12. L.-Cpl. A. Goldberg 12th London Regt.

1. Stoker M. Ford, H.M.S. *Arethusa*; 2. A/Cpl. H. Travis, Canadian Army Medical Corps; 3. Cpl. S. H. Bernstein, Highland L.I.; 4. Pte. R. Sandall, Cheshire Regt.; 5. Pte. J. Franklin, 1st Lincoln Regt.; 6. Pte. J. Lipman, 2/19th London Regt.; 7. Pte. P. Cohen, 38th Royal Fusiliers; 8. Dvr. A. Lowne, R.A.S.C.; 9. A.M. A. Pearlman, R.A.F.; 10. Cpl. N. Kronenberg, M.M., 6th Welch Regt.; 11. Gnr. M. Gosschalk, South African Heavy Artillery; 12. Gnr. E. M. Bernstein, M.G.C.

1. Pte. C. M. Lazarus, M.M., 2nd S. African Inf.; 2. A.M. I. Chalfen, R.A.F.; 3. Pte. M. Goldstein, R.A.S.C.; 4. Pte. S. Kremner, Middlesex Regt.; 5. Sergt. C. Gluckstein, Tank Corps; 6. Rfn. N. M. Brilliant, 15th London Regt.; 7. Gnr. C. N. Jacobs, 3rd Bty. Australian F.A.; 8. Cpl. S. Cahm, R.A.S.C.; 9. C.Q.M.S. M. Landaw, 1/4th Wilts Regt.; 10. Sergt. C. Aaron, 2/7th Welsh Regt.; 11. Pte. L. Kaplinsky, 1st Oxford & Bucks L.I.; 12. Gnr. H. Izen, R.H.A.

1. Rev. H. SHANDEL and group of soldiers.
2. Jewish soldiers, 1/7th Royal Warwick Regt. in Italy.
3. A Calais group, Royal Engineers with Rev. L. GEFFEN C.F.
4. Three Jewish soldiers.

1. 1st-A.M. Arthur Michaelson, R.A.F.; 2. Bdr. Sam Rosenbloom, R.F.A.; 3. Stoker J. Marks, H.M.S. *Hindustan*; 4. Rfn. H. Brod, Rifle Brigade; 5. Pte. A. Bloom, R.A.M.C.; 6. S.-Sergt. A. Weinstein, Middlesex Regt.; 7. Flight-Sergt. J. Jacobs, M.M., R.A.F.; 8. Sig. A. Most, R.F.A.; 9 L.-Cpl. J. Lubel, 2/5th Suffolk Regt.; 10. Pte. S. Shane, Argyll and Sutherland Highlanders; 11. 2nd-A.M. E. Esterson, R.A.F.; 12. Pte. J. Bloom, Argyll and Sutherland Highlanders.

1. Sergt. J. HAFT, 17th H.L.I.; (*seated*) Cpl. S. HAFT, 17th H.L.I. (killed in action).
2. Pte. H. LEVY, 2nd S. Wales Borderers (killed in action); (*standing*) C.Q.M.S. E. LEVY.
3. Pte. H. HERMAN, 1/5th West Yorks Regt. (*sitting*) (killed in action); and Brother, West Riding Regt.
4. "Judeans" on active service: Pte. S. GREYMAN, 38th Royal Fusiliers (*with pipe*) (killed in action).

Top.—Jewish Warrant Officer of the Royal Marines as Instructor of Gunnery on a Battleship.
Bottom.—The 17th London Regiment in training—Hatfield, 1914.
  Standing.—Dvr. A. JACKS, R.A.S.C.; Rfn. J. SHERN, Rfn. J. PIETERS, Rfn. M. MORRIS, Rfn. M. NORTON.
  Seated.—Rfn. S. SALMON, Rev. M. ADLER, Rfn. D. HARRIS, Sgt. M. M. GORDON (later killed in action), Rfn. S. POLLACK.
  Kneeling.—Cpl. H. BLOM, Rfn. J. LEVY.

1. Pte. M. Leschinsky, 4th Northumberland Fusiliers; 2. Pte. R. Fifer, 23rd Northumberland Fusiliers; 3. Sergt. A. I. Levy, 2nd K.R.R.C.; 4. Pte. C. Levy, 70th F.A., R.A.M.C.; 5. Pte. M. Croop, 18th Manchester Regt.; 6. Pte. L. Myers (Smith), 9th Royal Fusiliers; 7. L.-Cpl. H. M. Jacobs, 3rd South African Infantry; 8. Pte. M. Blackstone, 7th Seaforth Highlanders; 9. Pte. J. Freedman, 7th Rifle Brigade; 10. Pte. H. Coster, 101st Labour Battn.; 11. Pte. J. Lewis, 2nd H.A.C.; 12. Pte. Issy Jackson, 7th Durham L.I.

1. Cpl. J. I. Davis, 1st Border Regt.; 2. Rfn. A. Benjamin, 1st Rifle Brigade; 3. Pte. G. Myers, 7th London Regt.; 4. Rfn. E. Tragheim, 8th Rifle Brigade; 5. Pte. Isaac E. Balon, 7th Manchester Regt.; 6. Cpl. Aaron Macaborski, R.E.; 7. Pte. Harry Marks, 4th Middlesex Regt.; 8. L.-Cpl. H. Solomon (Sullivan), 1st Border Regt.; 9. L.-Cpl. J. Bender, 8th Royal Fusiliers; 10. Pte. Sol Littmann, M.M., 51st Australian Infantry; 11. Pte. E. Staal, 2nd Royal Scots; 12. Sergt. Myer E. Berkson, 1/4th Cheshire Regt.

5. Pte. M. Levene, Pte. F. Solomons, Labour Corps.
6. Pte. H. Dembofsky, Pte. M. Cohen, Labour Corps.
7. Pte. A. Levine, Pte. B. Scalnick, 38/40th Royal Fusiliers.
8. L.-Cpl. E. Rapaport, Pte. A. Bass, and Pte. A. Dufresnoy, 4th London Regt.

1. Pte. H. PERLMUTIER, London Scottish; 2. Pte. L. HICKMAN, Australian Infantry; 3. Pte. S. HARRIS, 8th Canadian Regt.; 4. Pte. L. CHART, Canadian Infantry; 5. Pte. A. BIERMAN, 39th Royal Fusiliers and 16th Rifle Brigade; 6. Rfn. B. PERKOFF, 12th K.R.R.C.; 7. L.-Cpl. D. GOLDSTON, 38th Royal Fusiliers; 8. 2nd-Cpl. N. PERLMUTTER, R.E.; 9. Pte. S. SUCHARD, Seaforth Hrs.; 10. A.B. S. R. LEVY, H.M.S. *Victorious*; 11. Cpl. M. PERLMUTTER, R.A.P.C.; 12. Cpl. H. N. MOSES, R.E.

1. Capt. WALTER LEWIS, M.C., 23rd London Regt.; 2. 2nd-Lieut. G. HYMAN, Royal Fusiliers; 3. Lieut. P. H. EMANUEL, F.R.G.S., 2nd Battn. County of London Regt.; 4. 2nd-Lieut. LEONARD RAPAPORT, 9th Manchester Regt.; 5. Capt. B. M. WOOLF, M.C., Tank Corps; 6. Lieut. A. F. POLACK, Royal Engineers; 7. Lieut. M. BRISCOE, R.A.M.C.; 8. Capt. B. B. SAMUEL, R.A.M.C.; 9. Capt. J. MERVYN GOLBIE, 6th Welsh Regt.; 10. Major M. GLUCKSTEIN, O.B.E., Royal Engineers; 11. Lieut. M. BESSO, R.A.F.; 12. Capt. MYLES COLT, R.A.M.C.

1. Pte. S. Sanofsky, 9th Welsh Regt.; 2. Pte. C. A. Marks, 3rd Canadian Inf.; 3. Sergt. W. Mack (Kurtzman), 2nd Seaforth Highlanders; 4. Dvr. L. Berzance, D/82nd Bgde. R.F.A.; 5. Pte. H. Ross (Rosenberg), 2nd West Riding Regt.; 6. Pte. S. Maginsky, 1/5th King's Liverpool Regt.; 7. Sergt. M. Bamberg, 1st Northumberland Fusiliers; 8. Pte. M. L. Steinberg, R.A.S.C.; 9. Pte. W. Marks, 2nd Manchester Regt.; 10. Rfn. A. L. Strauss, 17th London Regt.; 11. Pte. L. Bernstein, R.A.M.C.; 12. Pte. N. C. Solomon, 15th Royal Welsh Fusiliers.

Top.—Group at Canterbury, 1916.
Lower.—Australian Jewish Service on Salisbury Plain. Chaplain DANGLOW (centre), Lieut. HAROLD BOAS (back row).

1. Pte. E. Levy, R.A.M.C.; 2. Rfn. M. Levene, 25th K.R.R.C.; 3. 1st A.M. R. Nelson, R.A.F.; 4. Pte. A. E. Lipman, Australian Army Medical Corps; 5. L.-Cpl. L. M. Jonas, M.M., 21st Canadian Infantry; 6. Pte. B. Latner, R.A.O.C.; 7. C.Q.M.S. H. Moscow, 19th Cheshire Regt.; 8. Rfn. C. Kauffmann, 1/16th London Regt.; 9. Pte. J. Goldman, 8th Royal Fusiliers; 10. Pte. M. Plotsky, Labour Coy.; 11. Spr. S. Joseph, R.E.; 12. Pte. L. Joels, 71st Canadian Infantry.

1. A.M. A. Levy, R.A.F.; 2. Gnr. M. Mendelson, R.H.A.; 3. Pte. C. Shapero, 5th Royal Scots; 4. Cpl. S. Lightstone, R.N.A.S.; 5. Rfn. J. M. Wyler, 1/15th London Regt.; 6. Rfn. M W. Spurling, 1st L.R.B.; 7. Rfn. A. Pampel, 11th K.R.R. Corps; 8. Petty Officer A. Cowan, Anson Battn., R.N.V.R.; 9. Rfn. M. Spero, 17th London Regt.; 10. Pte. J. Winstone (Wainstain), R.F.A.; 11. Pte. D. Phillips, 2nd Border Regt.; 12. Pte. I. Morell, 2/24th London Regt.

In Memoriam

1. Rfn. J. Levy, 12th Royal Irish Rifles; 2. Pte. S. Finstein, Worcester Regt.; 3. Rfn. F. Franklin, 11th Rifle Brigade; 4. Pte. S. Lippman, 7th Border Regt.; 5. Pte. J. Manhoff, 2/10th London Regt.; 6. L.-Cpl. M. Sugarman, 17th Manchester Regt.; 7. L.-Cpl. A. Silver, 2nd (Garrison) Battn. Bedford Regt.; 8. Sergt. L. Barnard, 5th King's Liverpool Regt.; 9. Cyclist E. Schwartz, 6th Corps Cyclists; 10. Sergt. J. Myers, 1/21st London Regt.; 11. Gnr. M. Fishman, A/64 Brigade R.F.A.; 12. Pte. H. Lewis, 51st M.G.C.

Pte. H. Lesser. Pte. L. Miller. Pte. G. L. Jacobs. Pte. H. Miller. Pte. H. S. Libstein.

Pte. E. Woolfe. Pte. H. Davies. Pte. M. Dainow. Pte. M. Mendes.

JEWISH SOLDIERS IN 9TH MIDDLESEX REGIMENT, INDIA, 1914.

1. Pte. S. Taylor, Northumberland Fusiliers; 2. Cpl. J. Williams, Royal Fusiliers; 3. Pte. J. Levy, Royal Fusiliers; 4. Pnr. H. J. Barnard, R.E.; 5. C.S.M.I. of M. J. M. Samuel, School of Musketry; 6. Pte. P. Silverman, Labour Coy.; 7. Pte. M. Silverman, Labour Coy.; 8. **Cyclist H. Wagner, 2nd Corps Cyclist Battn. (Killed in Action)**; 9. Pte. H. Phillips, 4th Northumberland Fusiliers; 10. Sergt. A. Matz, 4th Argyll and Sutherland Highlanders; 11. Sig.-Cpl. J. Salmon, 5th Scottish Rifles; 12. Pte. M. Phillips, 1st Loyal North Lancs; 13. Bglr. S. Tabatsky, 39th Royal Fusiliers; 14. Pte. M. Lazarus, Welch Regt.

1. Pte. A. Latter, R. Scots Fus. and 25th M.G.C. ; 2. Pte. J. Gillis, 4th Yorks Regt. ; 3. Pnr. L. Green, 1st Bn. Spec. Bgde. R.E. ; 4. Pte. B. Levine, 6th Duke of Cornwall's L.I. ; 5. Sergt. L. Solomons, 40th Royal Fusiliers ; 6. Gnr. J. Goodman, R.F.A. ; 7. Sergt. Jackson Stahl, 7th East Lancs Regt. ; 8. Pte. H. Stone, 1/6th Manchester Regt. ; 9. L/Cpl. M. Solomons, 1/8th Middlesex Regt. ; 10. Cpl. S. Herman, 10th Rifle Brigade ; 11. Pte. S. W. Lipson, 18th King's Liverpool Regt. ; 12. Pte. S. Littman, 23rd Royal Fusiliers.

1. Pte. J. Raitiff, R.A.M.C.; 2. Cpl. M. J. Jacobs, Royal Fusiliers; 3. Pte. L. Rosenbloom, 1/7th West Yorks Regt.; 4. Pte. A. Rosenbloom, King's Liverpool Regt.; 5. Pte. D. Shapero, R.A.O.C.; 6. Pte. L. Shapero, M.M., East Yorks Regt.; 7. Pte. J. Rosenbloom, 1/6th Manchester Regt.; 8. Cpl. M. Pickles, 313th Prisoner of War Coy.; 9. Bdr. B. G. Phillips, M.M., Canadian Artillery; 10. Pte. L. Phillips, 2/7th London Regt.; 11. L.-Cpl. G. Posner, 2nd Somerset L.I.; 12. Pte. S. Shapero, East Yorks Regt.; 13. Pte. I. Rosenbloom, King's Liverpool Regt.

RECORD OF HONOUR, LIVERPOOL OLD HEBREW CONGREGATION.

1. Pte. E. H. L. Davidson, 1/28th London Regt.; 2. Rfn. I. Lea (Levy), 11th Rifle Brigade; 3. Rfn. A. Cohen, 17th London Regt.; 4. Pte. H. Cossack, 2/7th Lancashire Fusiliers; 5. Pte. A. Kyte, 55th M.G.C.; 6. Sergt. F. Downs, 8th Royal Fusiliers; 7. Pte. S. Davies, 7th King's Liverpool Regt.; 8. Pte. M. Wollman, M.G.C.; 9. Pte. J. R. White, 4th South African Infantry; 10. Cpl. L. Garbutt, 199th Coy., R.A.S.C.; 11. Cpl. H. Cole, 1st South Wales Borderers; 12. Pte. M. Brown, 1st Coldstream Guards.

1. Pte. I. Steinberg, 1st Cameron Highlanders; 2. Pte. W. Spilg, 9th Highland L.I.; 3. Rfn. H. Levenson, 7th Rifle Brigade; 4. Pte. M. Sillberg, 9th West Riding Regt.; 5. Pte. C. Seramber, 38th Royal Fusiliers; 6. Flight-Sergt. A. S. Simons, R.A.F.; 7. Pte. H. Filar, 10th Roy. West Kent Regt.; 8. Tpr. F. Mendelsohn, S. African M. Transport; 9. Desp. Rider E. P. Hayman, New Zealand Forces; 10. Rfn. H. Goodfriend, 2/17th London Regt.; 11. Corpl. H. Geller, R.A.F.; 12. Pte. S. Greenberg, 1st K.O R. Lancaster Regt.

1. Pte. N. Gottlieb, 31st Middlesex Regt.; 2. Gnr. J. Cohen, R.G.A.; 3. Guardsman S. H. Mazarkoff, Grenadier Guards; 4. Spr. C. Bloom, 1st Canadian Signal Co.; 5. Pte. L. Park, 11th Royal Fusiliers; 6. L.-Cpl. S. Park, 2/10th London Regt.; 7. Pte. I. Franklin, The Buffs; 8. Pte. V. Gordon, R.A.M.C.; 9. Pte. N. Gordon, R.A.M.C.; 10. Sergt. O. Cohen, R.E.; 11. Pte. J. Kossick, 8th Yorkshire Regt.; 12. Pte. P. Bloom, R.A.M.C.; 13. Cadet A. Harrison, Tank Corps.

1. Three Jewish soldiers, including Pte. S. HARRIS, 3rd Wilts Regt. (without cap).
2. Pte. H. VELLEMAN, Cpl. H. JACOBS, Pte. A. BLITZ, R.A.M.C. (from St. John's Ambulance).
3. Pte. L. RAPAPORT, Pte. H. BEIN, Middlesex Regt.
4. L.-Cpl. G. TOFF, M.G.C.; Pte. H. LEVINE, 10th H.L.I.

1. Rfn. H. Breslau, Rifle Brigade; 2. Pte. P. Lazarus, 2nd South African Inf.; 3. Pte. S. C. Lazarus, Durban L.I.; 4. Pte. D. Cohen, R.A.S.C.; 5. Pte. L. Goldsmith, Middlesex Regt.; 6. Pte. D. Jacobs, R.W. Kent Regt.; 7. Sergt. D. Boodson, 6th Manchester Regt.; 8. Pte. B. Josephs, Indian Defence Force; 9. **L.-Cpl. J. Michaels, Somerset L.I. (Killed in action)**; 10. Tpr. S. Goodman, 1st Life Guards; 11. Pte. J. Gilbert, 11th South Lancashire Regt.; 12. Gnr. P. Levy, R.G.A.

1. Pte. A. Felix, Royal Fusiliers; 2. A.M. H. Goldstein, R.A.F.; 3. Gnr. L. Diamond, R.F.A.; 4. Pte. W. Harris, 2nd Notts and Derby Regt.; 5. Pte. J. Freeman, 1st K.O.S.B.; 6. Pte. B. Ellis, 2/9th King's Liverpool Regt.; 7. Pte. B. J. Freedman, Royal Fusiliers; 8. L.-Cpl. D. Hernberg, 17th London Regt.; 9. Spr. J. Glass, R.E.; 10. Tpr. D. Hardy, Queen's Bays; 11. Pte. M. Brown, R.A.M.C.; 12. Rfn. H. Goodman, 4th Rifle Brigade.

1. Lieut. A. E. Morris, R.E.; 2. Capt. L. I. Isaacs, 1st S. African Inf.; 3. Capt. N. Morris, R.A.M.C.; 4. Lieut. D. van den Bergh, R.A.S.C.; 5. Capt. A. Instone, Intelligence Dept.; 6. Capt. J. Salmon, Gen. List.; 7. 2nd-Lieut. F. J. Conway, R.F.A.; 8. Capt. and Q.M. L. L. Franks, R.A.M.C.; 9. 2nd-Lieut. C. de Pinna, 2/3rd London Regt.; 10. Lieut. H. L. Jacobs, M.C., 42nd Bty. Australian F.A.; 11. Capt. H. B. Samuel, West Yorks and 38th Royal Fusiliers; 12. Lieut. Glyn Barton, M.C., 15th Battn. Tank Corps.

GROUP OF JEWISH SOLDIERS, CURRAGH CAMP, IRELAND, 1915.

1. Dvr. J. MILLER, Hedjaz Armoured Car Battery ; 2. Pte. J. RUBENSTEIN, Scottish Rifles ; 3. Rfn. I. LAZARUS, 1/17th London Regt. ; 4. Sergt. J. H. WARSHAWSKY, R.A.S.C. ; 5. S.-Sergt. H. M. LION, R.A.M.C. ; 6. Sergt. J. GOOD, M.G.C. (Motors) ; 7. L.-Cpl. J. ROBERTS, 1st Royal Irish ; 8. Pte. R. Boss, Bedford Regt. ; 9. Sergt. M. WOOLF, 1st East Surrey Regt. ; 10. Rfn. S. WEINER, 1/12th London Regt. ; 11. Tpr. A. MYERS, 3/2nd County of London Yeomanry ; 12. L.-Cpl. L. H. SAXTON, 38th Royal Fusiliers.

1. Pte. I. Philips, Welsh Regt.; 2. Pte. I. Simmons, Australian Infantry; 3. Pte. M. Taylor, 39th Royal Fusiliers; 4. Cpl. D. Kleinfield, R.A.F.; 5. Sig. B. Vitofsky, 38th Royal Fusiliers; 6. Pte. I. Lewis, R.A.M.C.; 7. L.-Cpl. A. Schein, Middlesex Regt.; 8. Pte. M. Lance, Labour Corps; 9. Pte. D. Kollenberg, 2nd South African Infantry; 10. Pte. J. Turitz, Northumberland Fusiliers; 11. Tpr. M. Toomin, County of London Yeomanry; 12. Sergt. M. Black, M.M., 39th Royal Fusiliers.

1. Pte. D. Alexander, 16th Middlesex Regt.; 2. Pte. J. Harris, 1/6th Gordon Highlanders; 3. Rfn. D. Rowson (Rosenbaum), 16th London Regt.; 4. Pte. L. Rosenberg, 10th Royal Fusiliers; 5. Pte H. Hoepelman, R.A.O.C.; 6. Pte. S. Herman, 87th Canadian Infantry; 7. Pte. H. Revensky, 2nd Suffolk Regt.; 8. Pte. L. S. Rasky, 2/5th Manchester Regt.; 9. Rfn. P. Silverman, 18th K.R.R. Corps; 10. Pte. L. M. Rosenthal, 14th Roy. Warwick Regt.; 11. Pte. H. Alexander, 3rd East Surrey Regt.; 12. Pte. L. Hurwitz, 9th East Surrey Regt.

1. Gnr. J. Cushelson, B/330 Bgde. R.F.A.; 2. Pte. A. Goldstein, M.M., 2/10th London Regt.; 3. Rfn. P. Goldstein, 9th K.R.R. Corps; 4. Pte. M. Hornick, 23rd Middlesex Regt.; 5. Pte. J. S. Gerber, 1/8th A. and S. Highlanders; 6. Pte. P. Coor, 3/10th Middlesex Regt.; 7. Pte. M. Alexander, 39th Royal Fusiliers; 8. Pte. J. Chalfen, 1/13th London Regt.; 9. Pte. S. Aronheim, 1st Essex Regt.; 10. Cpl. D. Cohen, M.M., 6th Welsh Regt.; 11. Rfn. L. Cowan, 14th King's Liverpool Regt.; 12. Drummer M. Cohen, 1/9th Lancs Fusiliers.

1. Capt. E. D. Pinder Davis, 10th Essex Regt.; 2. Lieut.-Col. Isidor M. Heilbron, D.S.O., R.A.S.C.; 3. 2nd-Lieut. I. M. Balaban, D.C.M., 8th King's Liverpool Regt.; 4. Lieut.-Col. S. C. Stanley Cohen, 1/5th King's Liverpool Regt.; 5. Capt. H. Symonds, Australian Army Medical Corps; 6. Capt. J. Dulberg, R.A.M.C., M.D., J.P.; 7. Rev. V. G. Simmons, C.F.; 8. Capt. S. M. Adler, 13th Royal Fusiliers; 9. Lieut. A. Collins, M.G.C.; 10. 2nd-Lieut. Eric W. Flatow, 1/4th Duke of Wellington's Regt.; 11. 2nd-Lieut. Edwin H. Samuel, R.F.A.; 12. 2nd-Lieut. H. Claff, 4th Loyal North Lancashire Regt.

1. Dvr. R. Levy, R.A.S.C.; 2. Cpl. L. Werbeloff, South African Mounted Troops; 3. Pte. H. Idels, Labour Coy.; 4. L.-Cpl. G. Miron, M.M., 4th K.R.R.C.; 5. Cpl. L. Scareff, 38th Royal Fusiliers; 6. 3rd A.M. E. Besso, R.A.F.; 7. Pte. J. Beck, R.A.V.C.; 8. Pte. A. Voss, Middlesex Regt.; 9. L.-Cpl. P. D. Weisbloom, R.E.; 10. Sergt. F. I. Spielmann, Canadian O.T.C.; 11. Tpr. L. Israel, 3rd County of London Yeomanry; 12. Dvr. D. Lawgorse, Canadian Field Artillery.

1. L.-Cpl. J. Zeitlin, 11th Welsh Regt. ; 2. Pte. S. Rosenberg, K.O.Y.L.I. ; 3. Cpl. E. Shindler, 1/12th London Regt. ; 4. Cpl. P. Shindler, 1/12th London Regt. ; 5. C.S.M. J. Prooth, D.C.M., 13th Royal Fusiliers ; 6. Cpl. M. Silverman, 11th King's Liverpool Regt. ; 7. Gnr. J. Taylor, R.G.A. ; 8. Q.M.-Sergt. A. Jacobs, Cape Peninsular Regt. ; 9. Pte. D. M. Kurtz, 11th Australian Field Ambulance ; 10. Pte. W. S. Zeitlin, R.A.S.C. ; 11. Rfn. I. Kain, 1/6th London Regt. ; 12. Pte. D. Rosenfield, M.G.C.

HOME SERVICE: CHAPLAINS AND OFFICIATING CLERGYMEN IN ENGLAND, 1917.

Back Row (*left to right*) : Rev. H. Jerevitch, Cardiff ; Rev. L. Woolfe, Reading ; Rev. W. Levin, C.F. ; Rabbi B. I. Cohen, Sheffield ; Rabbi M. Abrahams, Leeds ; Rev. J. Phillips, Manchester.

Front Row (*left to right*) : Rev. A. Cohen, Birmingham ; Rev. V. G. Simmons, C.F., Aldershot ; Rev. S. Frampton, Liverpool ; Rev. S. Lipson, S.C.F. ; Rev. H. Shandel, Ramsgate ; Rev. N. Goldston, C.F., Salisbury Plain ; Rev. D. Wasserzug, Eastern Command ; Lieut. H. Boas, Australian Y.M.C.A.

1. Sig. S. Novinski, 20th Durham L.I. ; 2. Pte. H. W. Spiers, R.A.F. ; 3. Pte. C. Kleinfield, 2/20th London Regt. ; 4. Cpl. H. Stanley, M.M., 1/5th H.L.I. ; 5. Rfn. L. S. Lyons, 2nd K.R.R.C. ; 6. 2nd A.C. J. Morris, R.A.F. ; 7. Pte. A. Jay, R.A.M.C. ; 8. L.-Cpl. S. F. Phillips, R.A.S.C. ; 9. L.-Cpl. J. H. Lesnie, 39th Royal Fusiliers ; 10. Gnr. S. Mander, R.F.A. ; 11. A.B. S. G. Bloom, Royal Naval Division ; 12. Pte. H. H. Ognall, M.G.C.

1. Sergt. A. Jacobs, R.E.; 2. Pte. M. Newman, Middlesex Regt.; 3. Gnr. H. Opitz, Australian Field Artillery; 4. Sergt.-Major A. J. Nathan, H.A.C. (Arty.); 5. Bdr. B. M. Leon, R.G.A.; 6. Pte. S. Middleman, 61st Battn. M.G.C.; 7. Rfn. P. Porter, 17th London Regt.; 8. Bdr. V. J. Nathan, H.A.C. (Arty.); 9. Tpr. B. Pezaro, 4th Hussars; 10. Pte. H. Ossofsky, 10th Canadian Infantry; 11. Sergt. A. Leon, 6th Manchester Regt.; 12. C.S.M. M. Karo, 38th Royal Fusiliers.

1. Lieut. Douglas M. Ullman, 24th Royal Fusiliers; 2. Pte. I. E. Isaacs, 2/13th London Regt.; 3. 2nd-Lieut. P. E. Coote, 8th London Regt.; 4. Pte. Myer Cohen, R.A.S.C. and R.W. Kent Regt.; 5. Lieut. E. H. Josephi, R.A.S.C.; 6. Cpl. I. Glasstone, 1st Cheshire Regt.; 7. 2nd-Lieut. C. R. de Frece, R.A.F.; 8. Capt. J. A. Benjamin, 9th West Riding Regt.; 9. Lieut. P. B. Henriques, 8th K.R.R.C.; 10. Cadet J. H. Levene-Davis, Inns of Court O.T.C.; 11. Pte. R. Carolten, 2nd Yorks Regt.; 12. 2nd-Lieut. C. Owen Smith, R.F.A.

1. Rfn. S. Samuel, 3rd Rifle Brigade; 2. Pte. F. Bernard, 17th Australian Inf.; 3. Pte. H. Benjamin, 7th Norfolk Regt.; 4. Pte. S. Michaels, 1/5th Loyal N. Lancs Regt.; 5. Pte. M. Shatz, 3rd S. African Inf.; 6. Pte. James Becker, 2/5th Notts and Derby Regt.; 7. Pte. S. Solomons, 2nd Royal Fusiliers; 8. Pte. S. Showman, 1st K.O.R. Lancaster Regt.; 9. Pte. P. Myers, 47th Canadian Inf.; 10. L.-Cpl. H. H. Baum, 1st Border Regt.; 11. Pte. A. Boller, 8th East Lancs Regt.; 12. Pte. Joe Becker, 2/5th Notts and Derby Regt.

1. Pte. S. Shapiro, 38th Royal Fusiliers; 2. Pte. A. Sherman, 1st South African Infantry; 3. L.-Cpl. A. Lewis, 1/1st Hants Cyclist Battn.; 4. Pte. W. Cohen, 6th Wilts Regt.; 5. Pte. H. Spiers, R.M.L.I.; 6. Pte. M. Weitzenfeld, 38th Royal Fusiliers; 7. Bdr. G. Solomons, R.G.A.; 8. Pte. L. Conley, 5th Scottish Rifles; 9. Spr. J. Campbell, R.E.; 10. Pte. S. Schwartz, 7th London Regt. and Cyclist Corps; 11. Pte. B. Seftor, 39th Royal Fusiliers; 12. Pte. L. Lizar, 19th Manchester Regt.

1. 2nd-Lieut. R. H. Lazarus, 2nd South African Infantry; 2. Lieut. H. H. Kingsley, K.O.R. Lancaster Regt. and Indian Army; 3. Lieut. A. E. Marks, R.A.F.; 4. Capt. B. A. Salmon, 17th London Regt.; 5. Cpl. J. M. Harris, Australian Infantry (later Lieut. Australian Flying Corps); 6. Lieut. N. B. Freiman, Australian Flying Corps; 7. 2nd-Lieut. L. P. Solomons, R. W. Kent Regt.; 8. Adj. F. A. Joseph, Kilburn Volunteer Reserve; 9. Lieut. G. Nathan, 22nd D.L.I.; 10. Capt. S. M. Spira, 9th K.O.R. Lancaster Regt.; 11. Cadet B. Franks, Artists' Rifles; 12. Lieut. V. Jabotinsky, 38th Royal Fusiliers; 13. Pte. L. V. Barney, H.A.C. (later 2nd-Lieut. Royal Fusiliers).

1. Group at Canterbury; 2. Jewish soldiers in India; 3. Group of Leeds Jewish soldiers in India; 4. Jewish soldiers of Pembroke Yeomanry.

JEWISH WAR MEMORIALS ABROAD.

Grave of L.-Cpl. J. Bender, Houplines, near Armentieres. Grave of Pte. H. Brown, St. Omer Cemetery, erected by Rev. Dr. Kay, Presbyterian Chaplain. Grave of Capt. E. C. Simon, Lancashire Fusiliers, Millencourt Cemetery, near Albert.

Pte. W. Fisher (*standing*) (killed in action) and Jewish soldier, 1/1st Bucks Battn.

Brothers: (*standing*) L.-Cpl. F. G. Tasch, 1st Border Regt. (killed in action); Pte. M. A. Tasch, 7th Middlesex Regt.; (*sitting*) Pte. E. E. Tasch, 7th Middlesex Regt.

Pte. I. Harbour (bareheaded), 22nd Royal Fusiliers (killed in action), and Brother.

1. Pte. G. Vynar, King's Liverpool Regt.; 2. L.-Cpl. L. Joseph, M.G.C.; 3. Pte. A. H. Solomon, Australian Inf.; 4. Pte. Malinsky, 4th Hussars; 5. Gnr. Rothstein, Australian Artllery; 6. Pte. S. Lerman, Border Regt.; 7. Cpl. J. E. R. Samson, Poona Rifles; 8. Pte. H. Miller, 2nd Manchester Regt.; 9. Pte. A. Shorts, 38th Royal Fusiliers; 10. Pte. A. Samuels, Australian Inf.; 11. 2nd-A.M. H. Jacobs, R.A.F.; 12. Pte. L. Vancliffe, R.A.M.C.

1. L.-Cpl. J. Kramer, Labour Corps; 2. 2nd-A.M. A. Lewis, R.A.F.; 3. Pte. J. Morris, Northumberland Fusiliers; 4. Pte. M. Green, Labour Corps; 5. Pte. S. J. Lazarus, R.A.M.C.; 6. Pte. I. J. Levy, New Zealand Inf.; 7. Pte. E. Gottlieb, Northumberland Fusiliers; 8. Sig. P. Black, R.G.A.; 9. Pte. I. Benzimra, Labour Corps; 10. Pte. E. Jacobs, R.A.S.C.; 11. Pte. H. Bader, R.E.; 12. Pte. J. Koopchick, Labour Corps.

1. Lieut. H. Schaffer, 7th Canadian Engineers; 2. Lieut. I. H. Greenwood, 8th Middlesex Regt.; 3. Lieut. R. H. Montagu, 15th Hampshire Regt.; 4. 2nd-Lieut. E. H. Lifetree, 16th Notts and Derby Regt.; 5. 2nd-Lieut. Harry G. Raphael, 10th East Lancs Regt.; 6. 2nd-Lieut. H. Levi, 9th Royal Fusiliers; 7. Lieut. Solomon King, 23rd Northumberland Fusiliers; 8. 2nd-Lieut. Leonard Fleet, R.A.F.; 9. Lieut. Alec H. Hyams, 3rd Royal Fusiliers; 10. 2nd-Lieut. A. M. Levy, R.A.S.C. attached 4th Bedford Regt.; 11. 2nd-Lieut. H. Lewinstein, 1st R.W. Kent Regt. and Coldstream Guards; 12. Lieut. S. Stern, King's African Rifles

In Memoriam

1. Rfn. D. Van Ryn, Q.V.R.; 2. L.-Cpl. H. J. Tresman, 2nd West Yorks Regt.; 3. Pte. A. Finkelstein, 3/4th The Queen's; 4. Pte. S. Woolf, 17th K.R.R. Corps; 5. L.-Cpl. L. Pestka, 61st Labour Coy.; 6. Rfn. R. Schilling, 8th K.R.R. Corps; 7. Rfn. M. Fresco, 12th London Regt.; 8. A.B. Louis Kossick, Hood Battn., Royal Naval Division; 9. Sergt. H. Fromer, 24th Australian Inf.; 10. Sig. J. Solomon, 4th (Reserve) Seaforth Highlanders; 11. A.B. L. H. Salaman, Hawke Battn., Royal Naval Division; 12. Sergt. J. Sarfaty, R.A.M.C.

1. Rev. A. Barnett, S.C.F.; 2. Lieut. M. Abrahams, 16th Cheshire Regt.; 3. Lieut. Maurice Besso, R.A.F.; 4. 2nd-Lieut. G. M. Frampton, 5th King's Liverpool Regt.; 5. 2nd-Lieut. M. Blumberg, 3rd York & Lancaster Regt.; 6. Lieut. R. M. Messulam, R.A.F.; 7. Lieut.-Col. F. D. Samuel, D.S.O., Royal Fusiliers; 8. Rev. J. Danglow, C.F. Australia; 9. Major R. Tuck, 3rd County of London Yeomanry; 10. 2nd-Lieut. M. G. Finsburg, M.C., Tank Corps; 11. Lieut.-Col. J. H. Levey, D.S.O., Gordon Highlanders; 12. Lieut. W. R. Beddington, Queen's Bays (2nd Dragoon Guards).

Top.—Rev. A. BARNETT, S.C.F., and group of soldiers, Lille Synagogue, 1918.
Bottom.—Group of soldiers, Passover, Bombay, 1918.

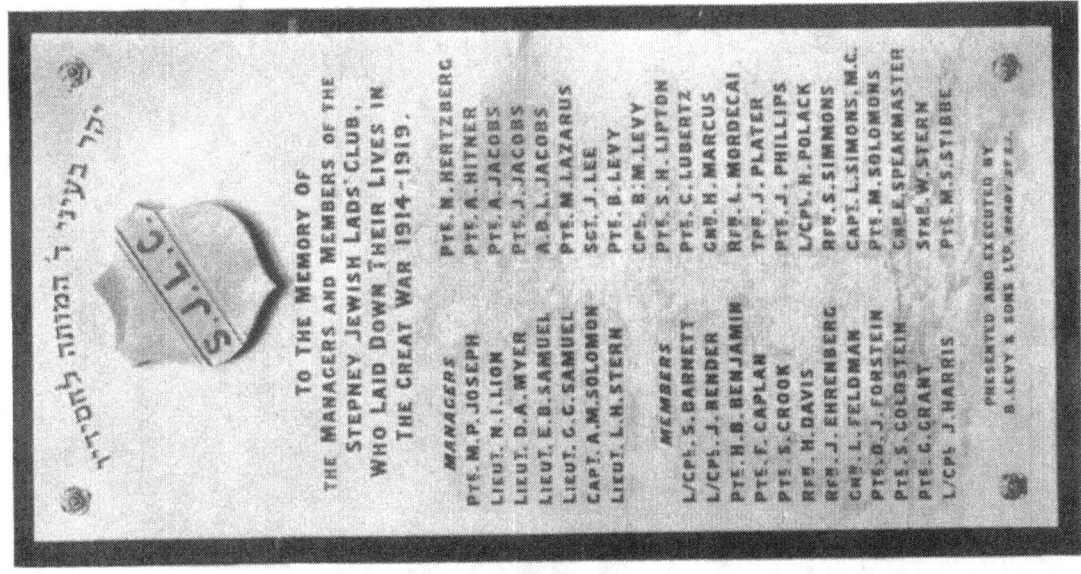

ROLL OF HONOUR
STEPNEY JEWISH LADS' CLUB.

WAR MEMORIAL
BRIGHTON SYNAGOGUE.

1. Lieut. ALBERT A. ROBINSON, M.C. and Bar, D.F.C., 7th King's Liverpool Regt. and R.A.F.; 2. Lieut. LEONARD H. LAZARUS, 4th Leicester Regt.; 3. 2nd-Liuet. A. LYONS, Manchester Regt.; 4. 2nd-Lieut. G. GREEN, W. Yorks Regt.; 5. Lieut. ISIDORE HARRIS, K.R.R.C. and R.A.F.; 6. Capt. SAUL H. HARRIS, R.A.M.C.; 7. 2nd-Lieut. S. JAY, 19th London Regt.; 8. Lieut. ERWIN W. FLATOW, 1/4th Duke of Wellington's Regt.; 9. Lieut. C. MARSDEN, R.A.F.; 10. Lieut. MYER LEVY, Royal Fusiliers (Jewish); 11. 2nd-Lieut. E. V. WHITE, Tank Corps; 12. Lieut. EDGAR JACKSON, R.F.A.

GROUP OF JEWISH SOLDIERS, BAGHDAD—NEW YEAR 1918.

1. Lieut. V. B. Barnett, 12th Northumberland Fusiliers; 2. 2nd-Lieut. L. Solomon, 1st King's Own Scottish Borderers; 3. Capt. E. C. Simon, 2/5th Lancashire Fusiliers; 4. Lieut. Joshua Levy, 1/5th Norfolk Regt.; 5. Lieut. A. M. Lyone, M.C., 11th Northumberland Fusiliers; 6. 2nd-Lieut. W. G. A. Joseph, 1/5th Norfolk Regt.; 7. Capt. D. Ezra, R.G.A.; 8. 2nd-Lieut. E. A. Rudell, 16th Royal Warwick Regt.; 9. 2nd-Lieut. D. E. Krauss, 1/5th North Staffs Regt.; 10. Major Evelyn A. de Rothschild, Bucks Hussars; 11. Major Ernest Alex Myer, 6th London Regt.; 12. 2nd-Lieut. E. J. Solomon, 2nd South Lancs Regt

1. Pte. H. Cohen, 10th Lancashire Fusiliers; 2. Cpl. M. Gillies, 5th Scottish Rifles; 3. Pte. B. Levy, 23rd Middlesex Regt.; 4. Pte. L. Cohen, 2/2nd London Regt.; 5. Rfn. E. Travers (Tragheim), 8th Rifle Brigade; 6. Pnr. Cpl. E. Tragheim, 4th Spec. Bgde. R.E.; 7. Pte. F. J. Jonas, 26th Royal Fusiliers; 8. Pte. B. Collins, 51st M.G. Battn.; 9. Rfn. J. Dobkin, 2/11th London Regt.; 10. Pte. J. Emden, 16th Middlesex Regt.; 11. Pte. C. Julius, 13th R. Sussex Regt.; 12. Pte. A. Cowan, 13th Hampshire Regt.

1. Major E. J. Davis, 1/19th London Regt.; 2. Capt. C. Jacobs, M.C. and Bar, R.A.M.C.; 3. Lieut. C. M. Davis, R.A.F.; 4. Lieut. C. T. Gordon, S. Staffs and M.G. Corps; 5. Lieut. C. Aserman, M.C., R.G.A.; 2nd-Lieut. D. Aserman, R.A.F.; 6. Capt. L. Levene, R.A.M.C.; 7. Lieut. V. R. Andrade, British West Indian Regt.; 8. Lieut. A. R. Cowan, 5th Royal Fusiliers; 9. Capt. S. R. Moss-Vernon, M.C., 12th London Regt.; 10. Lieut. D. L. Davis, M.G. Corps; 11. Lieut. H. H. Marks, M.C., 10th Durham L.I.; 12. Rev. Michael Adler, D.S.O., S.C.F.

Top Group.—Thirty Jewish Soldiers of 60th Divisional Ammunition Column, R.F.A.
Lower Group.—Rev. L. GEFFEN, C.F., and Rabbi C. WEIL, with Group of Soldiers at Boulogne, 1919.

1. Pte. J. Samuels, Welsh Regt.; 2. Rfn. L. J. Rudolf, P.P.C.L.I.; 3. Spr. A. Landstone, R.E.; 4. Pte. D. Salmon, 2/8th Argyll and Sutherland Hrs.; 5. Pte. P. Caller, 9th Black Watch; 6. Pte. F. A. Woolf, R.A.F.; 7. Pte. D. L. Woolfe, H.A.C. and Royal Fusiliers; 8. Pte. B. Golgowsky, R.A.S.C.; 9. Pte. G. Ward, R.A.M.C.; 10. Cpl. M. Raymon, 1st Durham L.I.; 11. Bdr M. Selby, R.F.A.; 12. Rfn. M. E. Rudolf, 9th London Regt.

GROUP OF JEWISH SOLDIERS: 1/4TH LONDON REGIMENT, MALTA, DECEMBER 1914.

1. L.-Cpl. S. Glynn, M.M., 38th Royal Fusiliers; 2. Pte. L. Sugerman, 2nd The Queen's; 3. C.S.M. Jack Gilbert, D.C.M., 16th Manchester Regt.; 4. Pte. Harry Robinson, 7th Scottish Rifle's; 5. Pte. G. Morris, R.A.F.; 6. Special Constable D. Cohen; 7. Pte. M. Morris, 13th Middlesex Regt.; 8. Pte. Alfred de Meza, Yorkshire Regt.; 9. A.B. Louis Jacobs, H.M.S. *Lord Nelson* (*killed in action*); 10. Gnr. F. D. Rissidore, 8th Canadian Field Artillery (*killed in action*); 11. Rfn. M. Barnett, 1/12th London Regt. (*killed in action*); 12. Pte. Isaac Lensnor, 6th Dorset Regt. (*killed in action*).

1. Pte. A. SNIPPER, 2nd Welch Regt.; 2. Dvr. SAM SNIPPER, R.A.S.C.; 3. Pte. I. SNIPPER, 3rd Royal Welch Fusiliers; 4. Pte. JACK GOLDMAN, Labour Battn.; 5. Lieut. M. TURIANSKY, R.A.M.C.; 6. Spr. JULIUS GOLDMAN, R.E.; 7. Sergt. MENDEL SHNEERSON, 40th Royal Fusiliers; 8. Pte. S. EPSTEIN, 1st Garr. Battn. Worcester Regt.; 9. Lieut. LIOVA SHNEERSON, O.B.E., Intelligence Corps; 10. Pte. I. VERBLOWSKI, 148th Canadian Infantry; 11. Pte. S. SCHARFF, 4th Middlesex Regt.; 12. 2nd-Lieut. M. J. FINKLESTONE, R.A.F.

In Memoriam

1. Pte. S. Rosenberg, 9th Royal Welsh Fusiliers; 2. Pte. A. P. Green, 14th Royal Warwick Regt.; 3. Pte. M. Zimmerman,* 39th Royal Fusiliers; 4. Spr. I. J. Hershon (W. D. Harris), R.E.; 5. Cpl. H. E. Hart, 3rd Wellington Regt., New Zealand Infantry; 6. Pte. S. Zimmerman,* 5th Oxford and Bucks L.I.; 7. Pnr. H. L. Woolf, Special Brigade R.E.; 8. Pte. Nat Zimmerman,* 2nd Yorkshire Regt.; 9. Dvr. A. Hyman, R.A.S.C.; 10. Gnr. H. R. Hovsha, C/232 Brigade R.F.A.; 11. Rfn. Joe Zimmerman,* 16th K.R.R.C.; 12. Cpl. A. Harris, 1st Duke of Cornwall's L.I.

* Brothers.

1. Pte. P. Leizerbram, 2/8th West Yorks Regt.; 2. Pte. O. Cohen, 7th East Kent Regt.; 3. Pte. H. Pattie, 16th Royal Scots; 4. Rfn. E. Wollman, 1/17th London Regt.; 5. Pte. E. Goldstein, 1st Middlesex Regt.; 6. Pte. M. Wallack, 1/6th West Yorks Regt.; 7. L.-Cpl. J. Levey, 1/6th King's Liverpool Regt.; 8. Pte. M. Deitz, 38th Royal Fusiliers; 9. Pte. M. Leibovitch, 50th Canadian Inf.; 10. Pte. H. H. Gofberry, 20th Middlesex Regt.; 11. Rfn. H. Levy, 6th London Regt.; 12. Pte. E. Schaffer, 6th Somerset L.I.

1. Spr. A. J. Rosansky, R.E.; 2. Cpl. D. Sasieni, 3rd South African Infantry; 3. L.-Cpl. A. Simnock, 2/17th London Regt.; 4. Pte. J. Bokofski, Canadian Railway Troops; 5. C.S.M. C. Blasentein, Middlesex Regt.; 6. Pte. H. J. Reece, 2nd Northampton Regt.; 7. Pte. M. Levy, 45th Royal Fusiliers; 8. Pte. Mersky, Australian Infantry; 9. Pte. J. Levene, 38th Royal Fusiliers; 10. Dvr. J. Solomon, R.F.A.; 11. Sergt. M. Stall, Canadian Medical Corps; 12. Pte. J. Malles, Coldstream Guards.

1. Sergt. C. P. Millingen, Australian A.M.C.; 2. Pte. A. Moreberg, 40th Royal Fusiliers; 3. Pte. A. Morris, Dorset Regt.; 4. Sergt. M. Rosenbaum, 4th Canadian Engineers; 5. Pte. H. I. Roberts, South African Infantry; 6. Dvr. B. Salmon, R.A.S.C.; 7. Pte. C. Zang, 4th Lancashire Fusiliers; 8. L.-Cpl. J. Marks, 12th Royal Lancers; 9. L.-Cpl. P. Zimmerman, Scottish Horse; 10. Pte. L. Silverman, 39th Royal Fusiliers; 11. Pte. I. Myers, 38th Royal Fusiliers; 12. Pte. M. Pick, London Regt.

GROUP OUTSIDE ALDERSHOT SYNAGOGUE, SEPTEMBER 1914 (SHOWING REPLICA OF SOUTH AFRICAN WAR ROLL OF HONOUR).

JEWISH SOLDIERS, PASSOVER, 1918, OUTSIDE THE WALLS OF JERUSALEM.

JEWISH SOLDIERS, PASSOVER, 1918, IN JERUSALEM.

On steps—Rev. I. FRANKENTHAL, C.F., the Chief Rabbi of Jerusalem (centre), and Rev. S. GRAJEWSKY, C.F.
Standing (centre with cane)—Major N. DE M. BENTWICH, Imperial Camel Corps.
On his right—Lieut. J. HART, 2/4th Hampshire Regt., Lieut. WEBBER, Cyclist Corps, and 2nd-Lieut. N. I. MINDEL.
On his left—Lieut. EDWIN H. SAMUEL and Lieut. RICHARDSON.
Seated at foot—2nd-Lieut. G. ISAACS and 2nd-Lieut. C. ISAACS, 1/8th Hampshire Regt.

1. Pte. A. E. Beenstock, Royal Marines ; 2. A.B. S. Solomons, Royal Navy ; 3. Sig. M. Blatt, Royal Navy; 4. A.M. N. Phillips, R.N.A.S. ; 5. A.B. J. Rose, Royal Navy ; 6. W.O. Cecil Asher, New Zealand Field Artillery ; 7. Sergt. David Cansino, 1st Seaforth Hrs. ; 8. Seaman J. Gilbert, Royal Navy ; 9. A.M. L. Robinson, R.N.A.S. ; 10. Pte. B. Lewis, Australian Infantry ; 11. Pte. D. H. Goldstein, Australian Infantry ; 12. Cpl. A. Solomon, Australian Infantry.

GROUPS OF BROTHERS.

1. Five Brothers: *(standing)* Rfn. S. JACOBS, K.R.R.C.; Spr. B. JACOBS, R.E.; *(sitting)* 2nd-A.M. M. JACOBS, R.A.F.; Pte. J. JACOBS, R.A.M.C.; Gnr. M. JACOBS, R.G.A.
2. Three Brothers: Pte. E. PHILLIPS, 9th Royal Welsh Fusiliers; Sergt. A. PHILLIPS, Royal Fusiliers; Cadet S. S. PHILLIPS, Glasgow University O.T.C.
3. L.-Cpl. H. FINN, L.-Cpl. J. FINN, 5th Seaforth Highlanders.

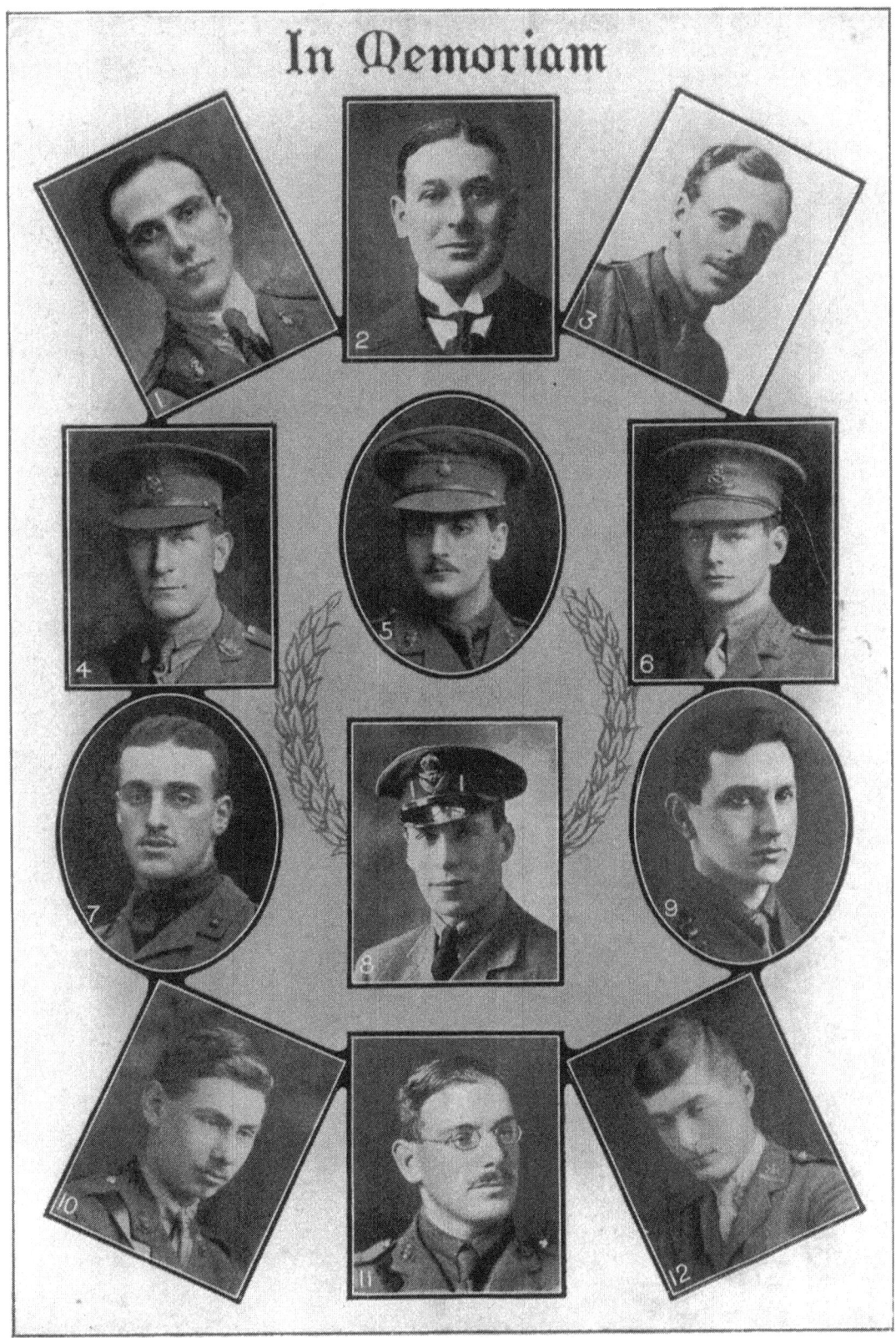

1. 2nd-Lieut. R. N. Cullen, 5th Royal Irish Fusiliers; 2. Lieut. A. Solomon, 87th Canadian Infantry; 3. Cadet W. H. Styer, 28th London Regt and Royal Fusiliers; 4. Capt. D. Piza, 1st East Yorks Regt.; 5. Capt. Seymour J. H. Van den Bergh, 1st County of London Yeomanry; 6. 2nd-Lieut. J. Kohnstamm, 54th M.G.C.; 7. Lieut. J. H. Van den Bergh, 6th London Bgde., R.F.A.; 8. Lieut. M. C. Sonnenberg, 35th Squadron R.A.F.; 9. Lieut. V. J. Hitner, R.A.S.C.; 10. 2nd-Lieut. V. S. Moses, R.F.A.; 11. Capt. A. M. Solomon, 2/10th (attached 19th) London Regt.; 12. Capt. N. Kohnstamm, 1/18th Manchester Regt.

1. Rfn. D. Goldstein, 1st Rifle Brigade; 2. Pte. A. Cohen, 1st Lincoln Labour Coy.; 3. Pte. L. Goldberg, 4th Canadian Inf.; 4. Gnr. W. Corper, R.H.A.; 5. Pte. R. Marks, 38th Royal Fusiliers; 6. Pte. D. Levy, 9th Norfolk Regt.; 7. L.-Cpl. A. J. Goldberg, 2nd S. Wales Borderers; 8. Pte. M. Lichtenstein, 46th M.G.C.; 9. Pte. P. M. Greenberg, 1/6th West Yorks Regt.; 10. Rfn. L. Nunes Vaz, 10th Rifle Brigade; 11. Pte. J. Cohen, 2/6th Manchester Regt.; 12. Pte. J. Levy, 38th Royal Fusiliers.

1. D. Marvin, Royal Navy; 2 Stoker B. Lewis, H.M.S. *Minerva*; 3. H. Hyman, Royal Navy; 4. P. Terry, Royal Navy; 5. Bdr. G. Leavey, R.F.A.; 6. Pte. I. Kronenberg, R.A.M.C.; 7. L.-Cpl. L. Lelyveld, Royal Warwickshire Regt.; 8. Pte. H. Solomons, 38th Royal Fusiliers; 9. L.-Cpl. W. Langdon, 12th H.L.I.; 10. Pte. Isaac Solomons, 20th King's Liverpool Regt.; 11. Pte. Victor Hamaui, Welsh Regt.; 12. L.-Cpl. Harry Epstein, D.C.M., 59th Field Coy. R.E.

1. Pte. A. Kronenberg, 6th Welch Regt.; 2. Pte. N. Kronenberg, M.M., 6th Welch Regt.; 3. Pte. L. Wender, 10th Canadian Infantry; 4. Pte. N. Spector, 10th Canadian Infantry; 5. Pte. J. Feldman, R.E.; 6. A.B. N. Lewis, Mine Sweeper; 7. Pte. I. Lewis, R.A.M.C.; 8. Pte. S. Brown, Royal Scots Fusiliers; 9. Pte. M. Barnett, Royal Scots Fusiliers.

R.A.F. AND 30TH MIDDLESEX AT READING SYNAGOGUE.

1. In France : *(standing, left to right)* Pte. D. CHESNEY, 1st Coldstream Guards (killed in action) ; Pte. A. A. LEWIS, 20th London Regt. ; Pte. S. SOLOMON, 4th Royal Fusiliers.
 (Seated, left) Pte. R. FRIEDLANDER, 7th London Regt. ; L.-Cpl. J. SAGMAN, R.A.M.C.
2. 30th Middlesex Regt. *(left to right)* Pte. A. SEELEY, Pte. R. LUNZER, L.-Cpl. F. LUNZER, Pte. A. LUNZER, Pte. A. BELL.
3. Chanucah Service held by Rev. H. SHANDEL, Ramsgate Synagogue, 1918.

1. Pte. D. Albert, Canadian A.M.C.; 2. Sergt. G. Mervish, King's African Rifles; 3. Pte. S. Holzberg, Canadian A.M.C.; 4. Sig. N. Horevitz, Manchester Regt. and 38th Royal Fusiliers; 5. Cpl. J. Hart, R.A.P.C.; 6. Pte. A. Levine, 38th Royal Fusiliers; 7. Pte. J. Levy, 2nd Northumberland Fusiliers; 8. L.-Cpl. S. Samuel, D.L.I. and R.A.O.C.; 9. Pte C. L. Morris, 8th Northampton Regt.; 10. Rfn. D. Adler, L.R.B.; 11. Pte. L. Levy, 38th Royal Fusiliers; 12. Rfn. M. Libstein, L.R.B.

244

1. Pte. J. S. Krailsheimer, 10th Royal Fusiliers and Norfolk Regt.; 2. Pte. L. Kossick, 26th Northumberland Fusiliers; 3. Pte. M. Rooms, 2nd Lincoln Regt.; 4. Pte. A. Guterman, 5th Durham L.I.; 5. Sergt.-Major S. Goldberg, South African S.C.; 6. Pte. J. Goldenberg, Lancashire Fusiliers and 38th Royal Fusiliers; 7. Pte. S. Rothblatt, 2/5th Royal Warwick Regt.; 8. Pte. C. Katz, 4th London Regt.; 9. Pte. R. Kossick, 13th K.R.R.C.; 10. Gnr. S. Kaye, M.M., R.F.A.; 11. L.-Cpl. Eli Gerber, 16th Lancashire Fusiliers; 12. Pte. H. Galinsky, 1st West Yorks Regt

In Memoriam

1. Pte. H. B. Woolf, R.A.F. and 2/2nd London Regt.; 2. Pte. M. Galinsky, 38th Royal Fusiliers; 3. Pte. S. Malinsky, 2nd Lancashire Fusiliers; 4. Pte. S. Cohen, 55th Australian Infantry; 5. Pte. A. Prins, 4th London Regt.; 6. Cpl. A. Glassman, 13th King's Liverpool Regt.; 7. Rfn. J. Bentley, M.M., 2/6th London Regt.; 8. Pte. L. Pinto, 15th H.L.I.; 9. Pte. W. Marks, 2/5th York and Lancaster Regt.; 10. Pte. A. Grower, 1/4th London Regt.; 11. Pte. A. Cohen, 2nd Honourable Artillery Company; 12. Pte. E. Blaubaum, New Zealand Infantry.

1. Sergt. D. Loverman, Lancashire Fusiliers; 2. Pte. J. Block, Royal Fusiliers; 3. 1st A.M. J. Cohen, R.A.F.; 4. Sergt. J. D. Goldstein, 47th Res. Battn.; 5. Pte. J. D. Jacobs, R.A.M.C.; 6. Pte. M. Gordon, Labour Corps; 7. Bandmaster B. Jellen, 40th Royal Fusiliers; 8. Gnr. H. Baker, R.H.A.; 9. Pte. A. Isaacs, 8th Manchester Regt.; 10. Pte. K. Kapshut, 38th Royal Fusiliers; 11. Cpl. E. Josephs, 13th Kensington Regt. and R.A.F.; 12. Pte A. Miller, Labour Coy.

1. Pte. H. Cohen, R.A.S.C.; 2. Pte. J. Perlstone, 39th Royal Fusiliers; 3. Pte. S. Cohen, R.A.O.C.; 4. L.-Cpl. W. Ellis, Rifle Brigade; 5. Cpl. H. Poorman, Labour Coy.; 6. Tpr. A. Elias, City of London Yeomanry; 7. Pte. B. Lewis, Royal Fusiliers; 8. Pte. J. Fordanski, 2nd Worcester Regt.; 9. Sergt. M. Ehrlich, 3rd London Regt.; 10. Pte. J. Davis, 2nd Manchester Regt.; 11. Pte J. Bennett, 3rd County of London Yeomanry; 12. L.-Cpl. A. L. Bentata, 3rd Hants Regt.

1. Pte. D. Woolf, R.A.M.C., awarded the Russian St. George's Cross, 4th class; 2. Cpl. R. Wansker, R.A.P.C.; 3. L.-Cpl. R. Myers, Military Foot Police; 4. Tpr. Alfred Shiers, Earl of Chester's Yeomanry; 5. Pte. H. Jeffrey, Lancashire Hussars; 6. Pte. W. Fine, Shropshire Light Infantry; 7. Gnr. R. Nordwind, R.G.A.; 8. Pte. Harold Shiers, R.A.M.C.; 9. Dvr. A. Singer, R.F.A.; 10. Pte. Jack Shiers, 2nd East Yorks Regt.; 11. Pte. J. Landanski, 7th Leicester Regt.; 12. Sergt. H. Wansker, 40th Royal Fusiliers.

Top (left).—Very Rev. the Chief Rabbi (Dr. J. H. HERTZ) on a visit to G.H.Q., France, 1915.
Top (right).—Rev. V. G. SIMMONS, C.F., and Rev. A. BARNETT, C.F., on active service.
Bottom.—Rev. MICHAEL ADLER, D.S.O., and Rev. V. G. SIMMONS, C.F., near Arras (note the "Mogen David" on the bonnet of the car).

1. 2nd-Lieut. M. A. MICHAEL, K.R.R.C.; 2. Surgeon Sub-Lieut. H. N. JAFFE, R.N.; 3. Lieut. M. W. DRUCQUER, 3rd Manchester Regt.; 4. Capt. HERSHEL HARRIS, Australian A.M.C.; 5. Capt. L. LAZARUS, R.A.M.C.; 6. Capt. MORDECAI JOSEPH, Indian Army; 7. Lieut. R. JOSEPH, R.A.S.C.; 8. Sub-Lieut. M. ABENSUR, R.N.V.R.; 9. Capt. E. A. FRANKLIN, 10th K.O.Y.L.I.; 10. Lieut.-Paymaster J. A. FRANKLIN, R.N.R.; 11. Lieut. A. H. DESMOND FREEMAN, 13th London Regt.; 12. Capt. M. ALEX MYER, 6th London Regt.; 13. Lieut. H. C. ROSENBLOOM, H.L.I. and Royal Fusiliers.

1. Cpl. E. MENDOZA, 2nd Grenadier Guards ; Pte. H. BRIGHTMAN, 1st Royal Berks Regt.
2. Corpl. S. GREEN, Pte. I. GREEN, Australian Forces
3. L.-Cpl. J. DEFRIES, Middlesex Regt. ; Dvr. A. HARMAN, R.F.A.
4. Group, Rifle Brigade : *(standing, left to right)* Rfn. LIPMAN, Rfn. ROSE, Rfn. S. CONWAY ; *(seated)* Rfn. J. BOOKER (killed in action), Rfn. H. SINGER.

1. Capt. B. L. Q. HENRIQUES, East Kent Regt. and Tank Corps; 2. Major A. C. ABRAHAMS, C.B.E., Administrator in France, British Red Cross; 3. Capt. S. SIMONS, 11th Lancashire Fusiliers; 4. Major C. D. ENOCH, T.D., 7th London Regt.; 5. Lieut. W. W. LUBELSKI, M.C. and Bar, R.A.F.; 6. Lieut. H. BLAIBERG, 5th Dragoon Guards and Royal Warwick Regt.; 7. Capt. LIONEL L. COHEN, 13th London Regt. and Staff; 8. 2nd-Lieut. I. E. LEVY, R.A.F.; 9. Capt. C. SINGER, R.A.M.C.; 10. Capt. JULIUS LEVENTON, General List attached R.A.M.C.; 11. Capt. E. BLAIBERG, South Lancs Regt.; 12. Capt. A. SCHOTTLANDER, East Yorks Regt.

INDIA: GROUP OF JEWISH SOLDIERS' CALCUTTA, PASSOVER, 1918, AT HOUSE OF Mr. D. EZRA.

Lieut. H. Loewe. Rev. E. M. D. Cohen.

1. Major Sir Herbert B. Cohen, Bart., 4th R. W. Kent Regt.; 2. Lieut. M. S. Lissack, 2/13th London Regt.; 3. Capt. E. R. Kisch, M.C., 2/13th London Regt.; 4. 2nd-Lieut. A. Silverstone, Royal Fusiliers; 5. Lieut. H. Wolfenstein, 40th Royal Fusiliers (Judeans); 6. Major Harold R. Mosenthal, R.A.F.; 7. Capt. and Adjt. I. Jaffe, 38th Royal Fusiliers; 8. Lieut. J. P. Myers, 229th Canadian Battn.; 9. Lieut. A. Hanbury, 38th Royal Fusiliers; 10. 2nd-Lieut. J. M. Rich, 39th Royal Fusiliers; 11. Major H. Dutch, M.D., T.D., R.A.M.C.; 12. 2nd-Lieut. B. Stone, 39th Royal Fusiliers.

1. Pte. A. Latter, 25th M.G.C.; 2. Pte. C. Boam, 8th York and Lancs Regt.; 3. Pte. L. Berman, 9th Royal Fusiliers; 4. Pte. I. Klein, 171st M.G.C.; 5. Sergt. A. Linde, 8th Norfolk Regt.; 6. Pte. J. Livingstone, 1/6th Manchester Regt.; 7. Pte. N. Segal, 10th Royal Welch Fusiliers; 8. Cpl. I. Shibko, 11th Welsh Regt.; 9. L.-Cpl. L. G. Marks, 17th Royal Sussex Regt.; 10. Pte. M. Bogard, 13th Royal Fusiliers; 11. Pte. H. Lewis, 10th Royal Fusiliers; 12. Pte. B. Phillips, 1/23rd London Regt.

In Memoriam

1. Pte. N. Isaacs, 1st Essex Regt.; 2. Pte. H. Franklin, 4th London Regt.; 3. L.-Cpl. H. Lazarus, 9th Royal Scots; 4. Rfn. B. Barnett, 12th London Regt.; 5. Pte. A. D. Levinson, 2/8th Lancashire Fusiliers; 6. Pte. J. A. M. Swede, 14th Royal Warwick Regt.; 7. Pte. H. Montsoff, 1/23rd London Regt.; 8. Pte. B. Lazarus, 10th King's Liverpool Regt.; 9. Pte. S. Larvey (Levy), 15th Canadian Infantry; 10. Pte. I. Slifkin, 17th King's Liverpool Regt.; 11. Pte. M. Marks, 2nd Royal Scots Fusiliers; 12. Rfn. J. Sackshiver, 9th Rifle Brigade.

257

REV. S. LIPSON, S.C.F., AND CANADIAN SOLDIERS.

1. Lieut. HAROLD J. FRASER, Royal Sussex Regt.; 2. Rev. WALTER LEVIN, C.F.; 3. Capt. J. JOELS, R.A.M.C.; 4. Lieut. F. ROWE, R.A.F.; 5. Lieut. B. M. COHEN, R.A.S.C., Indian Army; 6. Rev. DAVID I. FREEDMAN, Australian Chaplain; 7. Capt. A. P. MYERS, M.C., 1st K.O.R. Lancaster Regt.; 8. Lieut. J. LYNES, 1/23rd London Regt.; 9. Lieut. ELLIS E. JACOBS, R.N.V.R.; 10. Lieut. C. MARSDEN, Royal Navy; 11. Rev. M. GOLLOP, C.F.; 12. Lieut. H. P. LAWRENCE, 10th London Regt.

1. Pte. R. Pearlman, 38th Royal Fusiliers; 2. Pte. S. Moscovitch, Northumberland Fusiliers; 3. Rfn. J. Jeffreys, Rifle Brigade; 4. Rfn. A. Kass, 7th Rifle Brigade; 5. Pte. L. Myers, Australian Infantry; 6, Pte. S. Kutchinsky, R.A.F.; 7. Pte. S. Moscovitch, 39th Royal Fusiliers; 8. A.M. W. Podgus, R.A.F.; 9. Pte. A. Kutchinsky, Labour Corps; 10. Gnr. H. Jeffreys, R.F.A.; 11. Sergt. L. Jacobs, 39th Royal Fusiliers; 12. L.-Cpl. H. Jacoby, 7th Durham L.I.

Left to Right.—Sergt. M. Fleisig, M.M. and Bar; Sergt. J. Morris, 40th Royal Fusiliers, at Miss Sophie Pinto, V.A.D.; Miss Rosie Pinto, Sergt. S. Fleisig; Sig. D. Fleisig, Canadian Pyramids, Egypt. Canteen Worker; Pte. R. Pinto, H.A.C. and Infantry. O.T.C.

1. Pte. J. Phillips, 8th West Riding Regt.; 2. Rfn. E. Miller, K.R.R.C.; 3. Spr. J. Jacobs, R.E.; 4. Pte. G. Green, 4th Royal Fusiliers; 5. Pte. I. Haft, 18th Manchester Regt.; 6. Pte. J. Isaacs, R.A.S.C.; 7. Rfn. B. Goldstein, 13th Rifle Brigade; 8. L.-Cpl. J. O. Joseph, London Scottish (14th London Regt.); 9. Rfn. H. Woolf, 15th Royal Irish Rifles; 10. Gnr. B. Gordon (Woolf), 2nd Canadian Field Artillery; 11. Pte. J. B. Wyne, 19th Manchester Regt.; 12. Pte. L. Falk, 2/4th London Regt.

1. Pte. L. Farbstein, 2nd Lancashire Fusiliers; 2. Pte. S. Gilbert, 1/4th Royal Fusiliers; 3. Pte. G. J. Foster, 1st Norfolk Regt.; 4. Pte. A. Jacobs, 4th Middlesex Regt.; 5. L.-Cpl. M. Rood, 2nd Dorset Regt.; 6. Pte. V. M. Mendoza, R.A.O.C.; 7. Pte. B. Goldsmith, 6th Canadian Field Ambulance; 8. Pte. I. Jaffe, 9th K.O.Y.L.I.; 9. Pte. S. Rosenbaum, 1/1st Bucks Battn.; 10. Rfn. J. Bloom, 4th Rifle Brigade; 11. Pte. C. S. Beyfus, 2nd Honourable Artillery Company; 12. Pte. H. M. Davidson, 7th Oxford and Bucks L.I.

1. Pte. A. GOMPERTZ, R.A.M.C.; 2. Tpr. H. HESS, 1st County of London Yeomanry; 3. Pte. A. J. HESS, R.A.S.C.; 4. Sergt. H. S. HAYMAN, N.Z.M.C.; 5. Sergt. B. HYAMS, R.F.A.; 6. Pte. F. J. HESS, 16th London Regt.; 7. Cpl. S. S. GERSHON, Oxford and Bucks L.I.; 8. Sergt H. M. HAYMAN, N.Z.E.F.; 9. Cpl. M. GOLDBERG, 12th West Yorks Regt.; 10. 2nd A.M. R. COHEN, R.A.F.; 11. Pte. S. HARRIS, 5th Cameron Hrs.; 12. Pte. J. HARRIS, R.A.M.C.

1. 1st A.M. E. ROSKIN, R.A.F.; 2. Pte. M. ROSEBERG, Australian Infantry; 3. Cpl. I. J. LEVY, West Somerset Yeomanry; 4. Pte. S. WALTERS, 1st Gloucester Regt.; 5. Cpl. A. GOLDBERG, 10th Leicester Regt.; 6. Pnr. D. L. SAMUEL, R.E.; 7. Tpr. A. MORDECAI, Essex Yeomanry; 8. Sergt. JULIUS BERNSTEIN, 38th Royal Fusiliers; 9. Pte. L. M. SAMUEL, 51st Royal Sussex Regt.; 10. A.M. S. SAMSON, R.A.F.; 11. Gnr. M. MENDELSOHN, South African F.A.; 12. Pte. A. MATTHEWS, R.A.M.C.

AUSTRALIAN GROUP.

Officers.—Rev. J. Danglow, C.F.   Lieut. H. Boas.   Capt. H. Goldstein, M.C.

Top.—Group with Rev. H. SHANDEL, Westgate, 1917.
Bottom.—Group of Jewish soldiers at Northampton Synagogue.

1. Gnr. M. Wolfson, Royal Marine Artillery; 2. Cpl.-Drummer D. Markson, 40th Royal Fusiliers; 3. Rfn. B. Markson, 3rd Rifle Brigade; 4. Pte. I. Frankel, 39th Royal Fusiliers; 5. Pte. A. Baker, 9th Royal Scots; 6. Sig. L. Markson, R.F.A.; 7. Pte. H. Franks, East Lancs Regt.; 8. Pte. A. Nathan, 6th Dorset Regt.; 9. Pte. S. Hart, R.A.S.C.; 10. Dr. Raphael Levy, R.A.S.C.; 11. Pte. A. B. Mordecai, R.A.S.C.; 12. Art. Mech. W. Barnett, R.N.A.S.

1. Pte. H. Jessel, 1/4th Royal Berks Regt.; 2. Pte. S. Newman, Cyclists, attached 1st Scottish Rifles; 3. Pte. S. Marks, 1st Manchester Regt.; 4. L.-Cpl. A. Phillips, 22nd London Regt. (attd. 32nd R. Fusiliers); 5. Pte. M. Barback, Royal Scots; 6. Sergt. S. Morris, 2nd Oxford and Bucks L.I.; 7. Sergt. Harris Levy, 1st Royal Scots Fusiliers; 8. Pte. T. Solomons, 7th Royal Dublin Fusiliers; 9. Sergt. C. S. Whitefield, M.S.M., 4th Australian Infantry; 10. Pte. Baron Mendes da Costa, 1st Essex Regt.; 11. Rfn. M. Jay (Jacobs), 17th K.R.R.C.; 12. L.-Cpl. A. Lotsky, 2/1st Bucks Regt.

1. Pte. Sol Ellis, 2nd Yorks Regt.; 2. Pte. S. R. Lipchinsky (Lipman), 1/7th West Yorks Regt.; 3. Pte. J. Friend, 15th Cheshire Regt.; 4. Pte. P. S. Ellison, 3rd Royal Fusiliers; 5. Pte. I. Levey, 16th Manchester Regt.; 6. Pte. N. Ellis, 2/6th Sherwood Foresters; 7. Pte. J. Malkin, 38th Royal Fusiliers; 8. Pte. M. Foreman, 2/1st London Regt.; 9. Dvr. D. Michaels, 18th Batty, 3rd Brigade, R.F.A.; 10. Pte. S. Phillips, 9th Royal Fusiliers; 11. Cpl. R. F. Paterson, 8/10th Gordon Highlanders; 12. Pte. S. J. Ellison, 2nd Royal Irish Regt.

1. Pte. A. Lavender, 2/1st Oxford and Bucks L.I. ; 2. Pte. R. Nagavkar, Bangalore Rifles ; 3. Pte. I. Novinski, 1/4th East Yorks Regt. ; 4. Rfn. J Nyman, 2nd Rifle Brigade ; 5. Cpl. G. Norris (Nossek), 2nd Royal Scots ; 6. Pte. H. Naphtali, 1/13th London Regt. ; 7. Pte. E. Kaufman (Elias), Imperial Camel Corps ; 8. Sergt. A. F. Sampson, 4th British West Indies Regt. ; 9. Spr. B. Stander, R.E. ; 10. L.-Cpl. H. Levy 9th Devon Regt. ; 11. Cpl. S. Barnett, 1st Rifle Brigade ; 12. L.-Cpl. Isaac A. Stodel, 16th K.R.R.C.

1. Pte. M. Cooper, 42nd Royal Fusiliers; 2. Cpl. H. Hollander, 2nd Dragoons; 3. Pte. Woolf Fisher, 1st Middlesex Regt.; 4. R.S.M. M. Harris, 4th London Regt.; 5. Pte. S. Morris, Labour Coy.; 6. Pte. S. Portrait, 1st Royal Dublin Fusiliers; 7. Bdr. M. Raisman, R.G.A.; 8. Pte. J. Davis, 38th Royal Fusiliers; 9. Pte. L Seltzer, Labour Coy.; 10. Pte. H. Michael, 9th Manchester Regt.; 11. Pte. A. Bromberg, 1st Royal Berks Regt.; 12. Cpl. L. Schonfield, 40th Royal Fusiliers.

1. Pte. A. Brodie, "Judeans"; 2. Pte. C. S. Joseph, 3rd Grenadier Guards; 3. Gnr. R. Harris, R.G.A.; 4. Sergt.-Major S. Schottlander, M.M., 11th East Yorks Regt.; 5. Miss Florence J. Trenner, V.A.D.; 6. Gnr. H. Jacobs, A/178th Brigade R.F.A.; 7. S/Sergt.-Major B. Lyons, R.A.S.C.; 8. Pte. J. Bresler, South African Scottish; 9. 1st A.M. A. Lewis, R.A.F.; 10. Pte. H. Park, 40th Royal Fusiliers; 11. A.M. M. Marchant, R.N.A.S.; 12. Pte. Jules Singer, City of London Volunteer Corps.

WAR MEMORIALS ABROAD.

1. Pte. I. Lurie, 4th South African Infantry: Ploegsteert Cemetery.
2. Pte. H. M. Levy, 8th Australian Infantry: Estaires Cemetery.
3. Capt. L. J. Davis, 1/19th London Regt.: High Wood, near Albert.
4. Pte. H. Markus, 19th Canadian Infantry: Voormezeele, near Ypres..
5. 2nd-Lieut. R. Herman, 1st Canterbury Regt., New Zealanders: Armentières.

1. A group of Jewish soldiers of the Middlesex Regt. in France.
2. 11th Royal Fusiliers at Colchester, 1914: (A) Pte. S. PHILLIPS (killed in action), (B) Pte. S. BENSON (killed in action), (C) Sergt. P. ADLER, M.M. (killed in action).

1. Rfn. P. Benjamin, 1/17th London Regt.; 2. C.S.M. N. Eagle, 39th Royal Fusiliers; 3. Gnr. L. Moses, 208th Batty., R.G.A.; 4. Pte. S. Phillips, 2/5th R. Warwick Regt.; 5. Pte. B. Edgar (Ettinger), 1st Hampshire Regt.; 6. Rfn. S. Newman, 17th K.R.R.C.; 7. Pte. R. Woolf, 3/5th Lancashire Fusiliers; 8. Pte. J. Schein (Warner), 9th Worcester Regt.; 9. Pte. N. Primhak, 1st Essex Regt.; 10. Rfn. H. Lewis, 10th Royal Irish Rifles; 11. Pte. R. Levy, 6th Royal West Surrey Regt.; 12. Pte. A. Posenor, 11th Tank Corps.

1. Cpl. H. ERDMAN, 1st King's Liverpool Regt.; 2. Pte. M. AVNER, R.A.S.C.; 3. Rfn. M. M. GREEN, 1/5th London Regt.; 4. Pte. A. BERNSTEIN, 2/10th King's Liverpool Regt.; 5. L.-Cpl. S. APTER, 8th Oxford and Bucks L.I.; 6. Pte. J. COSTER, 2/8th Worcester Regt.; 7. Sergt. M. M. GORDON, 17th London Regt.; 8. Pte. M. ARONSON, 9th Royal Fusiliers; 9. A.B. A. KARLISH, 63rd M.G. Battn., Royal Naval Division; 10. L.-Cpl. S. BARNARD, 1st Royal Munster Fusiliers; 11. Pte. A. B. GREEN, 3rd South African Infantry; 12. Pte. H. MEISEL, 4th Northumberland Fusiliers.

Top Group.—Group of 40th Royal Fusiliers, Saltash Camp.
Bottom Group.—(*Standing.*)—Cpl. ISRAEL ABRAHAMS, Bucks Battn.; L.-Cpl. JACK ABRAHAMS, 38th Royal Fusiliers; Physical-Training Instructor LOUIS ABRAHAMS, R.N.A.S.
(*Seated.*)—Q.M.S. JULIUS ABRAHAMS, R.A.F.; Pte. J. ABRAHAMS, St. John's Ambulance; Pte. SID. ABRAHAMS, R.A.F.

GROUP OF JEWISH OFFICERS AND MEN, SIALKOT, PUNJAB—PASSOVER 1917.

In Centre Capt. SEFTON COHEN and Capt. H. ROSKIN.

1. Lieut. R. GOLDREICH, R.N.; 2. Lieut. S. DIAMOND, D.C.M., Croix de Guerre, Australian Infantry; 3. Lieut. B. JOSEPH, General List; 4. 2nd-Lieut. J. BLOOM,* M.G.C.; 5. Lieut. I. V. GLUCKSTEIN, R.A.F.; 6. Lieut. H. BLOOM,* R.A.P. Corps; 7. Lieut. L. V. COHEN-HENRIQUES, British West Indian Regt.; 8. Surgeon H. SINGTON, R.N.; 9. Flight Cadet M. BLOOM,* R.A.F.; 10. Major B. ISAACS, R.A.S.C.; 11. Lieut. A. LANG, Paymaster, H.M.S. *Columbella*; 12. Capt. W. M. GUTTMAN (M.C.), 10th Middlesex Regt.

* Brothers.

1. Cyclist B. LIPTON, 19th Corps Cyclist Battn.; 2. Pte. M. LEVY, R.A.M.C.; 3. Bdr. A. MORRIS, R.H.A.; 4. L.-Cpl. C. PINTO, M.F.P.; 5. Rfn. D. COLLINS (SHAPIRO), London R.B.; 6. Gnr. J. SOLOMONS, R.F.A.; 7. Gnr. A. LOVEGUARD, R.F.A.; 8. Cpl. W. WARSCHAWSKI, R.A.F.; 9. Pte. N. BENJAMIN, Oxford and Bucks L.I.; 10. Pte. S. R. SPURLING, K.O.Y.L.I.; 11. Spr. S. PEZIM, Canadian Engineers; 12. Cpl. L. WHITE, M.M., 10th Manchester Regt.

SOLDIERS OF VICTORIA WORKING LADS' CLUB, LONDON, E.

1. Pte. H. S. SMITH, R.A.M.C.; 2. Pte. S. LEVY, 2/7th Lancashire Fusiliers; 3. Sig. A. E. SIMPSON, 1st King Edward's Horse; 4. Pte. M. ROSENSTERN, 1/8th Essex Regt.; 5. Pte. I. SANKERWITZ, 38th Royal Fusiliers; 6. Cpl. A. SCHIFF, 1/17th London Regt.; 7. Pte. M. SERENO, Middlesex Regt.; 8. Cpl. RUTNER, 2/4th London Regt.; 9. Sergt. T. REES, R.A.S.C.; 10. Pte. A. RAPAPORT, Kin'gs Liverpool Regt.; 11. Cpl. B. LEVY, 17th H.L.I.; 12. Pte. H. SCHATZ, 2/4th K.O.Y.L.I.

1. Jews of Royal Welch Fusiliers in Egypt.
2. Group of Labour Coy. in France: (*left to right*) Ptes. BRODIE, CROM, LEVY, LEVESON.
3. *Back row.*—(*Left*) Bdr. B. HYAMS, R.F.A.; (*end of row*) Gnr. SHERMAN, R.F.A.
   Seated.—(*Left*) Pte. DEFRIES, R.A.O.C · Sergt. HAAGERMAN, R.N.A.S.; Pte. LITTMAN, R.A.O.C.
4. Group of men of Middlesex Regt.
5. Group of Jewish soldiers in Belgium.
6. Pte. G. SPILG, M.M. and Bar; Pte. R. SPILG, Glasgow Highlanders.

1. Pte. H. T. Myers, 1/5th Royal Warwick Regt.; 2. Pte Ralph A Strauss, 2/2nd London Regt.; 3. 2nd-A.M. J. Lubinsky, R.A.F.; 4. Rfn. H. Silverman, 1/21st London Regt.; 5. Pte. M. Berman, 9th Royal Scots; 6. Pte. P. Samuels, 7th Royal Fusiliers; 7. Pte. L. Marks, 9th South Lancs Regt.; 8. Spr. J. Slonemsky, Canadian Engineers; 9. Pte. H. Rosenbloom, 12th Manchester Regt.; 10. Rfn. J. Kopinsky, 8th Rifle Brigade; 11. Pte. S. Krohn, 2nd Lincoln Regt.; 12. Pte. A. M. Belman, 2/7th Lancashire Fusiliers.

In Memoriam

1. Rfn. S. Phillips, 8th K.R.R.C.; 2. Pte. A. Marshofsky, 723rd Labour Coy.; 3. Rfn. A. J. Cohen, 17th K.R.R.C.; 4. Pte. A. Solomons, 10th Royal Dublin Fusiliers; 5. Pte. L. Benjamin, 23rd Cheshire Regt.; 6. Pte. I. Lipman, R.A.S.C.; 7. Sergt. J. Monty, 2/10th London Regt.; 8. Rfn. S. Bazinski, 1/21st London Regt.; 9. Pte. L. Levy, 1st South Wales Borderers; 10. Cpl. M. Brodie, 520th Labour Coy.; 11. Pte. B. Chart, 4th London Regt.; 12. Dvr. I. Delinsky, R.A.S.C.

1. Pte. E. Mentel, Middlesex Regt.; 2. Cpl. M. D. Lazarus, 38th Royal Fusiliers; 3. L.-Cpl. A. Cohen, 17th London Regt.; 4. Pte. V. Joseph, R.A.S.C.; 5. Pte. M. Joseph, 3/4th Queen's (R.W. Surrey Regt.); 6. Pte. M. J. Jacobs, D.C.M., R.A.M.C.; 7. Pte. H. R. Lazarus, 40th Royal Fusiliers; 8. 1st A.M. E. Malinsky, R.A.F.; 9. Cpl. H. Morris, R.A.M.C. and Labour Corps; 10. Pte. C. Kosky, 38th Royal Fusiliers; 11. Dvr. E. Joseph, R.F.A.; 12. Pte. H. L. Isaacs, 5th Royal Warwickshire Regt.

JEWISH AUSTRALIAN Y.M.C.A. HUT, STRAND, LONDON, 1919.

Top Group.—SEDER SERVICE, AUSTRALIAN Y.M.C.A. HUT, LONDON, PASSOVER, 1919.
Lower Group.— Ditto. Ditto.

Sergt. Issy Smith, V.C., placing Wreath on the Cenotaph, November 11th, 1920, in honour of the Jewish Dead.

Memorial to L.-Cpl. M. Comor, 1st Newfoundland Regt., Blackpool.

1. Group at Clacton.
2. Group of Jewish soldiers.
3. Group in France with Rev. H. L. Price, C.F.
4. Group of regulars in R.A.M.C.: (sitting) Pte. J. Sagman, Pte. R. Sidney; (standing) Pte. S. Joseph, Pte. S. J. Lazarus.

Top.—1. Pte. L. ABRAHAMS and friend, R.A.S.C.; 2. Sergt.-Instr. P. SHTITZER, Inns of Court O.T.C.; Sergt.-Instr. D. SHTITZER, St. John Ambulance; Pte. B. SHTITZER, R.W. Kent Yeomanry; 3. Private 38/40th Royal Fusiliers at Saltash Depot.

Bottom.—Leading Aircraftsman A. MUSIKANSKY, R.A.F. Testing propellor.

In Memoriam

1. Rfn. I. S. Samson, 2nd K.R.R.C.; 2. Rfn. J. Isaacs, 21st K.R.R.C.; 3. L.-Cpl. C. Loveguard, R.A.S.C.; 4. Rfn. H. Solomons, 1/12th London Regt.; 5. Pte. S. Fink, Duke of Lancaster's Own Yeomanry and Manchester Regt.; 6. Pte. E. Geffen, Artists' Rifles and 2/13th London Regt.; 7. Gnr. J. Bloom. R.F.A.; 8. Pte. B. Shalgosky, 9th York and Lancaster Regt.; 9. Rfn. A. Franks, 17th K.R.R.C.; 10. L.-Cpl. D. Berson, 2/7th West Yorks Regt.; 11. Pte. N. Lewis, 1/7th Argyll and Sutherland Hrs.; 12. Pte. S. Levy, 2nd Middlesex Regt.

1. Pte. J. Marks, 4th London Regt.; 2. Pte. J. Pomerantz, 2nd Leicester Regt.; 3. L.-Cpl. M. Comor, Newfoundland Regt.; 4. Gnr. J. Savitz, 232nd Siege Battery R.G.A.; 5. Pte. M. Solomon, 23rd Northumberland Fusiliers; 6. Rfn. S. Hart, 1/5th London Regt.; 7. A.B. A. L. Hyman, Nelson Battn., R.N.D.; 8. C.P.O. E. Allen, H.M.S. *Mignonette*; 9. Cpl. M. Beckerwick, 4th Middlesex Regt.; 10. Pte. J. Silver, 2/4th York and Lancaster Regt.; 11. Pte. H. Rosenthal, 16th Northumberland Fusiliers; 12. Pte. H. Selcovitch, 1st South Wales Borderers.

1. L.-Cpl. G. Boyars, 40th Royal Fusiliers; 2. Sergt. H. Horowitz, 15th Northumberland Fusiliers and R.A.P.C.; 3. Sergt. N. Horowitz, R.A.F.; 4. L.-Cpl. M. Sherwin, M.M., Rifle Brigade; 5. Spr. D. Hyams, R.E.; 6. Pte. H. Levey, R.A.M.C.; 7. L.-Cpl. H. Davis, 38th Royal Fusiliers; 8. Sergt. H. Michaelson, 1st Welsh Regt. and 39th Royal Fusiliers; 9. Spr. J. Goodman, R.E.; 10. Pte. B. Marcus, 8th King's Liverpool Regt.; 11. Pte. H. E. Pearlman, 2/4th King's Shropshire L.I.; 12. Pte. M. Newman, Middlesex Regt.

1. Pte. B. Miller, Essex Regt.; 2. Pte. M. Pemzech, 38th Royal Fusiliers; 3. Sergt. L. Nathan, M.M., 1/9th London Regt.; 4. L.-Cpl. A. Nieberg, R.E.; 5. Pte. M. Olswang, 1/4th York and Lancaster Regt.; 6. Pte. D. Rosenberg, M.G.C.; 7. Pte. A. Phillips, 9th H.L.I.; 9. Rfn. M. Kay, L.R.B.; 9. Pte. E. Lenbie, Canadian Scottish; 10. Pte. T. M. Lippman, R.A.M.C.; 11. Dvr. F. R. Jacobs, R.A.S.C.; 12. Pte. M. Norton, R.A.M.C.

GROUP OF JEWISH SOLDIERS (LIVERPOOL REGIMENTS) WITH REV. S. FRAMPTON.

GROUP OF OFFICERS OF THE JEWISH LADS' BRIGADE, DEAL CAMP, 1911.

All served in the War—twelve died, viz: 1. Capt. C. L. HART; 2. Lieut. V. B. BARNETT; 3. 2nd-Lieut. A. R. HENRY; 4. 2nd-Lieut. L. SOLOMON; 5. Lieut. V. V. JACOB; 6. Capt. E. M. GREEN; 7. 2nd-Lieut. DENZIL G. A. MYER; 8. Capt. ARTHUR SOLOMON; 9. 2nd-Lieut. EDGAR KAHN; 10. Cadet WILFRED B. STYER; 11. Lieut. H. A. TELFER; 12. Lieut. E. B. SAMUEL.

1. L.-Cpl. P. Lyons, 7th Welsh Regt.; 2. Sergt. I. King, S. African Inf.; 3. 2nd-A.M. J. Annenberg, R.A.F.; 4. Pte. R. Grover, Princess Patricia's L.I.; 5. Spr. M. Cohen, R.E.; S.-Sergt. B. Cohen, R.A.O.C.; 6. Sergt. H. Himmel, M.M., 22nd Northumberland Fusiliers; 7. Cadet L. C. Marks, R.A.F.; 8. C.Q.M.S. J. Cohen, 16th King's Liverpool Regt. and Labour Corps; 9. L.-Cpl. R. Friedlander, 1/7th London Regt.; 10. Cpl. L. Gillis, 38th Royal Fusiliers; 11. S.-Sergt. F. M. Marsden, Queen's Westminsters; 12. Pte. L. W. Flatow, M.T., R.A.S.C.

JEWISH SOLDIERS OF THE K.R.R. CORPS AND RIFLE BRIGADE WITH REV. H. SHANDEL.

1. Sig. J. Klein, 26th Australian Infantry; 2. Bdr. S. O. Benjamin, 21st Howitzer Brigade, Australian F.A.; 3. Spr. H. Gorfunkle, R.E.; 4. Pte. S. Goodman, 1/1st Bucks Battn.; 5. Pte. I. Polikoff, 1/5th West Yorks Regt.; 6. Pte. M. Lubinsky, 2/22nd London Regt.; 7. L.-Cpl. H. Rosenthal, 2nd Manchester Regt.; 8. Pte. D. K. Davis, 13th London Regt.; 9. Pte. Godfrey C. Marks, R.A.S.C.; 10. Rfn. J. Cohen, 1st Rifle Brigade; 11. Pte. M. Lazarus, 38th Canadian Infantry; 12. Gnr. J. Cohen, 185th Hy. Baty. R.G.A.

1. Pte. G. Levy, 15th Royal Scots; 2. Pte. M. Wein, 1st R.W. Kent Regt.; 3. Pte. Abram Jacks, 49th Australian Infantry; 4. L.-Cpl. M. Perlman, 3rd Northumberland Fusiliers; 5. Pte. F. Solomon, 23rd Royal Fusiliers; 6. Pte. A. Loftus, 134th Field Ambulance, R.A.M.C.; 7. Pte. L. B. Silverstein, 1/23rd London Rgt.; 8. Tpr. J. Plater, 11th Hussars attached M.G. Squad.; 9. Rfn. L. Lightstone, 2nd Rifle Brigade; 10. Pte. S. R. Trotskey, R.A.M.C.; 11. A.M. M. Felperin, R.A.F.; 12. Pte. A. Isaacs, 1st Worcester Regt.

1. 1st-C. Stoker J. PRESSMAN, H.M.S. *Majestic* ; 2. Stoker ISAAC DE FRIEND, H.M.S. *Curacoa* ; 3. Leading Stoker B. JACOBS, H.M.S. *Lord Nelson* ; 4. 1st-C. Stoker H. SILVERSTONE, H.M.S. *Implacable* ; 5. 1st-C. Stoker J. KEESING, H.M.S. *Illustrious* ; 6. PHILIP COHEN, R.N.A.S. ; 7. P. TERRY, R.N.A.S. ; 8. Lieut.-Commdr. R. SAUNDERS, D.S.O. ; 9. Capt. S. C. JOSEPH, D.F.C. and Bar ; 10. Stoker J. SIMMONS, H.M.S. *Triumph* ; 11. A.B. S. CORNBLATT, H.M.S. *Colossus* ; 12. C.P.O. LOUIS WEINBERG, H.M.S. *Patrol*.

1. Pte. Isaac Valinsky, R.A.S.C.; 2. Pte. A. Cohen, R.A.S.C.; 3 Pte. Morris Valinsky, 30th Essex Regt.; 4. Dvr. A. Carlish, R.A.S.C.; 5. Pte. Alf Valinsky, 9th Loyal North Lancs; 6. L.-Cpl. C. Diamond 40th (Palestine) Royal Fusiliers; 7. Pte. Phil Valinsky, Cyclist Corps; 8. L.-Cpl. A. Cramer, Cheshire Regt. and Royal Scots; 9. Pte. Percy Valinsky, Royal Welsh Fusiliers; 10. Pte. S. Valinsky, 9th Yorkshire Regt.; 11. Gnr. C. Casher, R.F.A.; 12. Pte. Barnet Valinsky, 5th Manchester Regt.

JEWISH SOLDIERS IN FRANCE, 1918, WITH REV. H. SILVERMAN, C.F.

Capt. J. M. Cohen, S. African S.C. 2. Lieut. R. L. Michaelis, R.G.A.; 3. Lieut. G. Harris, 2/6th London Regt.; 4. Capt. J. Breckman, R.A.F.; 5. Lieut.-Col. J. S. Marks, 19th Royal Welsh Fusiliers; 6. Lieut. A. Abrahams, M.G. Corps; 7. Capt. S. Davis, M.C., 1/4th London Regt.; 8. Capt. K. L. Spiers, M.C., 3rd Worcestershire Regt.; 9. Sub-Lieut. S. D. Barney, R.N.V.R.; 10. Capt. J. J. Goldston, 10th London Regt.; 11. Lieut. A. Stiebel, 6th Royal West Kent Regt.; 12. Capt. A. Montagu Lyons, 16th Durham L.I. and General Staff.

1. Pte. FISCHER, Australian Inf.; 2. L.-Cpl. E. ABRAHAMS, M.F.P.; 3. Pte. J. DAVIS, R.A.M.C.; 4. 3rd Writer M. LEVY, R.N.; 5. Pte. H. DRAPKIN, 2nd Middlesex Regt.; 6. P.O. L. FRANKS, R.N.; 7. Pte. DRAGOVITCH, 38th Royal Fusiliers; 8. Pte. A. BOORMAN, R.A.S.C., M.T.; 9. Pte. H. HARRIS, 38th Royal Fusiliers; 10. Pte. P. FIELDMAN, 2nd Northampton Regt.; 11. L.-Cpl. J. ASHFIELD, 25th Rifle Brigade; 12. Pte. J. DA COSTA, 13th Essex Regt.

1. Pte. J. Himmel, R.A.M.C.; 2. Sergt. J. E. Jaye, 7th Buffs; 3. Pte. L. Himmel, R.A.S.C.; 4. Pte. S. Jacobs, 5th Middlesex; 5. Spr. M. Gallewski, R.E.; 6. Pte. S. Moss, R.A.S.C.; 7. Pte. S. Lipton, R.A.M.C.; 8. Gnr. M. Himmel, R.G.A.; 9. Pte. S. Joels, 7th Seaforth Highlanders; 10. Pte. I. Cohen, K.R.R.C.; 11. Gnr. S. Gerson, R.G.A.; 12. Pte. A. Joels, 2nd Seaforth Highlanders.

In Memoriam

1. Pte. J. J. Seline, 26th Royal Fusiliers; 2. Pte. J. Butman, 1st Somerset L.I.; 3. Rfn. H. Beyfus, L.R.B.; 4. Rfn. M. Magnus, 7th Rifle Brigade; 5. Pte. A. H. Sternheim, R.A.S.C.; 6. Pilot D. Best, Mersey Pilot Service; 7. Pte. H. B. Benjamin, 7th S. Wales Borderers; 8. Rfn. J. Malnick, 1/12th London Regt.; 9. Pte. M. Spear, 2/1st City of London Regt.; 10. Pte. S. Schneider, 5th Oxford and Bucks L.I.; 11. Pte. W. Berson, 13th Essex Regt.; 12. Pte. M. Black, 1st King's Liverpool Regt.

1. Rfn. J. Levy, 16th Rifle Brigade; 2. Pte. J. Krell, 1/7th Manchester Regt.; 3. Tpr. J. Jacobs, 2nd King Edward's Horse; 4. Pte. A. Daskel, 3rd Canadian Infantry; 5. Pte. B. Goldstein, 8th London Regt.; 6. Rfn. W. Green, 1/8th London Regt.; 7. Ptc. H. Galinsky, 2/20th London Regt.; 8. Rfn. A. Levy, 7th Rifle Brigade; 9. Pte. S. Sniders, Royal Bucks Hussars; 10. Bdr. A. Van Leer, D/331 Bgde. R.F.A.; 11. Pte. A. Galinsky, 16th K.R.R.C.; 12. Rfn. J. Lumer, 2/15th London Regt.

1. Rfn. L. Cohen, New Zealand R.B.; 2. Pte. A. Appleton, 1/8th Sherwood Foresters; 3. Sergt. M. Ash, Welsh Regt.; 4. Sig. I. Aschman, South African Expeditionary Force; 5. Dvr. H. Bernstine, R.A.S.C.; 6. Tpr. C. F. Heilbuth, 15th Hussars; 7. Sergt. J. Abrahams, 1/5th R.W. Kent Regt.; 8. Tpr. L. Barnard, Royal Horse Guards; 9. Bdr. L. Cornofsky, R.F.A.; 10. Pte. M. Goldstone, 13th East Lancs Regt.; 11. Pte. J. Bell, 19th Welsh Regt.; 12. Pte. H. Harris, Northumberland Fusiliers.

1. Pte. J. Sanders, Middlesex Regt.; 2. Cpl. S. Rapp, 4th South African Horse; 3. Pte. J. Levy, R.A.F.; 4. Tpr. C. Rosenberg, 6th Yorks Hussars; 5. Pte. L. Rosenbloom, 10th Royal Fusiliers; 6. Dvr. M. Bader, M.G.C.; 7. Pte. A. Morris, 5th Royal Fusiliers; 8. Pte. F. Wedell, Middlesex Regt.; 9. L.-Cpl. S. Mason, 4th South Lancs Regt.; 10. Pte. A. Lang, Middlesex Regt.; 11. Pte. H E. Samuels, Cheshire Regt.; 12. Tpr. L. Rapp, 1st Imperial Light Horse.

Left (top group)—Top row—*In Palestine*—2nd-Lieut. G. ISAACS, 1/8th Hampshire Regt.; 2nd-Lieut. J. HART, 2/4th Hampshire Regt.; 2nd-Lieut. C. ISAACS, 1/8th Hampshire Regt.; 2nd-Lieut. RICHARDSON.
2nd row—Lieut. WEBBER, Cyclist Corps; Rev. I. FRANKENTHAL, C.F.; Rev. S. GRAJEWSKY, C.F.; French Officer; and 2nd-Lieut. N. I. MINDEL.
Left (bottom group)—Group of Jewish Soldiers, London, Passover, 1915.
Right—1. Cpl. D. LEVINSON, 13th Welch Regt.; 2. Pte. A. DAVIES, 13th Welch Regt.; 3. Pte. P. MASON, 13th Welch Regt.; 4. Pte. I. TRAGEN, 13th Welch Regt.

Pte. N. Freshwater, R.A.M.C.,   Rev. M. Adler.   Lieut.-Col. J. H. Levey, D.S.O.   Sergt.-Maj. M. Nathan.
1st Jewish D.C.M.

GROUP AT FEAST OF CHANUCAH, LONDON—DEC. 13, 1914.

GROUPS OF BROTHERS.

1. Sig. L. Rubinstein, 39th Royal Fusiliers; 2nd-Lieut. M. Rubinstein, R.G.A.; Pte. Myer Rubinstein, 39th Royal Fusiliers.
2. Pte. C. Bader, Pte. M. Bader, Middlesex Regt.
3. New Zealand Forces.—Four Brothers: (left to right) Dvr. E. Boock, Field Artillery; L.-Cpl. S. Boock, Home Service; Pte. H. Boock, Medical Corps; Sergt.-Major B. Boock, Medical Corps (died on active service).
4. A.B. Phil. Simons, R.N.; Pte. S. Simons, M.M., 9th Essex Regt.

1. Pte. I. Wender, Labour Coy.; 2. Cpl. F. Stahl, 7th Manchester Regt.; 3. Pte. L. Swatski, 13th Devon Regt.; 4. Spr. Phillips, R.E.; 5. Pte. M. Potock, R.A.S.C.; 6. Pte. J. Rappaport, 2/4th Loyal North Lancs; 7. Pte. M. Woolfish, 38th Royal Fusiliers; 8. Pte. C. Schatz, 8th Canadian Infantry; 9. Cpl. M. E. Stahl, 8th Manchester Regt.; 10. Cpl. J. Bennett, R.A.O.C.; 11. Pte. A Rosenberg, Royal Fusiliers; 12. Gnr. S. Levine, R.G.A.

1. Rfn. J. Figgins, 2nd Rifle Brigade; 2. Pte. B. Falk, 8th Suffolk Regt.; 3. Pte. C. Fordanski, 10th Worcester Regt.; 4. Spr. H. Fitelson, 278th Railway Coy. R.E.; 5. Pte. I. Abrahams, 10th Northumberland Fusiliers; 6. Pte. H. Abrahams, 2nd Roy. Berks Regt.; 7. Pte. M. Freedman, M.M., 10th West Riding Regt.; 8. Pte. B. Fearn, 13th West Yorks Regt.; 9. Pte. M. Hart, 19th M.G.C.; 10. Pte. E. Reuben, 6th Manchester Regt. attd. 11th Lancs Fusiliers; 11. Pte. H. Finkelstein, 20th Australian Infantry; 12. Pte. D. Jacobs, 4th Middlesex Regt.

1. Sergt. M. J. BRONKHORST, South African Medical Service; 2. Pte. J. BERMAN, Royal Fusiliers; 3. Pte. A. MELNIK, R.F.A.; 4. Pte. S. SHAPIRO, 38th Royal Fusiliers; 5. Pte. N. LEVY, R.A.M.C.; 6. Pte. J. L. SCHWARTZ, B.R.C.S.; 7. Dvr. J. SIMLER, R.F.A.; 8. Pte. J. GARSON, R.A.M.C.; 9. Sergt. A. N. WITONSKI, Somerset L.I. and R.A.S.C.; 10. Pte. A. WOOLF, R.A.M.C.; 11. Dvr. L. WOOLER, R.A.S.C.; 12. Pte. H. GOLDMAN, 8th Royal Fusiliers.

1. 1st-Class Clerk E. PORTER, R.N.A.S.; 2. Pte. L. GOODMAN, R.A.O.C.; 3. A.C. B. LEWIS, R.N.A.S.; 4. Pte. S. GREEN, Labour Coy.; 5. Pte. A. CONLAN, 1st Dorset Regt.; 6. Pte. G. CRULEY, R.A.M.C.; 7. Sig. B. CHALFEN, 38th Royal Fusiliers; 8. Spr. J. ANNENBERG, R.E.; 9. Pte. M. HARRIS, Scottish Rifles; 10. Pte. S. ABRAHAMS, Labour Coy.; 11. Bdn. H. GARCIA, 1st Yorks Regt.; 12. Dvr. L. GINSBERG, R.E.

REV. A. BARNETT, S.C.F., AND JEWISH SOLDIERS IN DOUAI, 1919.

1. A.B. E. Miller, H.M.S. *New Zealand*; 2. Pte. M. H. V. Symonds, M.M., R.M.L.I.; 3. Cpl. Albert, Labour Coy.; 4. Pte. A. Davis, 13th Welsh Regt.; 5. Pte. B. Adler, M.T., R.A.S.C.; 6. Dvr. L. Harris R.F.A.; 7. Pte. M. Gotlob, Middlesex Regt.; 8. Sub-Conductor M. S. David, Indian Army; 9. Pte. I. Flack, Rifle Brigade; 10. Pte. M. Beirman, Royal Fusiliers; 11. Pte. E. Gordon, 1/6th Norfolk Regt.; 12. Pte. J. Feldman, 38th Royal Fusiliers.

REV. A. BARNETT, S.C.F., AND JEWISH SOLDIERS IN SYNAGOGUE, LILLE, 1919.

1. Spr. H. Freedman, Glamorgan R.E.; 2. Pte. B. Somers, 6th R. W. Kent Regt.; 3. Sergt. M. Kosky, 38/40th Royal Fusiliers; 4. Pte. M. R. Somers, 12th East Surrey Regt.; 5. Pte. H. Saunders, South African Infantry; 6. Gnr. Jacob Penn, R.F.A.; 7. Pte. F. Kosky, 2/13th London Regt.; 8. Rfn. M. Horevitz, 4th Scottish Rifles; 9. Leading Aircraftsman W. Kosky, R.A.F.; 10. L.-Cpl. L. Joseph, M.G.C.; 11. Pte. J. Horevitz, Manchester Regt.; 12. Pte. S. Wolf, Middlesex Regt.

GROUPS OF BROTHERS.

1. Sig. M. Berg, 12th North Staffs; 2nd-Cpl. S. Berg, R.E.
2. Bdr. R. Leslie, R.G.A.; Tpr. L. A. Leslie, 2nd Dragoon Guards.
3. Rfn. L. Pyser, London Rifle Brigade; 2nd-Lieut. M. Pyser, R.E.
4. Cpl. D. Samuels, 17th Lancs Fusiliers; Pte. E. Samuels, 7th Royal Fusiliers.

1. Pte. D. BURNETT (centre) and two Jewish soldiers, Royal Scots Fusiliers.
2. Pte. L. SHARP, Australian Infantry; and Asst. Vict. H. SHINEGOLD, H.M.S. *Glory*.
3. Group of Jewish soldiers.
4. Jewish soldiers of 12th London Regt., 1914.

1. Pte. C. Wise, 1st Dorset Regt.; 2. Pte. T. Miller, Manchester Regt.; 3. Gnr. M. L. Rosen, Australian Infantry; 4. Rfn. C. Moss, 1/12th London Regt.; 5. Tpr. E. Schneider, 20th Hussars; 6. Sig.-Cpl. J. Salmon, 15th Scottish Rifles; 7. Pte. H. Galizer, 3rd London Regt.; 8. Pte. S. Ampel, Royal Fusiliers; 9. Rfn. D. Moss, 1/12th London Regt.; 10. L.-Cpl. H. Middleman, 51st Rifle Brigade; 11. Pte. M. Solomons, Labour Coy.; 12. Pte. M. Levine, Labour Corps.

1. Nurse. R. Kreemer, V.A.D.; 2. Rosie Franks (Mrs. B. Alvarez), V.A.D.; 3. Mrs. Julian S. Marks, B.R.C.S.; 4. Nursing Sister Froomberg, South African Medical Corps; 5. Nurse B. Aschman, South African Military Nursing Service; 6. Miss Clara Baker, W.A.A.C.; 7. Mrs. M. J. Jonas, Headquarters Staff, V.A.D.; 8. Miss K. A. Woolf, V.A.D.; 9. Queenie Franks (Mrs. J. W. Myers), Red Cross Motor Transport; 10. Staff-Sister E. Ashberry (Annenberg), Q.A.N.S.; 11. Sister Bessie Baker, V.A.D.; 12. Nursing Sister S. Weiner, Nursing Service.

1. Sister FLORENCE OPPENHEIMER (Mrs. L. J. GREENBERG), Queen Alexandra's Imperial Military Nursing Service; 2. Orderly L. HERRING, B.R.C.S.; 3. Miss RACHEL ALVAREZ, V.A.D.; 4. Miss KITTY HUDSON, V.A.D.; 5. Capt. S. SAMUEL, M.D., R.A.M.C.; 6. Mrs. CARRIE LONDON, V.A.D.; 7. Mrs. MAY MARX, V.A.D.; 8. Capt. L. HADEN GUEST, M.C., R.A.M.C.; 9. Miss DORIS HIRSCHLAND, V.A.D.; 10. Miss G. VAN GELDER, V.A.D.; 11. ADOLPH RAPAPORT, B.R.C.S.; 12. Miss MINNIE HESS, V.A.D.

1. Mrs. Rosa Phillips, V.A.D.; 2. Miss Irene Rosenstein, V.A.D.; 3. Mrs. Madge Bolton, V.A.D.; 4. Miss Esther Cohen, V.A.D.; 5. Mrs. Rose Platnauer, V.A.D.; 6. Miss Jamilla Nahon, V.A.D.; 7. Mrs. O. A. Altman, V.A.D.; 8. Miss Hetty Harris, V.A.D.; 9. Miss Nita Roe, V.A.D.; 10. Miss Hilda Halford, V.A.D.; 11. Miss Muriel Bamberger, V.A.D.; 12. Miss Rose Selby, V.A.D.

Rev. V. G. Simmons, C.F.

GROUP AT HUT OF JEWISH NAVAL AND MILITARY ASSOCIATION, ALDERSHOT, 1918.

1. Engineer S. Benjamin, s.s. *Tayabi*; 2. Pte. J. Goldberg, Australian Infantry; 3. C.P.O. S. E. Zucker, R.N.; 4. Pte. M. Borisoff, Labour Coy.; 5. Pte. M. Aizin, R.A.M.C.; 6. Sig. W. Goldstein, R.H.A.; 7. Rfn. J. Cohen, 2nd Rifle Brigade; 8. Pte. J. Greenbery, 1st South Wales Borderers; 9. Pte. A. Greenstone, 38th Royal Fusiliers; 10. Pte. S. Gepstein, 9th Devonshire Regt.; 11. Pte. G. Green, Middlesex Regt.; 12. Pte. H. Gould, 38th Royal Fusiliers.

4. S.-Sergt. GINSBERG with his son, Trumpeter GINSBERG, Canadian Artillery.
5. Senior W.O. J. MISTOFSKY, H.M.S. *Gascony*; Senior W.O. M. MISTOFSKY, H.M.S. *Scalda*; (seated) Senior W.O. J. FELDMAN, H.M.S. *Ismailia*.
6. Pte. J. GERBER, 1st Queen's; Pte. J. DEMBOVSKY, K.O.R. Lancaster Regt.
7. Corpl. W. J. FRIEDLANDER, Pte. GERSHON, Pte. SIMMONS, Australian Forces.
8. Jews in 461 Field Coy., R.E., Spr. J. AVERBACK (left) killed in action.

1. Capt. J. Lumley-Frank, 1/19th London Regt.; 2. Lieut. A. L. Michaelis, R.G.A.; 3. Capt. S. Duparc, R.A.M.C.; 4. Lieut. B. M. Kauffmann, 1st M.G. Battn.; 5. Capt. P. P. Sabel, R.A.S.C.; 6. Lieut. H. Attwell, General List; 7. Lieut. S. M. Lipsey, 13th London Regt. att. 38th Royal Fusiliers; 8. Lieut. M. Salmon, General List; 9. Capt. A. Nathan, R.A.S.C.; 10. Rev. I. Frankenthal, C.F.; 11. Capt. S. S. Ansley, M.C., Berks R.H.A.; 12. Capt. A. Moss, Australian H.Q. Staff.

1. Spr. A. Freedman, R.E.; 2. Pte. M. Berman, Royal Fusiliers; 3. Pte. P. Boss, H.A.C.; 4. Cpl. J. Harris, R.F.A.; 5. Cpl. S. Carr, 7th Hussars; 6. Pte. E. Falk, 38th Royal Fusiliers; 7. Cpl. A. Fay, R.A.M.C.; 8. Pte. H. Alexander, R.A.M.C.; 9. Interpreter O. S. Abolafia, Egyptian Corps; 10. Gnr. P. L. Barnard, R.G.A.; 11. Pte. B. Diamond, M.G.C.; 12. Pte. J. Dyson, 2nd Manchester Regt.

1. Cpl. H. M. WACHOLDER, 10th East Yorks Regt.; 2. Pte. N. COHEN, 4th South African Infantry; 3. Pte. E. FRANKLIN, 2nd Royal Fusiliers; 4. Dvr. M. GREEN, R.A.S.C.; 5. Cpl. C. THOMAS, South Wales Borderers; 6. A.M. J. WHYL, R.A.F.; 7. Pte. M. CHELMINSKI, 38th Royal Fusiliers; 8. 1st A.M. A. D. ARONHEIM, R.A.F.; 9. Pte. S. EPSTEIN, 9th Russian Labour Coy.; 10. Pte. P. EPSTEIN, 38th Royal Fusiliers; 11. Sergt. L. J. LASKER, 38th Royal Fusiliers; 12. L.-Cpl. L. BAKER, Northumberland Fusiliers and R.A.O.C.

1. Sergt. D. Abrahams, 38th Royal Fusiliers; 2. Pte. L. Freedman, Royal Fusiliers; 3. Pte W. Fishman, Northampton Regt.; 4. Pte. H. Boekbinder, R.N.A.S.; 5. Pte. H. Barnett, R.A.M.C. (later Lieut. 39th Royal Fusiliers); 6. Pte. S. Fineburg, Royal Inniskilling Fusiliers; 7. L.-Cpl. J. Brown, Royal Fusiliers; 8. Dvr. D. L. Goldwater, New Zealand A.S.C.; 9. L.-Cpl. T. Gordon, 2/6th King's Liverpool Regt.; 10. C.S.M. M. De Friend, 1/17th London Regt.; 11. Cyclist J. Alexander, Cyclist Battn.; 12. Pte. A. Hoffmann, 15th K.O.Y.L.I.

336

1. Dvr. H. Woolf, R.A.S.C.; 2. Pte. J. Woolf, King's Liverpool Regt.; 3. Pte. S. Schein, Labour Coy.; 4. Pte. S. Reece, 1st K.O.R. Lancaster Regt.; 5. Pte. H. Rosenthal, Lancashire Fusiliers; 6. Pte. J. Woolf, Welsh Regt.; 7. Pte. M. Stone, 2nd Border Regt.; 8. Dvr. C. J. Rich, R.A.S.C.; 9. Pte. M. Levy, 1st K.O.R. Lancaster Regt.; 10. Pte. L. Silverman, Middlesex Regt.; 11. Pte. W. Weinberg, 39th Royal Fusiliers; 12. Pte. B. Ross, 2nd K.O. Scottish Borderers.

1. Lieut. C. G. Lotinga, 12th W. Yorks Regt.; 2. 2nd-Lieut. A. Abram, Tank Corps; 3. Capt. W. Stanford Samuel, 4th King's Liverpool Regt.; 4. Rev. H. L. Price, C.F.; 5. Lieut. D. H. Simmons, R.A.F.; 6. Capt. Baron H. Rothband, 2/5th Lancashire Fusiliers; 7. 2nd-Lieut. J. Marks, R.A.F.; 8. 2nd-Lieut. A. Olsberg, 9th A. & S. Highlanders; 9. Rev. L. A. Falk, C.F., 38th Royal Fusiliers (Jewish); 10. Lieut.-Col. E. J. Heilbron, 3rd K.O.Y.L.I.; 11. Lieut.-Col. E. H. L. Beddington, D.S.O., M.C., Staff and 16th Lancers; 12. 2nd-Lieut. J. C. Samuel, R.A.S.C., M.T.

1. Pte. D. Cohen, 7th Manchester Regt.; 2. Seaman M. Phillips, H.M.S. *Cornwallis*; 3. Pte. R. Freedman, R.A.O.C.; 4. Pte. I. Goldberg, Border Regt.; 5. P.O. S. Zeitlin, R.N.V.R.; 6. Pte. G. Arson, Royal Fusiliers; 7. Rfn. H. Feltbrodt, 12th London Regt.; 8. Pte. S. Goldstein, Somerset L.I.; 9. Dvr. B. Alexander, R.E.; 10. Pte. M. Ash, King's Liverpool Regt.; 11. 2nd A.M. H. Barnett, R.A.F.; 12. Sergt. P. Cohen, R.E., Nyasaland Field Force.

1. Lt.-Col. H. LIGHTSONE, D.S.O., M.C., R.A.M.C.; 2. Lieut. A. LEVY, M.G.C.; 3. Lieut. B. FLIGELSTONE, 3rd King's Liverpool Regt.; 4. Lieut. T. H. FLIGELSTONE, M.C., 38th Royal Fusiliers; 5. 2nd-Lieut. L. PEZARO, K.R.R. Corps; 6. 2nd-Lieut. A. BERNSTEIN, 39th Royal Fusiliers; 7. 2nd-Lieut. M. M. KAYE, R.A.F.; 8. Major M. BARNETT. R.A.S.C.; 9. Capt. M. LEWIS, M.C., 44th Australian Infantry; 10. Lieut. J. KATZ, Zion Mule Corps and Egyptian Labour Corps; 11. Capt. V. JOSEPH, General List; 12 Lieut. Harold BOAS, Australian Y.M.C.A.

1. Pte S. Rosenthal, 21st Lancashire Fusiliers; 2. Gnr. A. N. Levy, R.G.A.; 3. Pte. E. Nathan, 2nd Australian Infantry; 4. Pte. C. S. Kozminsky, Australian Medical Corps; 5. Rfn. S. A. Pezaro, New Zealand R.B.; 6. Pte. J. Pitch, 38th Royal Fusiliers; 7. Cpl. A. Krantz, Australian Infantry; 8. Sergt. J. L. Morris, M.M., 2nd Canadian M.G.C.; 9. Pte. A. A. Kempner, Middlesex Regt. and Royal Fusiliers; 10. Pte. P. Goldsmith, 38th Royal Fusiliers; 11. Pte. H. Levine, Labour Coy.; 12. Pte. B. Levi, 10th West Yorks Regt.

1. Lieut. I. A. Franks, 20th Divl. R.A.S.C.; 2. Capt. P. W. Simonson, Australian H.Q. Staff; 3. Lieut. A. Sniders, 2/8th Rajputs; 4. Lieut. G. S. Lindo, 11th British West Indian Regt.; 5. Lieut. M. Cohen, M.C., R.E.; 6. Lieut. W. S. Samuel. H.A.C. and General List; 7. Capt. G. F. Hyams, D.F.C., R.A.F.; 8. Capt. Ellis, Australian Medical Corps; 9. Capt. W. Sebag-Montefiore, M.C., R.G.A.; 10. Lieut. S. Joseph, R. Irish Regt.; 11. Capt. S. Spero, Croix de Guerre, R.E.; 12. Major I. Salmon, O.B.E., General List.

1. Pte. E. M. Fraser, Labour Corps; 2. Pnr. H. Bernstein, R.E.; 3. Pte. J. Henry, R.A.O.C.; 4. Pte. C. Abrahams, Essex Regt.; 5. Sergt. R. Aschman, Australian Expeditionary Force; 6. Sergt. C. L. D. Bes, 38th Royal Fusiliers; 7. A.M. L. Cornofsky, R.A.F.; 8. Sergt. L. Alexander, Interpreter; 9. Gnr. H. Brown, R.G.A.; 10. Sergt. L. M. Boock, Australian Army Medical Corps; 11. Rfn. J. Harris, 4th K.R.R.C.; 12. Pte. A. Cohen, Royal Fusiliers.

1. Capt. SIDNEY SALOMON, 8th Manchester Regt.; 2. Lieut. M. ALEXANDER, R.N.V.R.; 3. Flight Sub-Lieut. L. ROSENBAUM, R.N.A.S.; 4. 2nd-Lieut. S. THOMAS, R.A.F.; 5. Capt. P. Q. HENRIQUES, Cheshire Field Coy. R.E.; 6. Lieut. H. SALMON, R.N.V.R.; 7. Capt. I. FELDMAN, R.A.M.C.; 8. 2nd-Lieut. S. LOTHEIM, M.C., 7th Royal Sussex Regt.; 9. Major W. Q. HENRIQUES, 8th The Queen's and M.G.C.; 10. Lieut.-Col. Sir EDWARD D. STERN, 1st East Surrey Volunteer Battn.; 11. Major A. ABRAHAMS, O.B.E., R.A.M.C.; 12. Lieut. Hon. STUART A. S. MONTAGU, 2nd Grenadier Guards.

344

1. Cpl. J. Guterman, 9th Royal Fusiliers; 2. Cpl. S. Ellen, 17th London Regt.; 3. Pte. C. Ferber, 13th West Riding Regt.; 4. Sergt. M. Harris, 28th M.A.C., R.A.S.C.; 5. Pte. Bowson, Australian Infantry; 6. Pte. H. Ferber, 19th Lancashire Fusiliers; 7. Pte. M. Christie, 11th King's Liverpool Regt.; 8. Pte. A. Brown, King's Liverpool Regt.; 9. Sergt. M. Hyams, Welsh Regt.; 10. Pte. M. Ferber, 1/5th Buffs; 11. Pte. H. Davis, 11th Queen's; 12. Cpl. J. Drukker, 1/16th London Regt.

1. Rev. D. Hirsch, C.F.; 2. Lieut. Coleman P. Hyman, A.P. Corps; 3. Major J. Kemper, O.B.E., R.A.F.; 4. Capt. H. M. A. Woolf, R.A.S.C.; 5. 2nd-Lieut. W. Posener, Notts and Derby Regt.; 6. Lieut. G. Saxton, Royal Sussex Regt.; 7. Lieut. H. Littman, 2nd Essex Regt.; 8. Capt. L. Freedman, Military Representative at Tribunal; 9. Lieut. S. M. Gluckstein, M.C., R.F.A.; 10. Lieut. G. C. Ancill, 14th Royal Scots; 11. 2nd-Lieut. J. A. Grave, Interpreter, Special List; 12. Capt. M. W. Geffen, R.A.M.C.

1. Pte. A. Aitken, 2nd Royal Scots; 2. Pte. B. S. Boas, R.A.M.C.; 3. Pte. B. Epstein, Labour Coy.; 4. Pte. P. Fine, Tank Corps; 5. Pte. A. Finesilver, 38th Royal Fusiliers; 6. Pte. D. Altman, 13th Royal Scots Fusiliers; 7. Cpl. F. W. Flatow, M.M., 11th East Yorks Regt.; 8. Gnr. J. Driver, R.F.A.; 9. Pte. H. Erlstein, South African Infantry; 10. L.-Cpl. J. Berns, Cyclist Battn.; 11. Bdr. P. Couplan R.F.A.; 12. Cpl. A. Couplan, Duke of Wellington's Regt

1. Lieut. J. LAZARUS, R.F.A.; 2. Lieut. E. SELINGER, R.A.M.C.; 3. Capt. LEWIS G. R. HARRIS,* M.C., 7th West Riding Regt.; 4. Surgeon-Lieut. G. E. SPERO, R.N.V.R., H.M.S. *Manners*; 5. 2nd-Lieut. A. C. R. HARRIS,* 11th East Yorks Regt.; 6. Capt. A. GOLDSTEIN, R.G.A.; 7. Midshipman L. P. SPERO, R.N.V.R., H.M.S. *Prince*; 8. Capt. M. P. ARNOLD, London Regt.; 9. Lieut. C. L. R. HARRIS,* Tank Corps; 10. Lieut. C. E. R. HARRIS,* Tank Corps and East Yorks Regt.; 11. Rev. N. GOLDSTON, C.F.; 12. Capt. S. H. R. HARRIS,* M.G.C.

* Brothers.

1. Pte. H. Cohen, Suffolk Regt.; 2. L.-Cpl. L. Delow, 39th Royal Fusiliers; 3. Tpr. A Godfrey, R.A.V.C.; 4. Pte. M. Herwald, R.A.M.C.; 5. Pte. P. Cohen, 1/8th Worcester Regt.; 6. Cpl. R. Herwald, Labour Corps; 7. 1st A.M. A. Boskin, R.A.F.; 8. Sergt. A. Costa, M.T., R.A.S.C.; 9. 2nd A.M. L. Freedman, R.A.F.; 10. Bandsman S. Davis, R.G.A.; 11. Tpr. M Green, 2nd K.E.H.; 12. Pte. I. H. Bentwitch, Australian Infantry.

1. Sergt. L. C. Cohen, R.A.M.C.; 2. Pte. H. Rubin, 8th The Buffs; 3. Tpr. A. Solomon, 1st Life Guards; 4. Cpl. M. Wesansky, A.P. Corps; 5. Pte. J. Wattsman, R.A.S.C., M.T.; 6. Pte. R. Levy, 23rd Manchester Regt.; 7. Gnr. M. H. Levi, Canadian Artillery; 8. Gnr. M. Solomons, R.F.A.; 9. Pte. A. Rose, R.A.M.C.; 10. Pte. S. Woolf, South Wales Borderers; 11. Spr. S. Coleman, R.E.; 12. Pte. M. Levitski, Labour Coy.

1. Pte. E. Feldman, 38th Royal Fusiliers; 2. Pte. S Brill, R.A.M.C.; 3. Dvr. M. Freeman, R.F.A.; 4. Pte. L. Cohen, 39th Royal Fusiliers; 5. Pte. J. Baker, 2nd Scottish Rifles; 6. L.-Cpl. A. Davis, 14th Cyclist Battn.; 7. Pte. M. J. Chelen, 40th Royal Fusiliers; 8. Pte. H. Cash, 38th Royal Fusiliers; 9. Spr. M. Benjamin, 2nd Australian L.R.O. Coy.; 10. Sergt. V. Dubens, Middlesex Regt.; 11. Pte. L. Freeman, R.A.M.C.; 12. Cpl. M. Dorfman, 9th H.L.I.

1. A.C.I. H. Levine, R.A.F.; 2. Pte. S. E. Galician, R.A.S.C.; 3. Dvr. H. Cohen, R.A.S.C.; 4. Dvr. J. Levine, R.A.S.C.; 5. Cpl. H. Jacobi, 39th Royal Fusiliers; 6. S.-Sergt. B. S. Abrahams, Gloucester Regt.; 7. Pte. L. Birinberg, 10th Australian Infantry; 8. Gnr. A. Meropolsky, R.G.A.; 9. Pte. L. Lyons, 11th South Lancs Regt.; 10. Pte. A. Lewis, 18th M.G.C.; 11. 2nd A.M. S. Korn, R.A.F.; 12. Pte. M. Gavson, R.A.S.C.

1. Lieut. S. Levy, Tank Corps; 2. 2nd-Lieut. S. Breckman, General List; 3. Lieut. Conrad Samuel, R.F.A.; 4. Mr. Henry Franks, British Red Cross; 5. Lieut. F. J. Benzimra, M.C., M.G.C.; 6. Lieut. L. H. Gluckstein, Suffolk Regt. att. Intelligence Corps; 7. Lieut. W. Price, M.C., Royal Inniskilling Fusiliers; 8. Cadet T. Ockman, O.T.C.; 9. Capt. B. Chaikin, R.A.M.C.; 10. 2nd-Lieut. J. Cohen, Suffolk Regt. att. Bedfordshire Regt.; 11. Capt. H. Joseph, M.B.B.S., I.M.S.; 12. Capt. A. L. Mendoza, 1/7th Rajputs, Political Magistrate, Baluchistan.

ZION MULE CORPS.

1. Pte. A. MOLIN; 2. Lieut. S. ZLOTNIK; 3. Pte. M. GOLDSWEIG; 4. Soldiers from Zion Mule Corps, transferred to 3/20th London Regt.

ZION MULE CORPS.

1. Pte. J. APTER, 2. Pte. A. GODANSKY, transferred from Zion Mule Corps to 3/20th London Regt.
3. Capt. J. TRUMPELDOR, Zion Mule Corps.
4. Cpl. M. GROUCHKOWSKY, D.C.M., Zion Mule Corps.
5. Soldiers of Zion Mule Corps transferred to 3/20th London Regt.

1. Pte. D. Cohen, 12th Gloucester Regt.; 2. Gnr. S. Boorman, R.G.A.; 3. Pte. S. Allan, 2nd Northumberland Fusiliers; 4. Pte. S. Harris, 18th York and Lancaster Regt.; 5. Pte. D. Abrahams, 2/23rd London Regt.; 6. 2nd A.M. E. Cohen, R.A.F.; 7. L.-Cpl. H. Collock, 2/5th K.O.R. Lancaster Regt.; 8. Gnr. N. Frieze, R.G.A; 9. L.-Cpl. J. Freedman, R.A.M.C.; 10. Pte. H. Freedland, 24th Manchester Regt.; 11. Pte. L. Collock, 61st M.G.C.; 12. Pte. S. Goldman, R.M.L.I.

1. 2nd-Lieut. A. CHART, 16th London Volunteer Regt. and Sergt. 2nd South African Inf.; 2. Capt. A. WACHOLDER, 2nd Yorks Regt. and 38th Royal Fusiliers; 3. Lieut. D. GOODMAN, 40th Royal Fusiliers; 4. 2nd-Lieut. A. GOLDING, R.A.F.; 5. Lieut.-Col. Sir ALBERT STERN, K.B.E., C.M.G., R.E.; 6. Capt. and Adjt. L. BRILLIANT, 2/55th Coke's Rifles, Indian Army; 7. 2nd-Lieut. S. ABRAHAMS, King's Liverpool Regt. and 38th Royal Fusiliers; 8. Capt. A. S. MORLEY, R.A.M.C.; 9. Lieut. P. F. PHILLIPS, Northampton Regt.; 10. Capt. and Adjt. M. P. TUTEUR, R.F.A.; 11. Capt. C. H. MOCATTA, R.E.; 12. Lieut. D. SASSOON, Labour Coy.

1. Pte. S. Tannenbaum, Royal Welch Fusiliers; 2. Cpl. M. Sapper, R.E.; 3. Pte. J. Wolfson, 1/8th Inniskilling Fusiliers; 4. Pte. M. Levy, 12th Middlesex Regt.; 5. Pte. M. Barsofsky, Royal Fusiliers; 6. Drummer A. Teacher, Middlesex Regt.; 7. Pte. S. Palley, Royal Fusiliers; 8. Pte. Pam, Australian Infantry; 9. Sig. A. Barnard, 5th King's Liverpool Regt.; 10. Pte. R. Mordecai, Royal Dublin Fusiliers; 11. Pte. I. Rosenberg, 39th Royal Fusiliers; 12. Cpl. D. Speigel, R.A.F.

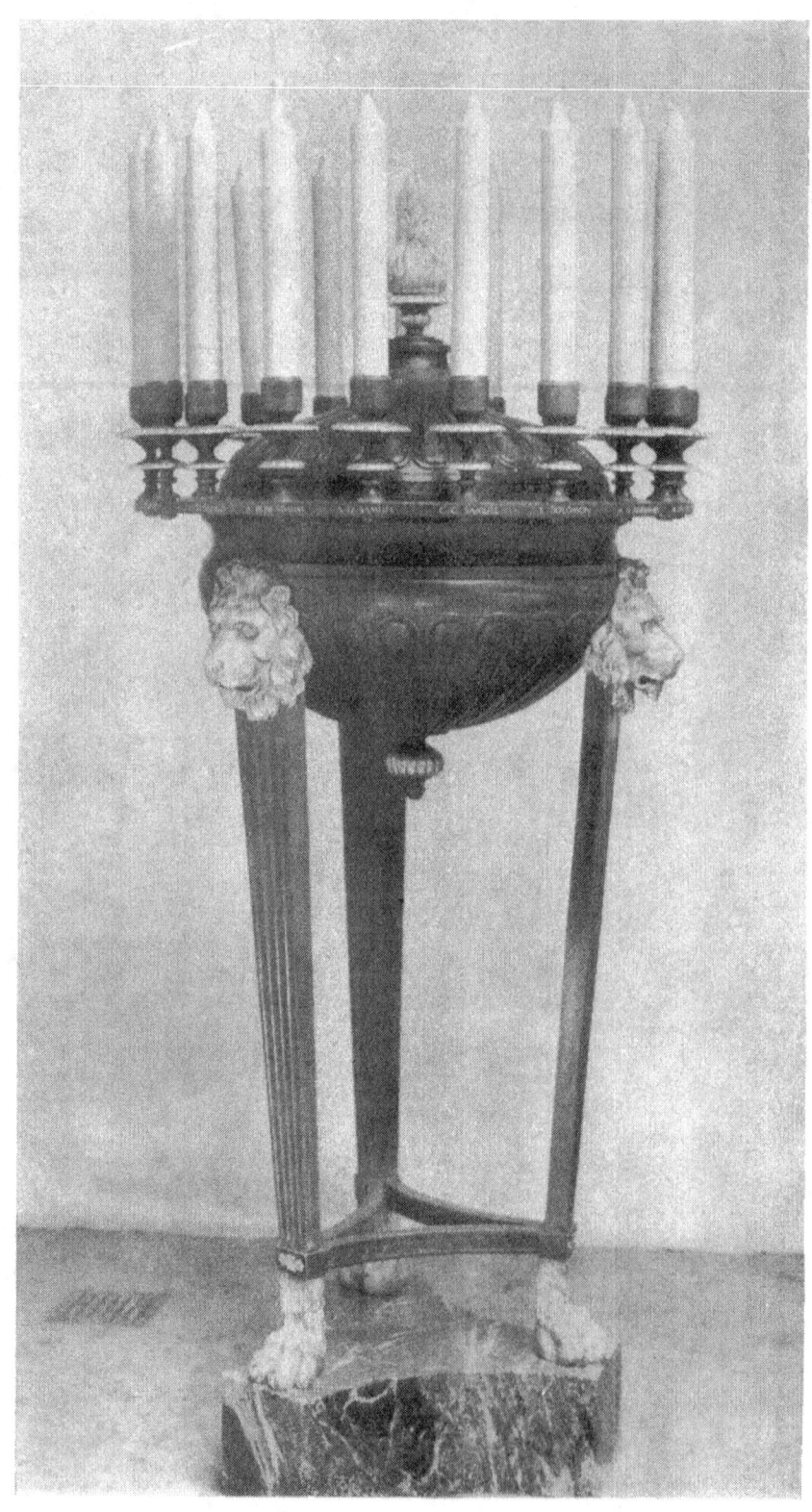

MEMORIAL CANDELABRUM, CENTRAL
SYNAGOGUE, LONDON, W.

1. Group of Labour Coy.
2. Group of R.F.A.
3. Pte. J. Cross, R.G.A.; Pte. H. Freedman, R.A.O.C.; Pte. R. Lattner, R.A.O.C.; Pte. C. Solomons, R.A.O.C
4. Four Jewish soldiers

ROLL OF HONOUR, CENTRAL SYNAGOGUE, LONDON, W.

ROLL OF HONOUR, ST. JOHN'S WOOD SYNAGOGUE, LONDON, N.W.

1. Lieut. A. L. C. Spiers, B.A., 7th King's Shropshire Light Infantry; 2. Capt. Cecil L. Hart, 2nd Duke of Wellington's Regt.; 3. 2nd-Lieut. F. J. Brooks, 4th South Staffs Regt.; 4. Lieut. E. E. Polack, 1/4th Gloucester Regt.; 5. Lieut. W. H. D. de Pass, 13th Middlesex Regt.; 6. Lieut. B. J. Polack, 9th Worcester Regt.; 7. Capt. L. Holt, 2/10th London Regt.; 8. Lieut. M. E. Kosminsky, 7th Australian Infantry; 9. 2nd-Lieut. M. Valentine, 2nd Queen's (Royal West Surrey) Regt.; 10. 2nd-Lieut. M. G. Selby, Artists' Rifles and Essex Regt.; 11. Lieut. H. V. Cleef, 8th Queen's (Royal West Surrey) Regt.; 12. 2nd-Lieut. H. Lewis, 1/7th King's Liverpool Regt.

1. Pte. H. Abrahams, 2nd Royal Welsh Regt.; 2. Pte. A. Goldstone, 16th Manchester Regt.; 3. Pte. J. Carey, 2nd Northampton Regt.; 4. Rfn. J. Cohen, Rifle Brigade; 5. Sergt J. M. Dresner, 4th Canadian Engineers; 6. Pte. N. Bloomfield, 7th Argyll and Sutherland Hrs.; 7 Pte Dalmer, Australian Infantry; 8. Pte. V. G. Carson, 2nd Royal Scots; 9. Gnr. H. Freedman, R.G.A.; 10. Pte. E. Gilbert, Middlesex Regt.; 11. Pte. J. Cooper, R.A.M.C.; 12. L.-Cpl. H Blitstein, R.A.F.

REV. S. LIPSON, S.C.F., AND GROUP AT PLYMOUTH.

www.ingramcontent.com/pod-product-compliance
Lightning Source LLC
Chambersburg PA
CBHW080827010526
44111CB00016B/2620